Welfare through Work

Welfare through Work

Conservative Ideas, Partisan Dynamics, and Social Protection in Japan

Mari Miura

Cornell University Press
Ithaca and London

Cornell University Press gratefully acknowledges receipt of a subvention from Sophia University, which aided in the publication of this book.

First published 2012 by Cornell University Press
Printed in the United States of America

Library of Congress Cataloging-in-Publication Data

Miura, Mari.
Welfare through work : conservative ideas, partisan dynamics, and social protection in Japan / Mari Miura.
        p. cm.
    Includes bibliographical references and index.
    ISBN 978-0-8014-5105-8 (cloth : alk. paper)
1. Job security—Political aspects—Japan.   2. Public welfare—Japan.
3. Economic assistance, Domestic—Japan.   4. Labor policy—Japan.
5. Conservatism—Japan.   6. Japan—Social policy.   I. Title.
    HD5708.45.J3M58   2012
    331.25'96—dc23   2012013340

Cornell University Press strives to use environmentally responsible suppliers and materials to the fullest extent possible in the publishing of its books. Such materials include vegetable-based, low-VOC inks and acid-free papers that are recycled, totally chlorine-free, or partly composed of nonwood fibers. For further information, visit our website at www.cornellpress.cornell.edu.

Cloth printing   10 9 8 7 6 5 4 3 2 1

For Koichi

Contents

List of Tables and Figures   *ix*

Acknowledgments   *xi*

Abbreviations   *xv*

A Note on Conventions   *xvii*

Introduction   1

1. Welfare through Work and the Gendered Dual System   12

2. Situating Japan's Social Protection System in Comparative Perspective   30

3. The Conservative Vision and the Politics of Work and Welfare   38

4. Reforming the Labor Markets   65

5. Who Wants What Reform?   93

6. The Neoliberal Agenda and the Diet Veto   114

7. The Double Movement in Japanese Politics   141

Conclusion   156

Notes   *165*
References   *187*
Index   *201*

Tables and Figures

Tables

1.1. Typology of work and welfare	13
1.2. Employment performance (1990s)	16
1.3. Major labor market policies	18
4.1. Labor market reform, 1986–2007	68
4.2. Dysfunction in social protection systems	89
6.1. The role of deregulation panels in labor law making	126
6.2. The ruling party's attitude toward the opposition	138

Figures

1.1. Mapping countries based on typology of work
and welfare (1990s) — 14
1.2. Share of non-regular workers by gender, age, and
type of employment (2000) — 26
3.1. Social expenditure by item per GDP (%) — 53
3.2. The LDP's share in the Diet — 54
4.1. Changes in employment protection indexes for
regular and temporary workers (late 1980s to 2003) — 67
4.2. Share of non-regular workers (1985–2010) — 75
4.3. Gini coefficient transition (1967–2004) — 87
5.1. Labor productivity and real wage indexes (manufacturing) — 101

Acknowledgments

People often ask me why I am interested in labor politics. Indeed, at first glance, labor may hardly seem the most appealing of subjects to scholars of Japanese politics given the declining influence of unions in policymaking. It is even less appealing, perhaps, to a (young) female researcher when one considers that unions are a traditional preserve of the "old-boy" network in Japan. It was while in Berkeley that I encountered the academic field of labor politics and found it intellectually stimulating and worthy of further exploration. The more I discovered of the critical role played by organized labor in shaping democracy in Europe and even in the United States, the more I felt the need to observe Japanese politics through the lens of labor politics. I am thus deeply indebted to the scholars who introduced me to this field and opened my eyes to its substance. I especially thank John Zysman, Steven Vogel, Jonah Levy, Chris Ansell, and Robert Cole for their generous support. Had I not had the opportunity to study at Berkeley, this book would certainly not have been written.

It is ironic that I have ended up researching and writing about the world of Japanese corporations, as it was in part their exclusion of women that originally led me to pursue an academic career. In this regard, I am greatly indebted to Sone Yasunori, one of my advisers at Keio University, who encouraged me to enter the academic discipline of political science and to commit to the improvement of representative democracy in Japan.

My initial interest in labor politics developed during my field research in Tokyo to include a specific focus on the social protection system. Sven Steinmo and Bruno Palier inspired me to choose this direction. My participation in a research project funded by the Shibusawa Eiichi Memorial Foundation convinced me that the linkage between party politics and the policy process should be empirically investigated and theoretically explored.

I thank Leonard Schoppa, Tanaka Aiji, and Robert Weiner for their stimulating input throughout the project. Many other scholars offered valuable advice on various occasions and helped me to develop my ideas. To mention just a few names, I thank Ōtake Hideo, Yamaguchi Jirō, Shinkawa Toshimitsu, Kume Ikuo, Charles Weathers, Kathleen Thelen, and Miyamoto Tarō.

This book would not have been accomplished without the institutional support that I have received. I am deeply grateful to the Institute of Social Science, University of Tokyo and its then director, Hirowatari Seigo, for providing me with a research fellowship during my field research and writing. I received invaluable feedback from Nitta Michio, Nakamura Keisuke, Hiwatari Nobuhiro, Ōsawa Mari, and Gregory Noble on the issues that I was researching. I also thank Rengō Sōken (Research Institute for Advancement of Living Standards), which organized and funded my research on Rengō's policy participation. Rengō Sōken also funded a research project on the policy-making process under the Democratic Party of Japan's government, and I was able to benefit greatly from the valuable comments of Itō Mitsutoshi and other project members. I am also grateful to Komoda Takanari, Suzuki Fujikazu, Ōmi Naoto, Tatsui Yōji, and Asō Yūko for advising me on Rengō's positions and involvement in politics. Two Kakenhi (Grants-in-Aid for Young Scientists (B) #16730078 and Grants-in-Aid for Scientific Research (C) #19530114) from the Japan Society for the Promotion of Science provided crucial financial resources for completing the research.

Sophia University has provided me with an ideal environment to concentrate on my work and write the book. My participation in the AGLOS (Area-Based Global Studies) project as well as in the activities of the Institute of Global Concern (IGC) kept me motivated to investigate the woes of Japan's social protection system from global perspectives. I thank Murai Yoshinori, Linda Grove, Terada Takefumi, Akahori Masayuki, Hataya Noriko, Shimokawa Masatsugu, Anno Tadashi, Mark Mullins, and Nakano Koichi for their encouragement and creative spirit. Their sincere dedication to others always inspires me to build a meaningful bridge between my academic work and real-life commitments.

I am deeply indebted to Nakano Koichi and John C. Campbell who gave me detailed and insightful feedback on each page of the book. I appreciate the reviews from two anonymous Cornell University Press readers who provided constructive advice and helped me polish my arguments. I also express my gratitude to Roger Haydon who was confident of the book's worth from the beginning and skillfully guided me to see it through.

Hamada Eriko, Shimada Reina, Kunieda Tomoki, Niikawa Shō, Takaba Haruka, and Hayakawa Miyako provided careful research assistance. Ian F. Martin proofread and provided superb editorial suggestions on the manuscript.

I acknowledge the kind permission granted by Taylor & Francis to draw on materials from my article published in *Labor History* (Miura 2008a) in chapters 3 and 5 of the book, as well as by the University of Toronto Press to draw on parts of Miura (2011a) in chapters 5 and 6.

Writing the book coincided with my pregnancy, the birth of my child, and child rearing. I especially thank Katō Kōzō, my colleague and friend at the Faculty of Law, for selflessly helping me take work reductions and leave, as well as my friends and peers Kasuya Yūko, Alisa Gaunder, and Jonathan Marshall for their encouragement and friendship. Their support has been incredibly important to me. Finally, I thank my parents, family, and extended family for tirelessly supporting and cheering me on. Hugo has made my life and work truly meaningful. Last, but not least, I thank Koichi. This book would have been intellectually, emotionally, and physically impossible without him. I dedicate it to him.

Abbreviations

CCRR	Council for Comprehensive Regulatory Reform (2001–2004)
CEFP	Council on Economic and Fiscal Policy (2001–2010)
CPRR	Council for the Promotion of Regulatory Reform (2004–2007)
CRR	Council for Regulatory Reform (2007–2010)
DPJ	Democratic Party of Japan
EEOL	Equal Employment Opportunity Law
JCP	Japan Communist Party
JSP	Japan Socialist Party
LDP	Liberal Democratic Party
MHLW	Ministry of Health, Labour, and Welfare (since 2001)
MHW	Ministry of Health and Welfare (until 2001)
MOL	Ministry of Labour (until 2001)
OECD	Organization for Economic Co-operation and Development
RRC	Regulatory Reform Committee (1998–2001)
TWAL	Temporary Work Agency Law

A Note on Conventions

Japanese personal names appear in the Japanese order—family name first—except when citing publications in English, in which the author's names appear in Western order. Macrons are used for long vowels except where the word in question appears commonly in English without macrons.

Introduction

Japanese society has long been considered egalitarian. High economic growth and relatively equitable distribution were among the most conspicuous characteristics of the postwar Japanese political economy, and their combined success brought the "Japanese model" under scrutiny throughout the world, especially in the 1980s and early 1990s. Where other affluent democracies suffered from slow economic recovery and mass unemployment after the oil crises of the 1970s, Japan enjoyed steady growth and low unemployment, thereby ensuring social and political stability. The success story of the Japanese economy was well researched worldwide and analyzed as a model of development. The lure of the Japanese model, however, has since faded. Japan has suffered two decades of economic stagnation since the collapse of the bubble economy in 1991 and the growing presence of the working poor can no longer be hidden. Growth is in short supply and equality a thing of the past.

Japanese society began to recognize the full extent of its poverty problem only in 2006. A series of TV documentaries broadcast by NHK (the Japan Broadcasting Corporation) brought to light the shocking reality of the "working poor"—a term that soon entered the Japanese lexicon. The subsequent impact of the *Haken* village affair was profound, revealing latent injustice in the labor market and deficiencies in the social protection system. "*Haken*" literally refers to dispatched or temporary agency workers and the *Haken* village was a temporary shelter camp for those who had lost both jobs and housing after being fired or refused renewal of contracts. Labor unions, lawyers, and nonprofit organizations (NPOs) set up the *Haken* village in Hibiya Park just in front of the Ministry of Health, Labour, and Welfare at the last day of 2008 so that the "village people" would be able to sleep safely in a tent and receive warm meals during the New Year's holidays. About 500 unemployed and homeless people gathered in the camp. All three rival national labor union centers also rallied, the first time they had rallied together since their reconfiguration in 1989. The physical presence of a significant number of people in need of temporary shelter pressured the government to respond: the village people were allowed to sleep in an auditorium hall inside the ministry, and plans were hastily drawn up to review the Temporary Work Agency Law, which was viewed by many as the main cause of the *Haken* workers' plight.

The *Haken* village affair shattered the widely shared perception of an egalitarian Japan, as poverty, all of a sudden, loomed large in the public eye. How did this situation develop? Why was Japan suddenly confronted with the problem of the working poor and mass dismissals? Was lifetime employment not a core tenet of the Japanese management system? Why was Japan unable to maintain equitable distribution? Put another way, why did Japan apparently elect to sacrifice social equality in an attempt to restore corporate profits? What political conditions allowed this choice? In order to understand the contemporary malaise of the Japanese political economy, it is essential to look in depth at its social protection system. This book, therefore, analyzes the characteristics of the Japanese social protection system, its historical development, and the political mechanisms that produced it, in an attempt to address these questions.

In this book, I contend that the Japanese social protection system should be understood as a system of "welfare through work," where employment protection has functionally substituted income maintenance. Although the government's social spending has generally been low by international standards and redistribution through taxes and social contributions has played only a marginal role in social protection, high employment rates for all categories of workers have served to reduce inequality. The welfare through work system appeared to have become dysfunctional by the mid-2000s. New market realities produced a large number of non-regular workers protected by neither their employers nor the state, and they now make up over one-third of the workforce in Japan. In a severely polarized labor market, welfare through work no longer functions as a social protection system, and the Japanese government has failed to update and modernize the system to cope with new social risks.

This book reveals how the welfare through work system functioned in the past and why it has ceased to function in recent years. Although it is generally thought that strong employment protection reduces employment rates, in the past Japan's welfare through work system combined robust employment protection mechanisms with high employment rates. I argue that flexibility provided by a "gendered dual system" in labor markets enabled Japan to achieve high employment rates. Under this system, male regular workers in large firms benefited from strong employment protection at the cost of long working hours and frequent relocations (internal flexibility); whereas women, played a critical, if unnoticed, role in sustaining employment protection, acting as primary caregivers and providing cheap and flexible labor as part-timers (external flexibility). Japan's highly gendered dual labor market thus included ample flexibility to support the coexistence of strong employment protection and high employment rates.

My research shows that labor market reforms since the 1990s altered the linkage between work and welfare and made the welfare through work system dysfunctional and unsustainable. Employment protection for regular workers essentially survived intact, whereas flexibility in both the internal and external labor markets was further enhanced. In other words, strong employment protection for a declining number of regular workers was maintained through the reinforcement of the gendered dual system. As far as deregulation of the temporary labor market was concerned, the extent of reform in Japan was modest by international comparison. However, the distributional consequences of labor market reform were particularly severe in Japan, as illustrated by the recent high poverty rates. That relatively modest labor market reforms led to high levels of poverty is due in large part to the fact that Japan neither strengthened security measures for non-regular workers nor expanded the social safety net. My focus on the linkage between work and welfare offers a coherent account of the mechanisms of the Japanese social protection system through the successful years of the postwar period to the agonizing social problems of the present day.

Ideas and Power in Making Social Protection Systems

Why did Japan follow such a path? The formation and transformation of the social protection system is a complex process. While accepting that a variety of factors affect policy outcomes, this book takes the position that *the political vision and values of the governing political party* greatly affect the design of the social protection system.

Power resource approaches that stress the importance of left-leaning parties in the construction and expansion of the welfare state provide classic explanations of the development of welfare states (Esping-Andersen 1985; Korpi 1974, 1983, 2006; Shinkawa 1993, 2005; Stephens 1974). This view regards the welfare state as an outcome of democratic class struggle pitting the pro-welfare, anti-market forces represented by labor against the anti-welfare pro-market forces of capital. As labor-based leftist parties are considered the sole driving force behind welfare expansion, the model holds that their strength directly affects the timing, size, and structure of welfare state. This theory seems adequate to explain Japan's low social spending. The Liberal Democratic Party (LDP) ruled Japan for thirty-eight years from 1955 through 1993. The prolonged exclusion from power of leftist parties surely capped the quantitative expansion of

Japan's welfare state. However, this model fails to explain why Japan has developed its own unique social protection system. Analysis of the role of the ruling party and its visions, ideologies, and values is indispensable, as it was the governing party rather than the Left that influenced more directly the way in which the welfare state was shaped in Japan. In other words, power resource approaches fail to take adequate account of the programs pursued by parties on the Right, which are assigned the role of gatekeeper against the tide of democratic desire for an egalitarian society.

What theories, then, account for the role of rightist parties? Three distinct lines of explanation offer theories as to what kinds of policies are preferred and proposed by the Right. The first one stresses the importance of employers and their positive role in the development of the welfare state. Studies have found instances of employer support for certain aspects of welfare programs and explain employer preferences in relation to the specific functions of a particular policy.[1] Because there are often aspects of welfare programs that are beneficial to employers, for instance in terms of controlling competition and externalizing costs that they would otherwise have to accept and address individually, welfare states can provide solutions in terms of coordination around problems that employers are eager to solve (Hall and Soskice 2001). This perspective has greatly advanced our understanding of the welfare state. It is important to recognize complementarities and positive relationships between capitalism and the welfare state, as it is a simple fact that welfare programs require the support of at least a portion of employers in a capitalist economy. Employers are, nevertheless, often resistant to new legislation, if not always actively hostile toward the welfare state and prefer to secure as much flexibility as possible (Huber and Stephens 2001; see also Korpi 2006). However powerful as they may be, employers do not always achieve their initial targets in terms of social policy and are often forced to accept second-best options due to internal divisions in the business community and unfavorable political environments. Welfare state programs should therefore be regarded as compromises resulting from political struggle between various actors with heterogeneous interests and resources.[2]

The second line of explanation regards welfare programs as part of pork-barrel politics and seeks the source of clientelism in electoral systems and constitutional structure.[3] Welfare politics is thus placed in the larger context of distributional politics. Among a rich array of literature on Japanese clientelism, recent studies have provided robust accounts of the institutional mechanisms behind distributional politics, revealing incentive structures provided by the electoral system (Scheiner 2006; Tatebayashi 2004). This line of argument cogently explains the political mechanisms by which the LDP created segmented welfare programs to court their constituencies (Estévez-Abe 2008). It also accounts for Japan's vast spending on public works, which has consistently contributed to job creation. It thus provides important correctives to the first line of explanation, which focuses almost exclusively on the role of social actors, paying scant attention to the independent role of politics. Political actors do not merely represent the interests of social actors, but in certain circumstances lead and shape public opinion, setting the agenda from above. Even powerful social actors need to strategize their political actions in accordance with the political environment they inhabit. Clientelism-based explanations usually emphasize institutional constraints and the electoral impact of the political calculations of the agents, thereby neglecting their ideational motivations. Political struggle aims not only at material gain as is implied by clientelism-based explanations but also at ideational goals. It may be useful here to recall that the advancement of social rights underpinned the development of the welfare state, as first theorized by T. H. Marshall (1950). Clientelism-based explanations do not adequately capture the politics of entitlement, a concept that crystallizes the acute political conflicts between political parties.

A third line of argument, which emphasizes the role of ideology, explains the politics of entitlement (Garon 1997; Ishida 1989; see also Béland and Cox 2010). The LDP, and Japanese conservatives in general, have never disguised their hostility toward the foreign concepts of human rights and citizenship, and have persistently resisted the establishment of social rights as a matter of entitlement.[4] The LDP's desire to revise the postwar constitution stems not only from its contempt for Article 9, which prohibits Japan from possessing military forces, but also from its fundamental abhorrence of gender equality (Art. 14 and Art. 24), social rights (Art. 25), and freedom of religion (Art. 20).[5] Although it is easy to spot conservative and even anachronistic discourses and ideologies that clash with the very concept of social rights, scholars disagree on the extent to which ideology matters in actual policymaking. Sheldon Garon (1997) holds the view that conservative ideology has greatly affected Japan's welfare state even in the postwar period as elites have manufactured ideologies to dampen popular expectations of state assistance and to encourage familial and communal support. Those who discount conservative ideology in this regard might point out that Japan has maintained a quantitative expansion of its welfare state in line with other affluent democracies even under conservative governments. In my view, the role of ideology is far from trivial.[6] In order to understand why Japan has not developed universal welfare programs and why the government has constantly implemented cutbacks in social assistance and public services, the conservative elite's rejection of citizenship-based entitlements should not be underrated. Ideology should not be treated as either static or essential to the political culture of a given country, because political actors periodically refashion and redefine their ideologies in order to build coalitions and gain electoral advantage in a particular political environment. What needs to be understood here is how the dynamics of partisan competition induces political parties to innovate with respect to their ideational foundation and how such policy repositioning ultimately produces policy change.

Bringing Political Parties Back In: Vision and Competition

Based on these critiques of earlier studies, I emphasize the role of the political vision and values of the governing party, the LDP, in shaping the social protection system. This is not to suggest that political actors, maintaining a consistent and coherent set of ideas, always behave strictly in accordance with their values. Nor is this to suggest that purposive actors dominate political processes through which their ideologies and intentions are coherently manifested in the architecture of policy. Political actors engage in the struggle for power in order to promote their preferred policies, but partisan competition constrains the potential achievements of the ruling party. The strategic behavior of political actors, which is largely shaped under a given configuration of political power, is also significant.

In more recent years, some scholars have stressed the role of ideas in welfare reform by applying discursive analyses (Béland and Cox 2010; Blyth 2002; V. Schmidt 2002; Taylor-Gooby 2005; see also Campbell 2002). My examination of the conservative vision can be positioned in terms of the literature on the power of ideas. However, I emphasize the agency of political parties in promoting policy change. Arguments that focus solely on the independent and causal role of ideas overlook the dynamic process according to which actors acquire power in order to shape the discourse of the day as well as by trying to influence it. Political actors "actively take up certain issues and espouse certain solutions *as weapons* in the power struggle" (Nakano 2010, 7; emphasis added). The struggle for power is inextricably linked to the battle of ideas. Instead of giving either one of these factors analytical primacy, I focus on the power politics played between purposive actors.

More specifically, I argue that three strands of conservatism—statism, productivism, and cooperatism—were fundamental to the establishment of Japan's welfare through work system. Traditionally, Japanese conservatives neither espouse free market ideology nor hold the state in contempt, in contrast to their counterparts in Anglo-American countries where liberalism has gained greater political currency. Japan modernized its political and economic systems under the leadership of state elites. Consequently, in conservative thinking, national interests are equated with the interests of the state, which are in turn defined by the conservative elite. In this context, the social protection system is justified in terms of the state's interests. I use the term "statism" to characterize this line of conservative thinking.

At the same time, some Japanese conservatives share a conviction with European Christian democrats that "conflicts of social interests can and must be reconciled politically in order to restore the natural and organic harmony of society" (Van Kersbergen 1995, 28; see also Korpi 2001). Class compromise and political mediation have been perennial characteristics of both Christian democrat and Japanese conservative policy. I employ the term "cooperatism" to describe the line of thinking that has advocated the creation of social institutions that would generate cooperation between employers and workers and the segmentation of workers into separate occupational communities in order to undermine the basis for collective action.[7] Indeed, the first legislation for social insurance was the conservative response to the growing political threat from the industrial working class and socialist parties. Likewise, cooperatism provided political support to the cross-class coalition, which made employment protection the nucleus of the social contract.

Productivism has also been an important element in postwar conservative thinking. Economic development being the sole national goal in postwar Japan, welfare programs had to be justified from the perspective of economic growth. Cooperatism was a reactionary solution to the social question at the time, but productivism provided a positive linkage between the social protection system and production strategy. Full employment policy was advanced in recognition of the fact that Japan needed to maximize the use of its human resources in order to increase national production power.

This conceptualization of Japanese conservatism is crucial to partisan explanations. The well-known typology of welfare regimes advanced by Gøsta Esping-Andersen—Liberal, Conservative/Christian Democrat, and Social Democrat—encounters difficulties when applied to the Japanese case (see chapter 2). Consequently, scholars tend to either view Japan as a hybrid of the Liberal and Conservative welfare regimes (e.g., Esping-Andersen himself) or jettison such partisan explanations altogether (Estévez-Abe 2008; Kasza 2006). The difficulties in applying partisan explanations to the Japanese case result in part from a lack of theoretical discussion of Japanese conservatism.[8] This book recuperates the essential tenet of partisan explanations by explicating the political vision of Japanese conservatives.

Moreover, I argue that the eventual shift in partisan dynamics brought about a gradual transformation of the LDP's ideologies through the rise of a fourth strand of conservatism: neoliberalism, which is an idea that puts the highest priority on the individual's freedom to make profit even at the cost of workers' rights and safety. It shifts the state's responsibility to individuals with respect to protecting people's welfare, but retains the state's role in creating and preserving an institutional framework appropriate to economic freedom. Neoliberalism thus fused with statist thinking, gradually replacing productivism and cooperatism between the 1970s and the 1990s.

The LDP's adoption of neoliberalism first took place in the-mid 1970s, in the form of a conservative backlash against welfare expansion earlier in the decade, with the main battlefield at the time being in the realm of public discourse. It was in the 1980s that the LDP found neoliberal policy electorally rewarding and thus pursued administrative reform and welfare retrenchment. Because employers were still praising cooperatism, only productivism disappeared from the conservative thinking. It was in the 1990s that the LDP embraced neoliberalism in a full-fledged fashion and carried out labor market reforms.

My conceptualization of the Japanese conservative vision is a heuristic device that also serves to evaluate the influence of the power alternation that resulted from the electoral victory of the Democratic Party of Japan (DPJ) in 2009. I argue that the DPJ aims to revive and redefine productivism and cooperatism in the contemporary context, while renouncing the statist tradition. This means that the party will not ultimately revert to dependence on welfare through work but will attempt to remake it in a more functional and productive fashion. My conceptualization provides useful analytical lenses through which to perceive the significance of power alternation.

In essence, my emphasis on the critical role of political parties should be understood in a broad sense as a variant of the power resource approaches. This is not because I focus on the power of labor-based parties and labor unions, but because I treat political parties as the agents of policy change and conceptualize the vision and values of the parties in power. However, as I examine the way in which partisan dynamics influences the strategic adaptation of parties' policy positions, I afford in my explanatory framework the ideational innovation of political parties a much greater importance than it received in the conventional power resource approach.

Plan of the Book

Welfare through work characterizes the Japanese social protection system: employment maintenance functionally substitutes for income maintenance. Chapter 1 explores the mechanism though which employment maintenance has been achieved despite the fact that legal employment protection is strong in Japan. The key to understanding the unusual coexistence of strong employment protection with high employment performance was the gendered dual system, which embedded a variety of flexibilities in the Japanese labor market.

In chapter 2 I provide an international comparison of social protection systems in order to highlight the specificity of the Japanese case, thereby locating my conceptualization of welfare through work in the theoretical debate. I demonstrate the strength and limitations of regime theory and introduce the merits of my partisan explanation.

Chapter 3 discusses the historical development of the welfare through work system from its genesis in the 1950s to the end of the 1980s and chapters 4–7 examine the transformation of the system since the 1990s. For both periods, I focus on (i) the development of the major policy programs that form the backbone of the welfare through work system, such as labor market policy, unemployment benefits, the minimum wage, social assistance, and gender equality policy; (ii) the involvement of major social actors, notably business organizations and, to a lesser extent, labor unions, exploring how they understand and define their interests; and (iii) the dynamics of partisan competition, which induces strategic adaptation by political parties through ideational renewal and policy repositioning.

More concretely, chapter 3 argues that the precedence given to statist, productivist, and cooperatist concerns in conservative circles influenced the genesis of welfare through work. The conservative blending of the three concerns resulted from the polarized partisan competition of the 1950s during which the Left posed a significant threat to conservative rule. The same threat also existed at the industrial level and by the early 1960s resulted in the formation of the social contract epitomized by employment protection as the cornerstone of a cross-class coalition. Whereas employment protection at the firm level and employment policy at the government level were mutually reinforcing, social safety nets to supplement full employment were not developed. Conservative denunciation of social rights precluded the creation of extensive social safety nets in Japan, and the level of the minimum wage, unemployment benefits, and social assistance have all remained low. It was this political dynamics that shaped the combination of strong employment protection for regular (male) workers and weak social safety nets for those without regular employment, which is the essence of welfare through work.

I also examine a brief period of welfare expansion during which the polarized party system was phased out as a result of both the LDP's declining popularity and the increased presence of centrist parties. This new party dynamics of the 1970s prompted the LDP to increase social spending, but a conservative backlash was not long in coming. Conservatives replaced productivism with neoliberalism, and pursued welfare retrenchment and administrative reform in the 1980s. Urban salaried workers were still well disposed toward cooperatism at the time, so they accepted the LDP's neoliberal policy: they insisted that their jobs be protected but preferred a small government with a limited tax burden.

Chapter 4 analyzes how the welfare through work system has been transformed since the 1990s. In examining the major labor market reforms during this period, I draw attention to the limits of welfare through work as a social protection system that became evident by the 2000s. This chapter also critically examines the development of gender equality policy and shows that progress was insufficient to counteract the effects of labor market flexibilization and avoid further stratification among women. I contend that this was not simply due to the inability of the welfare through work system to deal with new social risks that have emerged in a globalizing market economy. Rather, the policy framework of welfare through work has created these risks.

Why did the welfare through work system became dysfunctional? Chapter 5 examines the new policy demands made by business organizations and chapter 6 analyzes the political process through which those demands were translated into policy programs. By means of in-depth empirical research, chapter 5 reveals how employer preferences with respect to labor market reforms evolved in the new economic environment shaped by prolonged recession and globalization since the 1990s. My review of documents issued by major business organizations shows that Japanese employers have sought to abolish regulations viewed as obstacles to greater flexibility in the labor market, except in the case of employment protection for regular male workers. I argue that this was partly because employment protection was a token symbol of the postwar political settlement and partly because employment protection was useful to employers to be invoked to justify the creation of further flexibilities in other areas. Through this analysis of employer preferences, I conclude that the influence of cooperatism steadily declined throughout the 1990s.

Chapter 6 turns to political processes, exploring how neoliberalism gained political currency in Japan. Labor market reform to ensure greater flexibility was initiated by employers, but it was the new pattern of partisan competition that allowed neoliberal reform to appear on the political agenda. The split and consequent fall of the LDP from power in 1993 led to a new era of party politics. Instead of leading the alternative to the LDP, the political presence of the Japan Socialist Party waned, leaving a sizeable political space that was ripe for the taking by new political forces. Neoliberal reformers, many formerly from the LDP, moved in to dominate this new space, and this, in turn, prodded the LDP to enhance its own neoliberal stance. In addition to administrative reform and welfare retrenchment, neoliberal labor market reform also made it onto the public agenda because by then employers had abandoned the ideology of cooperatism. The creation of the deregulation panels and the Council on Economic and Fiscal Policy hastened the reform process. Ultimately, neoliberal labor market reform was not comprehensively implemented as the DPJ and labor unions succeeded in rolling back some of the more excessive deregulation. I conduct case studies of nine labor laws to identify the political conditions under which neoliberal reform was carried out.

Chapter 7 discusses what changes the election of the DPJ government in 2009 brought to the welfare through work system, which had already become dysfunctional by then. I place the DPJ's electoral victory in historical context, contending that it should be understood as a contemporary manifestation of the "double movement" advanced by Karl Polanyi (1944). A reaction against neoliberalism began to develop under LDP rule around 2005, but the DPJ accelerated the trend with its democratic mandate. Although it initially appeared that the DPJ might attempt to revive and redefine productivism and cooperatism, the party has been confronted with a political context of partisan dynamics that has not been conducive to implementing reform. By assessing the policy changes that the DPJ introduced in its first two years of governance, I show that it succeeded in strengthening the social safety net to a certain extent but failed to effectively strengthen labor market regulation.

I conclude with a summary of the political process through which welfare through work was undermined and "policy drift" took place. Then, I elaborate on my discussion of ideational factors, looking at the visions and values of political actors, the preference formation of social actors, discourse, as well as at the interaction between these conceptual elements. I also discuss how the dynamics of partisan competition determines which ideas are rewarding with respect to alliance formation and vote seeking. This book show that the interplay of ideas and partisan competition explains why Japan developed the welfare through work system and why this system became dysfunctional in recent years, and discuss the kind of political process that might enable Japan's social protection system to be reformed.

1

Welfare through Work and the Gendered Dual System

Employment protection is the core of the social protection system in Japan. This is a simple enough claim, but one that requires theoretical justification and situation in a comparative framework. This chapter discusses the basic traits of the Japanese social protection system from a comparative perspective and demonstrates that it can be characterized as a system of "welfare through work," where employment maintenance policies functionally substitute for income maintenance policies. While the government's social spending has generally been low by international standards and redistribution through taxes and social contributions has played only a marginal role in social protection, high employment rates for all categories of workers have served to reduce inequality.

My concept of welfare through work not only serves to highlight the characteristics of Japan's social protection system but also takes us a step further in the investigation of the mechanisms that link work and welfare. Although it is generally thought that strong employment protection reduces employment, in the past Japan's welfare through work system enabled high employment rates to be maintained despite the existence of robust employment protection mechanisms. I argue that a "gendered dual system" has provided a high degree of labor market flexibility, and that this was the key to the unusual coexistence of strong employment protection and high employment rates. Male regular workers in large firms benefited from strong employment protection, but in exchange they relinquished control over their jobs, consequently suffering the imposition of long working hours and frequent relocations. On the contrary, women assumed the role of primary caregiver while providing cheap and flexible labor as part-timer workers, thereby playing a critical role in sustaining strong employment protection for the male regular workers. The trade-off between strong employment protection and the existence of sufficient flexibilities embedded in the labor market sustained by the gendered division of labor enabled welfare through work to function as a social protection system at least until the 1980s.

The Typology of Work and Welfare

Social protection systems aim to protect individuals who experience poverty, unemployment, illness, injury, disability, and infirmity. There are many ways to achieve these aims and multiple actors—such as the state, communities, family, voluntary associations, and for-profit firms—engage in the process. Because it is primarily the role of the welfare state to redistribute resources for social protection, scholars have paid close attention to income maintenance programs in order to understand the different types of social protection system. It is certainly true that income maintenance is a core policy of welfare states, but labor markets also play a critical role in allocating individuals with jobs and income. Further, though the instruments for income maintenance are essentially ex post social policies, which aim to correct undesirable market outcomes, the instruments for employment maintenance consist of ex ante measures, which prevent poverty caused by unemployment. Labor markets are, in turn, regulated by the state. Therefore, the state's role as a welfare provider and as a regulator of the labor market needs to be systematically analyzed in order to fully understand its role in managing social protection systems.

In this book, I propose that we add the axis of employment maintenance when classifying welfare states because this is justified in theoretical terms and, empirically, this will help us comprehend the specific characteristics of Japan's social protection system.

TABLE 1.1

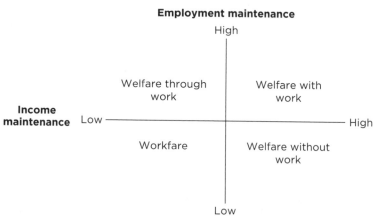

By adding the axis of employment maintenance to the axis of income maintenance, the two axes conceptually demarcate four categories of work and welfare (Table 1.1). A combination of high income maintenance and high employment maintenance can be characterized as "welfare with work," whereas a mix of low income maintenance and low employment maintenance can be regarded as a case of "workfare." A country that embraces high income maintenance but low employment maintenance can be classified as "welfare without work." In contrast, the classification of "welfare through work" consists of low income maintenance and high employment maintenance.

The data substantiate this conceptual categorization. Table 1.1 summarizes different patterns of unemployment and employment in the major Organization for Economic Co-operation and Development (OECD) countries and Figure 1.1 demonstrates national positions along the two axes of income maintenance and employment maintenance during the 1990s. Because most countries have since experienced welfare and labor market reform, the snapshot picture of the 1990s provides a baseline from which we can identify change and transformation in subsequent years. As a measurement of the degree of income maintenance, I use the share of public social expenditure per GDP (gross domestic product), as per the standard

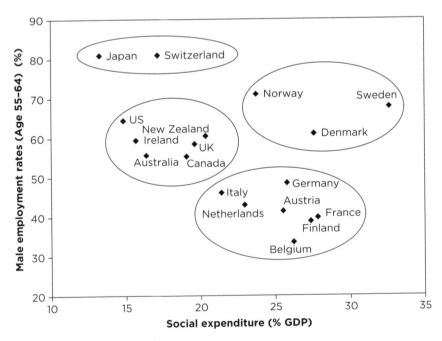

Figure 1.1. Mapping countries based on typology of work and welfare (1990s)
Source: OECD.Stat (http://stats.oecd.org).

practice.[1] I then use the employment rates of male workers ages 55–64 as an index of employment maintenance because the functional equivalence of income maintenance and employment maintenance was most prominent among this category of workers.

Figure 1.1 shows that four clusters of countries clearly emerge, which correspond to the conceptualized categories presented in Table 1.1. Sweden, Norway, and Denmark fit the welfare with work model, having high levels of social spending and high levels of employment. Six Continental European countries plus Finland exemplify the welfare without work model. Although levels of social expenditures are equally high in both models, employment rates are comparatively low in the latter one. The Anglo-American countries—United States, United Kingdom, Australia, New Zealand, and Ireland—can be categorized according to the workfare model, as they do not spend as much on welfare programs and maintain mid-level employment rate levels. Employment rates in these countries are higher than those of welfare without work countries, yet somewhat lower than in welfare with work countries. Japan and Switzerland stand apart in terms of employment maintenance, thus constituting a welfare through work regime. In this model, employment maintenance functionally substitutes for income maintenance, which stands in sharp contrast to welfare without work where generous income maintenance programs functionally substitute for the lack of employment maintenance in the labor market.

The introduction of the employment maintenance axis allows us to coherently situate Japan with respect to the Continental European countries. Figure 1.1 shows that employment maintenance also brings some of the key features of the Japanese social protection system into sharp relief.[2] In fact, the employment rates for Japanese male workers are higher in all age categories. Among male workers in their prime (25–54 years old), employment rates are 97.7% in Japan, 93.1% in Germany, 95.2% in France, and 89.7% in Italy. Cross-national differences increase for male workers ages 55 to 64 or older to 84.9%, 55.0%, 42.3%, and 44.0%, respectively. Moreover, Japan's high employment rates are most evident for elderly workers over the age of 65. Employment rates of male workers between the ages 65 and 69 are 52.9%, 7.3%, 3.3%, and 10.8%, respectively, in the countries mentioned above. The only country comparable to Japan is Sweden, which has even higher employment rates among elderly male workers at 54.5%.[3] High employment rates in Japan signify that Japan does not implement public policies to induce early retirement and that there are mechanisms that provide elderly workers with incentives to stay in the labor market.

Other indexes support the characterization of Japan as an example of welfare thorough work system (see Table 1.2). The country's average unemployment rate was 1.3% in the 1960s, 1.7% in the 1970s, 2.5% in the 1980s, and 3.1% in the 1990s.[4] Due to the prolonged economic downturn in the 1990s and early 2000s, the unemployment rate reached a record high level

TABLE 1.2
Employment performance (1990s)

	Unemployment		Male employment rates (55–64)	Female employment rates (25–54)	Youth unemployment rates (15–24)
	Standardized	Long-term			
Welfare with work					
Denmark	6.9	30.1	61.0	77.8	10.6
Norway	5.2	18.6	42.9	77.9	11.9
Sweden	7.2	23.3	67.7	82.7	16.5
Average	**6.4**	**24.0**	**57.2**	**79.5**	**13.0**
Welfare without work					
Austria	4.1	26.6	41.4	70.7	5.4
Belgium	8.5	60.8	33.5	60.3	18.8
Finland	11.9	28.4	38.8	76.8	24.8
France	10.6	39.2	39.8	67.1	24.4
Germany	7.6	44.7	48.5	66.4	7.7
Netherlands	5.4	47.8	42.9	60.7	9.9
Italy	10.3	63.2	46.1	47.5	31.4
Average	**8.5**	**46.4**	**41.7**	**63.7**	**18.2**
Workfare					
Australia	8.6	30.1	55.6	63.8	16.1
Ireland	12.1	60.4	59.4	48.3	18.6
United Kingdom	8.0	37.1	58.4	69.9	14.0
United States	5.8	8.9	64.4	71.9	12.0
Canada	9.6	13.9	55.3	69.9	15.4
New Zealand	7.9	24.9	60.5	67.1	14.9
Average	**8.6**	**28.6**	**58.9**	**65.2**	**15.2**
Welfare through work					
Japan	3.1	18.8	80.9	63.7	6.0
Switzerland	3.4	26.5	81.0	72.7	5.1
Average	**3.2**	**22.6**	**80.9**	**68.2**	**5.6**

Source: OECD.Stat (http://stats.oecd.org).

of 5.4% in 2002, with the average rate 4.9% between 2000 and 2005.[5] These numbers are quite high in view of Japan's performance in the past and surpassed the 4.0% figure of the United States, 2.9% of the Netherlands, 2.7% of Switzerland, and 3.4% of Norway (2000). Nevertheless, Japan's unemployment rates remain strikingly low by international comparison. The average rate in the 25 OECD countries is 6.8% and that of the OECD European countries is 9.2%. More important, Japan's figures diverge significantly from those of the welfare without work model. The average unemployment rate in

Belgium, France, Germany, and Italy was 10.1% in the 1990s and 8.3% in from 2000 through 2008.[6] The fact that persistent economic stagnation in Japan throughout the 1990s and early 2000s only pushed up unemployment rates to 5.4% is remarkable and suggests the existence of mechanisms preventing easy termination of employment of redundant workers and of mechanisms for swiftly creating new jobs.

The employment patterns of Japanese women also mark Japan as a different type. Japanese female labor force participation rates are low during the prime age brackets but are comparatively high for women ages 55–59 and even more so for women ages 60–64. Japanese women over 60 participate in the labor force to the same degree as their counterparts in the United States and Norway, and considerably more than in Italy, Germany, France, Belgium, and Austria. Similarly to Japanese men, Japanese middle-age and elderly female workers stay in the labor market longer than their counterparts in other countries.[7]

Employment Performance and Labor Market Policy

The main feature of Japan's social protection system, welfare through work, can be situated in a comparative context by adding the axis of employment maintenance. The question is how Japan has managed to keep high levels of employment maintenance. Because the axis of employment maintenance relates to ex ante measures as opposed to ex post income maintenance programs, the role of the state is indirect. Numerous factors affect employment rates, including levels of economic growth and public investment. Bearing in mind that efforts by the state to maintain employment do not necessarily have the desired results, it is nonetheless useful to focus on labor market policy as this area of policy reveals the extent of the state's efforts to create and maintain employment. Labor market policy affects the willingness of employers to retain redundant labor in the workforce as well as that of workers to remain in the labor market. Just as welfare states create new stratifications, so does labor market policy by influencing who is more likely to be (un)employed, rather than how many people will be (un)employed (Esping-Andersen and Regini 2000). As unemployment is one of the most significant factors in the generation of income inequality and poverty, the distributional consequences of labor market policy deserve serious attention.

Table 1.3 shows four components of labor market policy measured by the OECD: (1) protection of permanent workers against dismissal; (2) regulation of temporary employment; (3) safety nets for the unemployed; and (4) active labor market programs.

Protection against dismissal covers regular procedural inconvenience, notice, and severance pay for no-fault individual dismissals, and regulates the difficulty of enforcing dismissals. This protection is provided only to regular

TABLE 1.3
Major labor market policies

	Protection against dismissal[a]	Regulation of temporary employment[b]		Unemployment benefits[c]	Public expenditure on labor market programs (% GDP, 2005)[d]	
	2003	Late 1980s	2003	2003	Active measures	Passive measures
Welfare with work						
Denmark	1.5	3.1	1.4	50	1.74	2.51
Norway	2.3	3.5	2.9	34	0.75	0.87
Sweden	2.9	4.1	1.6	24	1.32	1.20
Average	**2.3**	**3.6**	**2.0**	**36.0**	**1.27**	**1.53**
Welfare without work						
Austria	2.4	1.5	1.5	32	0.62	1.51
Belgium	1.7	4.6	2.6	42	1.08	2.37
Finland	2.2	1.9	1.9	36	0.89	1.90
France	2.5	3.1	3.6	39	0.90	1.62
Germany	2.7	3.8	1.8	29	0.97	2.35
Netherlands	3.1	2.4	1.2	53	1.33	2.02
Italy	1.8	5.4	2.1	34	0.54	0.82
Average	**2.3**	**2.8**	**2.2**	**37.9**	**0.90**	**1.80**
Workfare						
Australia	1.5	0.9	0.9	22	0.45	0.61
Ireland	1.6	0.3	0.6	38	0.63	0.83
United Kingdom	1.1	0.3	0.4	16	0.32	0.19
United States	0.2	0.3	0.3	14	0.13	0.24
Canada	1.3	0.3	0.3	15	0.32	0.62
New Zealand	1.7	–	1.3	28	0.39	0.87
Average	**1.2**	**0.4**	**0.6**	**22.2**	**0.37**	**0.56**
Welfare through work						
Japan	2.4	1.8	1.3	8	0.25	0.43
Switzerland	1.2	1.1	1.1	33	0.76	0.93
Average	**1.8**	**1.5**	**1.2**	**20.5**	**0.51**	**0.68**

Sources: (a) indicates the overall strictness of protection against dismissal for regular workers (OECD 2004, table 2.A.2.1.); (b) indicates overall strictness of regulation of temporary employment (OECD 2004, table 2.A2.2.); (c) is measured by gross replacement rates of previous wages offered by unemployment insurance (OECD 2004); (d) OECD. Stat (http://stats.oecd.org).

workers under contracts of indefinite length or so-called permanent employees. For regulation with respect to non-regular workers, I use the overall strictness of regulation of temporary employment including regulation of fixed-term contracts and temporary work agencies. The third indicator is measured by gross replacement rates of previous wages offered by unemployment insurance and public expenditure on passive measures in labor market programs per GDP. These three indices partially indicate the flexibility of external labor markets and the relative ease of firing workers. Lastly, public expenditures on active labor market policies per GDP indicate the government's commitment to worker employability.

Wage regulation by means of a minimum wage and collective bargaining also affects employment rates and the degree of market segmentation. A high level of minimum wage in relation to the average wage of full-time workers constricts wage disparities among low- to middle-income workers, but creates a barrier obstructing low-skill workers from entering the labor market. Wage bargaining coverage includes not only the scope of collective bargaining between unions and employers but also legal extensions of such agreements by the government. This indicator shows the extent to which market segmentation is politically suppressed or rectified (see Table 4.2 on wage regulation).

The four types of welfare-labor market models form distinct clusters, but the main dividing line in terms of labor market policy seems to exist between the workfare model and the remaining models. The workfare model is typified by a low level of regulation with respect to both regular and temporary workers. The social safety net for the unemployed is not particularly well developed and active labor market policies are not regular policy options, except in Ireland. In contrast, the differences between the welfare with work model and the welfare without work model are not immediately evident. This observation is consistent with Scharpf and Schmidt's claim that welfare state model consists of "the extent to which welfare goals are pursued through the regulation of labor markets and employment relations or through the 'formal welfare state' of publicly financed transfers and services, and the extent to which 'caring' services are expected to be provided informally in the family or through professional services" (2000, 7). They argue that the first axis divides the Anglo-Saxon countries from Continental Europe and the Nordic countries, whereas the second differentiates Continental Europe from the Nordic and Anglo-Saxon countries.

However, a closer look at labor market policy reveals that there is also variation within models. In each regime, it is relatively easy to spot outliers, as already stressed by area specialists. For example, among the welfare with work countries, Denmark stands out in terms of the low degree of protection provided against dismissals and generous benefit levels for the unemployed. This stands in stark contrast to the Swedish welfare state, which offers a high degree of protection against dismissals and strong emphasis on active labor market policies as opposed to passive measures targeting the unemployed (Björklund 2000). Similarly, the Netherlands differs from other welfare without work countries in that it places far fewer restrictions on temporary employment. In addition, Italy stands out in terms of its weak unemployment insurance system and high level of minimum wage (Rhodes 1997). Among the workfare countries, Australia and New Zealand form a distinct cluster, characterized by comparatively higher regulation of labor markets and the strong role played by state arbitration courts in setting wages (Castles and

Mitchell 1993). Statutory minimum wages do not exist in Austria, Germany, or the Scandinavian countries where the high coverage rates of collectively agreed minimum wages set the wage floors. Indeed, the complexities of the effects of labor market policy urge us to broaden our perspective and explore how specific policies interact with other policies in producing certain market outcomes. In the following, I examine the Japanese case in more detail in order to identify the mechanisms used to achieve welfare through work.

Japan

The Japanese level of employment protection for regular workers is high by international standards. In terms of "Overall Strictness of Protection against Dismissals," Japan ranked fifth among the 18 OECD countries, scoring 2.4 in 2003, after the Netherlands (3.1), Sweden (2.9), Germany (2.7), France (2.5), and in sharp contrast to the United States (0.2) and the United Kingdom (1.1), which do not provide employment protection. This score is based on three factors: (i) difficulty of dismissal, (ii) regular procedural inconveniences, and (iii) notice and severance pay for no-fault individual dismissals. Japan ranked fourth in terms of the "Difficulty of Dismissal," following Sweden (4.0), Austria (3.8), and Norway (3.8).[8]

In terms of labor market programs, Japan spends almost the least among the major OECD countries. As of 2005, Japan spent the equivalent of 0.43% of its GDP on passive measures and 0.25% on active measures. The most conspicuous features of Japan's active measures in the labor market are its emphasis on employment maintenance and the underdevelopment of vocational training. The active measures included in the OECD statistics comprise a wide range of policies that aim to activate the unemployed or inactive workforce, such as public employment services and administration, labor market training, youth measures, subsidized employment, and services for the disabled. Among these, the share of "subsidized employment" has generally been quite large in Japan, whereas the share of "labor market training" has been negligible. From a comparative perspective, Belgium, Finland, and Japan are heavy spenders on subsidized employment programs, while the United States, the United Kingdom, and Canada spend less on subsidized employment but stress training programs. Japan's aversion to vocational training is demonstrated by its spending in this area: only 0.03% of GDP in 1995. In contrast, this figure was, 0.55% in Sweden, 0.69% in Denmark, 0.45% in Germany, 0.07% in the United States, and 0.09% in the United Kingdom.[9]

The other important aspect of unemployment policy is income support for the unemployed. Japan's gross unemployment benefit replacement rates are even lower than those in the United States and the United Kingdom (J. Martin 1996). Until 2003, monthly unemployment benefits in Japan were 60–80% of previous monthly earnings, depending on the income strata.[10] Net replacement rates depend on family type, income level, and duration of unemployment. The OECD data indicate that Japan's overall net replacement rates in the initial phase of unemployment are not low when viewed internationally. Rather, the striking feature of Japan's unemployment insurance is its short duration. The maximum length of provision was previously 300 days and only those taking a public vocational training course are entitled to continuously receive benefits until the end of the course.[11] Continental European countries usually provide unemployment benefits for the unemployed for over 60 months. If we take into consideration unemployment benefits for long-term unemployment, which are measured as the gross unemployment benefit replacement rate, in 2003 Japan's level is quite low at 8%, compared to 14% in the United States, 16% in the United Kingdom, 29% in Germany, and 39% in France.[12] Even compared to the workfare model, Japan's level appears low. Japan's weak social safety net for the long-term unemployed suggests that once caught in a situation of long-term unemployment, the individuals concerned are entirely and solely responsible for improving their circumstances.[13]

Combining Protection and Performance: The Gendered Dual System

Japan's comparatively high level of employment protection may have contributed to its high level of employment maintenance. However, other countries having the same levels of protection do not always achieve similarly high levels of employment maintenance. In fact, labor economists argue that high levels of employment protection actually reduce the level of employment because firms tend to recruit fewer regular workers than necessary during economic booms so that they can adjust to recessions without having to dismiss them (Lindbeck and Snower 1988, 2002; Saint-Paul 1996, 2000). This line of reasoning appears to be at odds with the reality of Japan's high employment rates coexisting with stringent regulation against dismissal. What explains this unusual combination?

Limited Coverage of Employment Protection

One way to resolve this enigma is to note that the high level of employment protection is applied to a rather limited range of workers. Japan's regulations against dismissal were formulated not by the legislature or the executive but by the judiciary (Foote 1996). This case law created a division between workers who benefit from employment protection and those who do not.

The Japanese civil code guarantees employers the liberty to terminate employment (Art. 627), but the courts have adopted the "doctrine of abuse of the right of dismissal" (*kaiko ken ranyō hōri*, or the "doctrine of abusive dismissal"), which precludes employers from dismissing their employees without objectively rational reasons. Moreover, with respect to dismissal for economic reasons, the courts have established the following requirements (*seiri kaiko no 4 yōken*): (1) that it is necessary to reduce the number of employees, (2) that the employers do their best to avoid implementing dismissals, (3) that the criteria and procedures for selecting the dismissed workers are fair, and (4) that the employers give appropriate explanations to, and hold meetings with, unions or workers. If the courts judge that an employer has abused the right to dismiss, the dismissal becomes ineffective and the dismissed worker is allowed to return to the workplace. In most countries, the courts simply order financial compensation for damages to dismissed workers, and the fact that Japanese courts are able to invalidate dismissals is seen as extremely problematic by corporations. Taken together, the four requirements make dismissal very costly and inconvenient for employers.

Numerous precedents have contributed to the gradual process of forming Japan's employment protection legislation into case law. In the early 1950s, the Tokyo District Court pioneered the formation of the abusive dismissal doctrine, which was then applied by other district courts. In 1975, the Supreme Court recognized the precedents of the district courts and officially adopted the doctrine.[14] Widespread economic adjustments after the oil crisis necessitated protective measures for workers and the courts responded to the social needs of the time. Based on the doctrine of abusive dismissal, the four requirements for dismissal for economic reasons had taken shape based on several precedents in the district courts in the late 1970s and early 1980s. The four requirements are not necessarily categorically applied to all cases of dismissal for economic reasons and the Supreme Court has not stipulated any specific standards for application. Indeed, the courts tend to only apply some of the four requirements in many cases.[15] Notwithstanding, the four requirements are often referred to in cases of dismissal for economic reasons, thereby constraining employers' management strategy. Unlike US employers who enjoy the right of "employment-at-will," Japanese employers are inhibited from utilizing downsizing as a proactive measure to improve competitiveness. Until a firm actually begins to fail, employers have an obligation to retain employees, and these binding institutions underpin Japan's high level of employment maintenance.

One way to reconcile Japan's high level of employment protection legislation with high employment rates is to consider that the scope of judicial protection is limited. Abundant evidence supports this hypothesis. Workers in small and medium-size firms, elderly workers, and non-regular workers are, in one way or another, excluded from the system of judicial protection. Whereas the courts actively engage in protecting jobs for male workers in their prime, they have regarded the dismissal of elderly workers (after 55 or even 53 years old) as rational and fair (Mori 2001). Likewise, the four requirements the firms must meet in order to implement dismissals for economic reasons are generally interpreted to include, as a prerequisite, the termination of contracts with non-regular workers. When the courts determine that part-time workers or fixed-term workers have worked under de facto contracts of indefinite length, these workers are granted the same legal protection as regular workers. Otherwise, Japan's stringent employment protection legislation actually encourages the dismissal of elderly workers and non-regular workers.

The degree to which courts protect workers in small and medium-size firms is not clear. Large firms tend to respect labor laws and administrative guidance, because violation damages their reputation and, in turn, their recruitment strategies. In contrast, employers in small firms, lacking ready access to sophisticated legal advice, are often simply not aware of legal codes. Indeed, more lawsuits regarding dismissals are filed against small- and medium-size firms than against large firms. However, without union support, it is difficult for individuals to seek redress for wrongful dismissal in the courts (Ōtake and Fujikawa 2001). Because unions tend to exist only in larger firms, workers in small and medium-size firms are less likely to be able to litigate. It is thus reasonable to conclude that while regular workers in small and medium-size firms are legally protected to the same extent as regular workers in large firms, the former are more likely to experience wrongful dismissal than the latter. When they have sufficient resources to file a lawsuit, they have a high chance of success; however, these resources are not available to many workers in smaller firms.[16]

Internal Labor Market Flexibility

Another way to interpret the coexistence of rigorous employment protection and high employment rates is to consider whether the burden shouldered by employers is sufficiently offset by labor market flexibilities. I argue that the flexibilities embedded in both the internal labor market and the external labor market have enabled Japanese firms to retain redundant workers while complying with strict judicial regulation against dismissals. A significant degree of labor market flexibility has thus underpinned Japan's system of welfare through work. The two dimensions of labor market flexibility are deeply intertwined, creating a duality in the labor market. This duality is highly gendered because of the prevailing male breadwinner regime.

Marino Regini (2000) classifies labor market flexibilities: (1) numerical or external flexibility, (2) functional or internal flexibility, (3) wage flexibility, and (4) temporal or working-time flexibility. Japanese employers enjoy a high degree of flexibility in all four categories. During recessions, employers first reduce or cut overtime (working-time flexibility). Then, they implement job transfers and relocations (functional flexibility). This is followed by the reductions in the salaries of top to middle management and the biannual bonuses for all employees (wage flexibility), and then by the restrictions on the recruitment as well as the dismissal of part-timers and temporary workers (external flexibility). At the last resort, they begin to encourage early retirement.

This pattern of employment adjustment had become widespread by the mid-1970s and has found legal support in the doctrine of abusive dismissal.

With regard to functional flexibility in the internal labor market, the fact that employers enjoy the right to transfer and relocate their employees at will in exchange for refraining from dismissing workers should not be underrated (Gordon 1985).[17] The freedom to relocate employees is critical for Japanese firms if they are to be able to offer employment security to costly elderly workers (Foote 1996; Mori 2001). By freely transferring workers to their subsidiaries and affiliated companies, Japanese firms are able to meet the demands of employment protection. Indeed, the four requirements for dismissal for economic reasons also regulate job transfers and relocations in order to protect employment. The courts have even concluded that employers are within their rights to dismiss workers who reject company orders pertaining to new job assignments and relocation.[18]

Conversely, regular workers are expected to accept overtime work and relocations as a price for employment protection. It is not unusual for frequent relocations to be scheduled as part of a standard career path. Such working conditions make it difficult to reconcile work and family responsibilities, thus reinforcing the dominant male breadwinner regime. In other words, the system is structurally biased toward the production of "corporate warriors." It is not that the Japanese are inherently workaholics or possess a highly developed work ethic; rather, "unlimited duties" at the behest of company directives and "total commitment" are part of the unwritten contract between employers and employees.[19] Not all workers are able or willing to make an unlimited commitment to the company. Those who must tend to their family responsibilities, mostly women, retreat from the labor market or accept part-time jobs.

External Labor Market Flexibility

Non-regular workers mainly provide external flexibility. Existing outside the framework of judicial protection, they function as shock absorbers during economic downturns, thereby sustaining the employment security of regular workers. The category of non-regular worker includes all workers other than full-time workers with open-ended contracts and covers various styles of work. They are characterized by one or more of the following features. (1) Part-time employment: their working hours are shorter than those of full-time workers. Generally, part-time workers work fewer than 35 hours a week. (2) Fixed-term contract: their employment contracts set a term limit, whereas regular workers conclude contracts for an indefinite duration, which means that they are expected to work until the mandatory retirement age. (3) Indirect employment: temporary agency workers, or dispatched workers, are employed by staffing agencies but work for client companies.

There are several varieties of non-regular workers according to different combinations of the above three features. The largest group consists of *pāto*, who comprise approximately half of non-regular workers. The term comes from part-timer (an abbreviation of *pāto taimā*), but company definitions of *pāto* do not always correspond to the definitions of part-time workers used by the government's surveys or the Part-Time Labor Law.[20] *Pāto* is a highly gendered terminology, and refers mostly to housewives working under particular employment conditions regardless of actual working hours. In 1985, 95.6% of *pāto* were women and the remained as high as 90.1% in 2005.[21] Most *pāto* work short hours—literally as part-timers—but a significant portion of them work as many hours as full-time workers, if not longer. The category of full-time *pāto* made up 13.9% of all *pāto* in 2001, and 16.8% in 2006.[22]

The second largest group of non-regular workers is that of *arubaito*, comprising approximately 20%. The term derives from the German word *arbeit* (labor). These are usually young people working part-time without taking on any substantial job responsibilities. The third largest group consists of full-time fixed-term workers, making up about 17% of the non-regular workforce.[23] Finally, the deregulation of the staffing industry both created new categories of and increased the numbers of workers dispatched by temporary agencies. In 2005, 6.5% of non-regular workers fell into this category.[24]

Figure 1.2 shows the share of non-regular workers by gender, age, and type of employment (2000). It illustrates that gender and age strongly affect the type of employment that one is likely to be offered with middle-age women mostly classified as *pāto*, and young people generally classified as *arubaito*. Dispatched workers are mostly young women, whereas entrusted workers tend to be older men.

Non-regular workers provide not only numerical flexibility but also wage flexibility, as the wage differential between regular workers and non-regular workers is substantial. Wages for *pāto* are usually determined by the local labor market and are barely higher than the minimum wage. Unlike in the case of regular workers, length of employment is scarcely taken into account when determining wage levels. *Pāto* are not guaranteed promotions or raises, even if they take on greater job responsibilities.[25] Macro-level data confirm pay inequalities between regular workers and non-regular workers. In terms of scheduled earnings per hour, a male part-time worker earns on average 55.3% of the base wage of a male regular worker and a female earns 44.5% (as of 1995). As for the earnings gap between female regular workers and female part-time workers, the latter earn on average 70.4% of the wages of the former.[26] If over-time payments and bonuses were included, the gap between regular workers and part-time workers would be much wider.

Pāto's low wage level reflects the function of the minimum wage. The ratio of the minimum wage relative to the median wage of full-time workers in 2000 was 32% in Japan, well below the figures of 59% in France, 58% in Australia, 47% in the Netherlands, 34% in the United Kingdom, and 36%

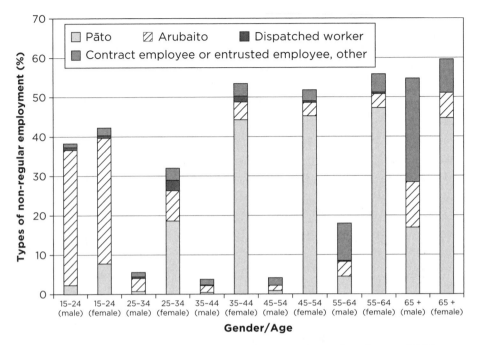

Figure 1.2. Share of non-regular workers by gender, age, and type of employment (2000) *Source:* Ministry of Internal Affairs and Communications, *Labour Force Survey* (February 2000). See http://www.stat.go.jp/data/roudou/. Each bar represents the overall share of non-regular workers within a particular age and gender group, further divided into the shares of each type of non-regular employment for that group.

in the United States (see Table 4.2). The low level of the minimum wage in conjunction with the low coverage of collective bargaining means that Japan does not effectively regulate the low wage structure, which provides wage flexibility in the external labor market.

Gender and the Dual Labor Market

Ample flexibility in both the internal and external labor markets has been key to Japan's high employment maintenance. Japanese employers essentially have a free hand in job transfers and relocations, as well as with respect to the use of non-regular workers, which counterbalances the rigidity of employment protection. These two areas of flexibilities intertwine and create what I call a "gendered dual system."

The internal and external flexibilities embedded in the Japanese labor market are highly gendered in the sense that the sexual division of labor allows the coexistence of the two types of flexibility. The male breadwinner regime predicated on the roles of male breadwinner and female caregiver is not in itself peculiar to Japan and can be found in other affluent democracies, at least until a certain point in postwar period (Crompton 1999; J. Lewis 1993; Orloff 1993; Sainsbury 1996, 1999). What separates Japan from other male breadwinner regimes is the way in which internal and external flexibilities intertwine in a gendered fashion. In a typical case of such a regime, male workers receive the level of family wages necessary to support their families. It is often pointed out that high family wages, in turn, become an obstacle preventing women from work, as most women lack sufficient skills to qualify for such high wages. Even though Japan's female employment rates are relatively high overall, it lags far behind in terms of wage levels. For example, Japan's Economic Planning Agency estimated in the 1990s that female regular workers earn 63.5% of the wages of male workers in Japan, which is well below the corresponding levels of 80.8% in France, 75.5% in the United States, and 74.2 % in Germany.[27]

Blau and Kahn (1995) present different figures, but indicate a similar trend. According to their calculations, Japanese female workers earn approximately half the wages of male workers, whereas female/male hourly pay ratios are about 65–75% in the United States, the United Kingdom, Ireland, and Germany, and 80–90% in France, Denmark, Australia, New Zealand, and the Scandinavian countries. Data for Italy are not calculated by the same method, yet their research using micro-data files shows that Italian women earn 82.3% of male earnings, followed by 77.2% for Swedish women, based on gender earnings ratios adjusted for hours. Moreover, Japan is the only country covered in their research that demonstrated a downward trend in female pay rates relative to those of men since the mid-1970s (Blau and Kahn 1995). Several variables, such as age, education, sector, firm size, and length of work, need to be controlled for in order to produce reliable figures. However, taken together, these statistics bring the internationally low wages of Japanese female workers into sharp relief.[28]

If these figures fairly portray the reality of the working conditions of Japanese female workers, this suggests that the Japanese version of the male breadwinner model is distinctive, where employment rates for women are high and their wages are low. This presents a sharp contrast, for instance, to the Italian version of the male breadwinner model, which features low female employment rates but highly equitable income distribution between the two sexes. This can be attributed to the fact that in Japan non-regular employment has mostly been taken up by women as a form of *pāto*. The low wages of non-regular workers become socially invisible and acceptable when the gender division of labor constitutes a social norm. High economic growth in the 1950s and 1960s greatly diminished the number of male non-regular workers such as temporaries (*rinjikō* or *kikankō*). Instead, it has been female *pāto* that have provided flexibility in the labor market since the mid-1970s.[29] The fact that *pāto* have predominantly been housewives conceals or, more precisely, has concealed until recently, the precarious circumstances of non-regular workers.

As external flexibility fortifies the gendered division of labor, so does internal flexibility. As already discussed, the freedom of employers to relocate employees makes it difficult for male workers to assume family responsibilities. In addition, the Japanese style of meritocracy also reinforces the total commitment of workers to corporations, thereby propagating the gendered division of labor. Contrary to conventional wisdom, which often assumes that seniority-based wages are ubiquitous in Japan, merit-based wages also played a vital role and, more important, individual merit ratings, or personnel assessments (*satei*), have been prevalent.[30] As of 1976, 72% of all types of firms, and 98% of firms employing more than 5,000, had introduced personnel assessment (Kumazawa 1997, 30).[31] Japanese wages for regular workers are not only based on the features of the job being performed by an employee but are also based on the characteristics of the employee, including objective criteria such as age, length of employment, and measurable skills or results, as well as subjective judgments on personal traits.[32] Insofar as subjective judgments on personality and attitude affect the wage level awarded to a worker, individual merit ratings induce workers to work longer, invest in skill formation even in their free time, and prioritize company obligations over their private life and family caregiving responsibilities.[33]

It is often argued that Japanese regular employees consider themselves to be members of their company rather than mere workers (Dore 1973; Gordon 1985, 410). The concept of membership helps explain sharp definitions in status differentials. Full members—regular male workers—benefit from employment security, but they relinquish control over their jobs. Consequently, their wages are not based on jobs they accomplish but on the level of commitments they show. In contrast, non-members, that is non-regular workers, are assigned clearly defined jobs, but denied the most important perk of employment security. Female regular workers are relegated to the rank of junior members because the personnel assessments function to their disadvantage. Gender bias can easily be slipped into assessments of an individual's commitment and endeavor.

There are many ways to achieve a high level of employment. Countries classified as operating systems of welfare with work such as Sweden, Norway, and Denmark, maintain high employment levels by expansion of the social service sector. In contrast, wage flexibility in countries classified as employing workfare systems contributes to job creation. In Japan, stringent employment protection has ensured employment security for regular workers, while also facilitating increases in functional flexibility in the internal labor market and employment and wage flexibility in the external labor market. In the system of welfare through work, the gendered dual system has provided a peculiar combination of labor market flexibilities, thereby ensuring that the high level of employment protection has not resulted in reductions of employment rates.

The limitations of this mechanism of employment maintenance became clear once the job creation capacity of the Japanese economy began to drastically decline after 1998. Gone are the times when part-time jobs were taken by housewives needing extra income to support their families. It is now increasingly the case that prime age male workers, not to mention the younger generation, can find only non-regular work. Economic stagnation and highly volatile market conditions since the late 1990s have meant that a disproportionate amount of the cost of employment adjustment has been borne by those who have been denied full membership. Yet, it is a mistake to embrace the view that pits full members (or insiders) against junior and non-members (or outsiders). Such view, often called the insider-outsider theory, only focuses on the unequal distribution of employment protection and hence overlooks the significant functional flexibility in the internal labor market as manifested, for example, in the regular employees' lack of control over job assignments and personnel assessments, which, in turn, fosters their "total commitment." These trade-offs inherent to employment protection reinforce the gendered division of labor, as they cannot be reconciled with family responsibilities. Therefore, welfare through work needs to be analyzed as a system that is sustained by a gendered dual system. The conjunction of internal and external flexibilities in the labor market, thus, perpetuates the male breadwinner regime in Japan.

Situating Japan's Social Protection System in Comparative Perspective

This chapter provides a brief theoretical discussion illustrating how my concept of welfare through work accurately characterizes Japan's social protection system by situating it in the welfare states literature. In so doing, I demonstrate the limitations and possibilities of "regime theory," thereby emphasizing the role of ideas and partisan dynamics.

Liberal, Conservative, or Hybrid?

Gøsta Esping-Andersen's (1990) seminal work categorizing welfare regimes provides an effective theoretical tool for the study of welfare states. Despite evident shortcomings in his concepts and methods, his typology has been repeatedly employed in the literature on welfare states. Esping-Andersen claims that welfare states can be categorized into three distinct kinds of welfare regime, which are underpinned by varying degrees of decommodification and modes of stratification. Decommodification takes place when a welfare state provides a service as a matter of right and thus a person is able to "maintain a livelihood without reliance on the market" (Esping-Andersen 1990, 22). Liberal regimes, which are often found in Anglo-American countries, tend to concentrate on needs-based social assistance and employ market mechanisms in underwriting risks. This results in minimization of the effects of decommodification and the creation of a dualism between welfare recipients and the working majority. In contrast, comprehensive risk coverage, generous benefit levels, and egalitarianism characterize social democratic welfare regimes. Scandinavia countries exhibit many of these traits, thereby achieving high levels of decommodification and low levels of stratification. The countries of Continental Europe are often labeled as corporatist, conservative, or Christian democratic regimes, characterized by status-segmented social insurance systems and familialism.[1] The provision of social rights is rarely contested, but status differences are preserved through the edifices of the welfare state.

Scholars of the Japanese welfare state view Japan as a hybrid of conservative and liberal regimes.[2] In fact, Japan embraces the traits of both regimes in its social protection system. Japan has developed a social insurance system that is segmented along occupational lines and largely financed by wage-based contributions, similarly to other conservative countries such as Germany, France, Austria, Belgium, and Italy. This is not surprising given the fact that the prewar Japanese government originally adopted a Prussian-style social policy. Japan also exhibits another key feature of the conservative regime, clearly embodying the ideology of familialism. While male breadwinners earn family wages, the underdevelopment of social services leads to low female employment rates and low fertility rates. Ōsawa Mari (2007) argues that Japan is the definitive example of the male breadwinner model.

The Japanese system, however, also incorporates liberal elements. Indeed, the country's low social spending per capita and per GDP have led many scholars to conclude that the Japanese welfare state is residual in character.[3] According to OECD (Organization for Economic Co-operation and Development) statistics, as of 1995 Japan used 13.9% of its GDP for social expenditure, which is markedly lower than 15.4% in the United States, 20.4% in the United Kingdom, 19.8% in Italy, 26.6% in Germany, 28.3% in France, and 32.5% in Sweden. Moreover, social assistance is strictly means-tested and stigmatizing. Transfer benefit levels—for pensions, sickness, disability, unemployment, and family allowance—are also low.[4]

This "service-lean and transfer-lean" feature of the Japanese welfare state makes Japan more liberal than the "transfer-heavy and service-lean" conservative welfare states. However, the crude level of expenditures per se does not signify the basic logic of the welfare regime. The principal analytical axis of Esping-Andersen's three typologies of welfare capitalism is the public-private mix. According to him, it is not the benefit levels of social programs but the relatively large share of private pensions that should give Japan residual attributes. However, Japan differs from liberal regimes in several important respects.

First, as Esping-Andersen points out, conservative attributes will be strengthened as the corporatist social insurance system matures and the population ages. In fact, there is already a general and steady decline in the share of private pensions in relation to public pensions in Japan.[5] Second, the low share of private sphere expenditure in Japan makes the label of liberal welfare regime problematic. For example, the share of gross public social expenditure in the total social expenditure is 94%; this is similar to most European countries, which vary from 91% (Sweden) to 96% (Norway, Denmark). Such a level is in stark contrast to the liberal welfare regimes: 64% in the United

States, 80% in Australia, 81% in Canada, and 85% in the United Kingdom (1997) (Adema 2001). Japan's minimal reliance on private social spending does not support categorization of Japan as a variant of the liberal welfare regime.

Third, if the social assistance bias is a more distinctive feature of the liberal regime than private pensions, then also Japan deviates from the liberal model (Esping-Andersen 1999, 77). Targeted social assistance as a percentage of total social expenditure amounts to approximately 100% in Australia and New Zealand, about 40% in the United States and Ireland, and 20–30% in the United Kingdom and Canada (Esping-Andersen 1999, 75). In Japan, the share of welfare, which includes family benefits, social assistance, unemployment benefits, and survivors, accounted for 16.8% in 1970, 14.5% in 1980, 10.2% in 1990, and 14.0% in 2000.[6] Moreover, Japan is the only country among the twenty-four OECD countries that experienced a decrease in its spending on per GDP social assistance cash allowances between 1980 and 1992 (Uzuhashi 1999). The small share of means-tested relief programs for the poor makes it difficult to classify Japan as a liberal welfare state.

One of the factors contributing to Japan's low level of spending on social assistance is the low level of the take-up rate, which indicates the proportion of social assistance recipients among those considered eligible. Estimates of the take-up rate range widely depending on the researchers, from 40% in 1989 (Hoshino 1995), to 24–32% in 1972–1982 (Sohara 1985), to 5.7% in 1994 (Ogawa 2000). Komamura Kōhei (2002) estimates that it was 24.3% in 1984, 54.8% in 1989, 16.9% in 1994, and 19.6% in 1999.[7] The low take-up rate in part results from strict eligibility criteria such that people of working age with financial savings equivalent to more than one month's worth of minimum livelihood costs are unable to receive social assistance. Yet, even among those with a lower amount of savings, only 32.0% receive social assistance (Yoshinaga et al. 2010). Although estimations of the take-up rate vary significantly, at most only about half of those eligible have received social assistance.

Japan deviates from the conservative model in several important regards. First, the level of social transfers is markedly lower in Japan than in other conservative welfare states.[8] Although the share of public pensions has increased due to the maturity of the system and an aging society, other social transfer programs such as unemployment insurance and disability insurance remain very limited in scope. If "transfer-heavy and service-lean" features are intrinsic to the conservative model, Japan's low social spending does not support the view that the country is simply a variant of the conservative welfare state.

Another important difference between Japan and the conservative model lies in the role of the labor market, which is the central concern of this book. Conservative welfare regimes are often associated with negative characteristics, as implied by the phrase "welfare state without work" (e.g., Esping-Andersen 1996; Hemerijck, Manow and Van Kersbergen 2000). This kind of system guarantees high family wages to male breadwinners, which results in the containment of job creation. This situation caused "negative spirals" after the 1973 oil crisis because industrial restructuring was implemented by the (over)use of early retirement and disability programs. The use of social insurance programs to deal with labor market problems, in turn, weakened the financial foundation of pension programs. The extent to which this downward spiral actually prevailed in different countries is debatable, and scholars have highlighted more positive aspects of conservative regimes (e.g., Levy 1999; Rhodes 1997, 2001). Insofar as Japan is compared with the conservative regimes, it is remarkable that it did not develop a system of welfare without work.

Lastly, Japan differs from conservative regimes in the way its male breadwinner model is sustained. In Japan, the government relies less on direct cash benefits to caregivers than on indirect means such as tax expenditures. This tendency can be confirmed by the share of cash benefit family allowances as a percentage of GDP: 0.1% in Japan, 0.8% in Germany, 1.2% in France, 1.1% in the Netherlands, and 2.0% in Belgium (1990) according to OECD statistics. The low level of family allowances is partly compensated by family wages, which offer high wages to male breadwinners to support their families. Family wages, however, preclude the realization of pay equity between the two sexes. Moreover, the government's use of indirect means puts a cap on earnings that housewives might rather prefer to earn, thus consolidating the low wage structure (for more on this, see chapter 4).

A System of Work and Welfare

Japan cannot be neatly categorized as either a liberal or a conservative regime. If we categorize welfare states based on type rather than size, Japan should be considered a variant of a conservative regime because the Japanese system employs occupationally segmented wage-based social insurances. If Japan's low level of social spending is the only factor that makes Japan anomalous with the conservative regime, Giuliano Bonoli's (1997) two dimensions of welfare states provide a useful perspective. Bonoli classifies welfare states according to Bismarckian and Beveridgeian models. He also adds the axis of the level of social spending, thereby creating four categories of welfare state: the high-spending Beveridgeian model (Scandinavian countries), low-spending Beveridgeian model (United Kingdom, Ireland), high-spending Bismarckian model (Continental Europe), and low-spending Bismarckian model (Switzerland, Southern Europe). This model effectively captures Japan's combination of a Bismarckian social insurance system and low social expenditure. If one aims to situate Japan's income maintenance policy in relation to other industrialized countries, Bonoli's typology situates Japan more precisely than Esping-Andersen's three typologies of welfare capitalism.[9] However, income maintenance policies constitute only one aspect of welfare regimes. The two principal traits of conservative regimes—high levels of public social expenditure and low employment rates—are, indeed, highly connected. The availability of social insurance programs for the termination of work caused by unemployment, disability, and retirement, has allowed conservative countries to induce early retirement, which has resulted in low employment rates. The fact that welfare and work are interconnected suggests that we need to include consideration of the labor market into welfare when reconceptualizing the typology of welfare states.

In order to overcome the shortcomings of typologies offered by Esping-Andersen and Bonoli, I proposed that an axis of employment maintenance should be added to the conventional models (see chapter 1). Although conventional studies on welfare states have narrowly focused on income maintenance policies, employment maintenance policies can be functionally equivalent to income maintenance policies, if it preempts the need for poverty-relief programs or redistribution of wealth by public welfare programs. It is often the case that the level of income maintenance policies and that of employment maintenance policies highly correlate—for instance, Sweden pursues to achieve both, whereas the United States does neither (see Esping-Andersen 1990). However, only by treating work and welfare in a separate fashion and then exploring the link between them allow us to comprehend the Japanese model in relation to the other three established categories of welfare capitalism.[10]

This perspective is not new. For example, Uzuhashi (1997) calls attention to the possibility that the Japanese labor market provides a functional equivalent for welfare provision. He argues that the relationship between the labor market and the welfare state is "complementary" in a social democratic regime but functionally "equivalent" in Japan. Likewise, Castles and Mitchell (1993) argue that, in Australia, the role of the courts in setting wage levels is often viewed as an integral function of the welfare state. Recently, scholars have more assertively stressed the functional equivalence of, or elective affinities between, welfare states and labor market policies in Europe (e.g., Bonoli 2003; Goodin 2001; Iversen 2005).[11] Moreover, Estévez-Abe (2008) has identified a wide range of functionally equivalent policies that exist in Japan, including not only labor market policy but also financial, public works, anti-competitive, trade, and other policies.

My explicit focus on the labor market-welfare nexus allows us to delineate Japan's unique features and differentiate them from those of liberal and conservative regimes in a systemic fashion.[12] It is particularly important to situate Japan in relation to the conservative regimes rather than liberal ones, as they share the same basic social insurance system framework. I have conceptualized four distinct types of work and welfare system: welfare through work, welfare with work, welfare without work, and workfare (for details, see chapter 1). My concept highlights Japan's heavy reliance on the labor market, in stark contrast to the conservative regime's system of welfare without work. As long as employment rates were sufficiently high, the Japanese state has been able to control the gross amount of social expenditure and concentrate its welfare efforts on the elderly, who tended to stay in the workforce until relatively late.[13]

Because the axis of employment maintenance is an ex ante measurement, several factors affect employment maintenance. Although public works and anti-competitive policy certainly play a role, this book focuses on labor market policy because it is concerned with a particular pattern of distributional consequences among wage earners, which is produced by a system of work and welfare. This analytical focus also enables us to comprehend Japan's distinctiveness and commonalities in relation to other male breadwinner models.[14]

Beyond Regime Theory: A Dynamic Partisan Approach

Thus far, I have argued against simple application of Esping-Andersen's typology to Japan. Although the Japanese welfare state certainly contains elements of both regimes, labeling Japan as a hybrid of liberal and conservative regimes is theoretically problematic. Nonetheless, Esping-Andersen's emphasis on the role of political parties in formulating the welfare state deserves another serious consideration.

Characterizing the Japanese welfare state as a hybrid regime is theoretically inconsistent. As the terms liberal, conservative/Christian democratic, and social democratic imply, the political forces that were in power in the formative and developmental stages of welfare states affected the characteristics of the respective regimes. The core of regime theory is that the power resources of class-based political parties ultimately shape different types of welfare states. The concept of a hybrid regime only works when more than one political force has influenced the development of the welfare state. For example, strong labor protection in Australia and New Zealand led Castles and Mitchell (1993) to argue that Australasian welfare states substantially differ from liberal regimes. These two countries can be viewed as hybrids of liberal and social democratic regimes, created by Lib-Lab political forces or by both the Liberal Party and the Labor Party. Huber and Stephens (2001), following this line of logic, classify Australia and New Zealand as "wage earner" welfare states.

If Japan is indeed a hybrid case, we would expect power alternation between liberal and conservative parties to have shaped its hybrid characteristics. However, postwar Japan has only been ruled by conservative governments. The enduring absence of rule by political forces that would have otherwise left the imprint of liberal traits on the Japanese welfare state might militate against the Japanese welfare state as a hybrid type.[15] Or, perhaps, regime theory itself is flawed, as political parties do not actually dominate welfare policy-making process. State bureaucrats, interest groups, and international organizations also play important roles. For instance, Gregory J. Kasza criticizes the regime theory so popular among welfare scholars, claiming that "there is not a single industrialized country whose welfare programs represent the work of one political party or even one political tendency" (2006, 153). Similarly, other Japan specialists point out the limits of power resource approaches when applied to the Japanese case because it is hard to identify purposive actors who have shaped the Japanese welfare state. Tominaga Ken'ichi stresses that state bureaucrats have played a crucial role in introducing other countries' experiences in a rather ad hoc fashion without any concomitant long-term vision, which has inevitably resulted in the apparent inconsistencies in the attributes of the Japanese welfare state (Tominaga 2001, 207–212). In a similar vein, John C.Campbell argues that "in telling the story of the Japanese welfare state, we can feature neither a consistent champion nor a consistent opponent, at least not to the extent such helpfully dominating characters can be employed in explaining the welfare state in Europe or even the US" (Campbell 1992, 371).

Although these critiques are not without merit, there remains much to learn from the insights of regime theory. Values and ideologies espoused by dominant political forces should not be dismissed out of hand.[16] Although, admittedly, no welfare state is designed by a single coherent value system, the political processes of competing ideas concerning the appropriate role of the state in shaping people's welfare deserve special attention. Recent studies of welfare retrenchment have rediscovered the importance of political forces behind the formation and transformation of regimes (Béland 2007; Huber and Stephens 2001; Levy 1999). What need to be examined are the ideological tendencies of Japan's Liberal Democratic Party in relation to liberal and Christian democratic political forces in other affluent democracies. The scarcity of measured theoretical discussion of Japanese conservatism has made it difficult to apply partisan explanations to the Japanese case. I aim to recuperate the essential tenet of partisan explanations by explicating the political vision of Japanese conservatives. I argue that four strands of conservatism—statism, productivism, cooperatism, and neoliberalism—were fundamental to the establishment and transformation of Japan's welfare through work system.

It should also be emphasized that analysis of the philosophy of the dominant political actor alone does not provide a full account of the characteristics of a welfare state. Dynamics of partisan competition needs to be taken into account. It was the electoral threat from the Left that pressured conservatives to develop the welfare state (Wilensky 1975). The ascendance of the Left then paved the way for a conservative backlash and eventually led to their repositioning toward neoliberalism. Political actors fashion and reformulate ideas in their struggle for power, and ideas need to be analyzed in the context of political conflict. My treatment of ideas, therefore, is dynamic rather than static. Rather than looking at the independent role of ideas affecting policymaking, I examine the dynamic process according to which actors acquire power in order to shape the discourse of the day as well as by trying to influence it. In other words, political actors engage in politics in order to realize their agenda. At the same time, they acquire power by espousing new agendas. As the struggle for power is inextricably linked to the battle of ideas, we should pay due attention to the interactive relationship between actors and ideas in the context of power struggle.

Treating ideas in a dynamic fashion may not be a mainstream approach in contemporary political science. Conventional partisan theory tends to regard democracy as a political market in which electorates play a similar role to consumers, with parties delivering policies in order to acquire support from the electorate. According to this approach, parties matter because they have different policy priorities that mirror the distinctive preferences of their social constituencies.[17] In my view, this is only half of the story. Politicians not only contest for votes but also struggle to alter the public mind. They influence, rather than merely reflect, the distribution of preferences among voters. Thus, both parties and ideas matter because the way in which they interact determines policy priorities.

My dynamic partisan explanation is also useful in terms of understanding why policy takes "the specific form and content that it does." Jal Mehta (2011) points out that this question has received insufficient attention in welfare state literature dominated by institutionalist perspectives. Institutional explanations that emphasize the role of veto players and the number of veto points are instructive as to why a certain welfare state may be small or less developed, but do not offer an account of why it takes a particular form (Mehta 2011, 26). The role of veto players in obstructing welfare expansion is undeniable. However, in order to understand the specific content of the welfare state, we need to analyze proponents rather than contenders. Likewise, recent studies on policy agenda ignore the content of ideas. Frank Baumgartner and colleagues' (2009) project on policy agendas is a rare example dealing with how new ideas may or may not be accepted in the political system. However, they focus on temporal changes of issue attention and thus stress the role of external pressure in triggering policy change. I am more concerned with the content of ideas than the prospects of policy reform. To this end, conservative ideas on the purpose of the welfare state must be unraveled, which is the task of the next chapter.

The Conservative Vision and the Politics of Work and Welfare

We now turn to the questions of why and how Japan developed a social protection system based on welfare through work. I take the position that the ideology and vision of the governing party—the Liberal Democratic Party (LDP) in Japan's case—strongly affected the way in which the welfare state was designed and constructed. However, two caveats are necessary here. First, a political party does not subscribe to a single coherent set of ideas and values. Multiple streams of ideas coexist under the umbrella of a single party's philosophy and sometimes compete with each other, generating ideational development and transformation. Analyses of partisan ideologies need to consider this dynamics. Second, political parties behave strategically in a given political environment as they pursue multiple, often conflicting goals. Although ideas matter, the struggle for power takes precedence over ideological purity. Therefore, the dynamics of partisan competition, which shapes partisan strategy, also merit close attention.

This chapter examines the formation and development of the welfare through work system during three separate periods corresponding to different stages in the evolving party system.[1] The first section examines the formative period of the welfare through work system in the 1950s and early 1960s. I argue that in the political context of polarized partisan competition, the ideas of statism, productivism, and cooperatism justified the LDP's commitment to full employment and a small state. The second section analyzes further development of the welfare through work system from the mid-1960s to the 1970s. Important policy shifts occurred during this period: from welfare retrenchment to expansion as well as from labor transfer to employment stability. As a result, state responsibility was reduced with respect to employment policy but enlarged with respect to social welfare. I show that the new dynamics of partisan competition at this time—the fragmentation of the opposition and the decline of LDP popularity—resulted in the selective nature of state intervention. The final section analyzes the impact of neoliberalism along with the conservative resurgence in the 1980s. I show that neoliberalism coupled with statism laid the ideational foundation for welfare retrenchment, while the impact of cooperatism reached its zenith during this period.

Polarized Partisan Competition: Defining the Conservative Welfare State

The first half of the 1950s was a period of party realignment during which the interplay between competing political visions played an important role in shaping the ideological boundaries between political parties. During this period, the concepts of the "welfare state" and "full employment" were viewed as promising cornerstones for the political program of a sector of conservative political forces ideologically situated between the Liberals and the Socialists. These conservatives eventually formed the Japan Democratic Party, which then formed the LDP in 1955 by merging with the Liberal Party. The influence of this group was decisive in the formation of welfare through work.

The policy orientation of the Japan Democratic Party sharply differed from that of the Liberal Party led by Prime Minister Yoshida Shigeru. Whereas the Liberal Party, as the governing party, supported the US-Japan Security Treaty and planned to reconstruct the Japanese economy based on liberal market ideology, the Japan Democratic Party advocated relatively progressive social policy on the domestic front in combination with hawkish foreign and security policy, seeking constitutional revision and military independence. In its policy platform issued in 1954, the Japan Democratic Party claimed that it aimed to establish an independent economy by comprehensive planning, thereby stabilizing people's lives and constructing a welfare state.[2] Yoshida's foreign policy position of relying on US military forces, which is often called the "conservative policy line" (*hoshu honryū*), became LDP's mainstream position (Muramatsu and Krauss 1987), but in terms of economic and social policy it was the Japan Democratic Party that left a lasting impact on LDP policy (Kouno 2002).

The members of the Japan Democratic Party were essentially anti-Yoshida conservatives. They included members who subscribed to cooperatism, like Miki Takeo, as well as the members of the prewar Minseitō Party, such as Machida Chūji, who formed the Japan Progressivist Party in 1945. This latter party inherited the concept of "reformed capitalism" from the wartime Imperial Rule Assistance Association and sought to create a safety net for the dispossessed. When these groups formed the People's Democratic Party together with anti-Yoshida conservatives like Ashida Hitoshi in 1950, the new party adopted a progressive stance and pledged to construct a welfare state through the establishment of a large-scale social security system, holding up the UK as a model welfare state (Amamiya 1997, 76). The People's Democratic Party metamorphosed into the Reform Party (Kaishin-tō) in 1952 after including other anti-Yoshida politicians such as Hatoyama Ichirō and Kishi Nobusuke, who had been purged from public posts during the occupation. The new members of the party invoked nationalistic sentiment and called for constitutional revision and rearmament. The aggregation of these anti-Yoshida conservatives naturally gave the Reform Party a hawkish outlook, but social reformism nevertheless occupied a central position in its policy orientation.[3] Journalists succinctly portrayed the Reform Party as calling for "both butter and guns," in contrast with the Liberal Party's "guns after bread" policy.[4]

These politicians, who eventually formed the Japan Democratic Party in 1954 promoted a distinct brand of conservatism that blended statism, productivism, and cooperatism in varying degrees. These three concepts provided the justification for the welfare state in different ways. Statism called for welfare provision in the interests of the state; that is, the interests of the governing apparatus and the ruling elite. Welfare is a tool of rule. Statists expect the welfare state to consolidate social unification and national identity thereby facilitating popular mobilization. Kishi's views on the welfare state were rooted in this state-oriented perspective. In contrast, productivism justified the welfare state from the standpoint of economic growth. Some welfare programs are both conducive to, and contribute to, improved productivity. Ishibashi Tanzan, for example, was a vocal advocate of productivism. Although statism and productivism are separate concepts, they were effectively combined in conservative thought, as production increase was an important resource contributing to state strength.

Cooperatism is an ideology that rejects class struggle and emphasizes the importance of harmony and cooperation, providing a less radical alternative to communism and socialism. This idea was essentially a conservative response to the growing threat from the flourishing labor movement, providing justification for various social institutions that fostered cooperation between labor and capital. However, cooperatism was not necessarily the exclusive domain of conservatives and some labor unions also espoused it. For instance, "harmony and cooperation between Labor and Capital" was first advocated by the Yūaikai (Friendly Society), the most successful early labor organization founded by Suzuki Bunji in 1912. Yūaikai's stance was inherited by Sōdōmei (the Japan General Federation of Labor) in the prewar period, then by Dōmei (abbreviation of Zen Nihon Rōdō Sōdōmei or the Japan Confederation of Labor) in the postwar period, and is currently upheld by Rengō (Nihon Rōdō Kumiai Sōrengōkai; the Japanese Trade Union Confederation). Some businessmen also supported the idea of a constructive role for unions, like Shibusawa Eiichi in the prewar period and Gōshi Kōhei in the postwar period. In political circles, Machida Chūji, for instance, founded the liberal newspaper *Tōyō Keizai Shimpō* (Eastern Economic Journal), a consistent advocate of labor rights in the 1910s. Cooperatism and productivism were fused in conservative thought, providing an ideational justification for the productivity movement.

As discussed in the book's introduction, cooperatist thinking has some affinity with certain aspects of Christian social democracy in Europe. This is not surprising given the fact that Suzuki was a Christian (Unitarian) and that many Christian socialists and unionists joined Sōdōmei. Although Christianity was too weak to form a confessional party in Japan, the views of its adherents were incorporated into the conservative and social democratic parties they joined.

Statism, productivism, and cooperatism, taken together, justified state intervention in order to achieve full employment or provide public support to those who are willing to work, but did not encourage the establishment of social welfare programs for those who declined to engage in low-wage contingent work. Ishida Takeshi, analyzing the historical development of the concept of the welfare state as defined by Japan's political elite, argues that conservatives continuously undermined the concept of social rights as enshrined in the postwar constitution. Instead, they viewed welfare as the state's paternalistic endowment to the people (Ishida 1989). Conservatives certainly abhorred the idea of social rights, which were considered a Western value that had been brought to Japan by the occupation forces. However, it was not simply paternalistic concern that induced the conservatives to construct the welfare state. The concepts of statism, productivism, and cooperatism justified the conservatives' commitment to the construction of the welfare state, thereby creating a distinct type of social protection system that I call welfare through work.

In the political context of the 1950s, the conservatives regarded the construction of a welfare state as an essential project, and one that showed continued promise for the future, in order for them to both secure and retain power in domestic politics. Three political forces—liberals, anti-Yoshida conservatives, and socialists—were competing in the party system in the early 1950s, when the possibility still existed of an alliance between the anti-Yoshida conservatives and moderate socialists. Such an alliance had already materialized under the Katayama and Ashida cabinets, which were born from a coalition between Ashida's Democratic Party, Katayama's Socialist Party, and the National Cooperative Party in 1947–1948. Although this Center-Left coalition ultimately failed for a number of reasons, an attempt to repeat such a coalition was not ruled out until 1955. The construction of the welfare state was a program on which both camps could agree. To reiterate, the People's Democratic Party and the Reform Party repeatedly called for the creation of a welfare state, and were often more vocal with respect to this issue than the socialists.[5]

The issue cleavage of international security and the constitution was so overwhelming that the left-wing Socialist Party and the right-wing Socialist Party joined in 1955 to form the Japan Socialist Party (JSP), triggering the conservative camp merger of the Liberal Party and the Japan Democratic

Party a month later. The party system after 1955 was thus characterized by polarized partisan competition in which the main contender, the JSP, systemically opposed LDP rule (Curtis 1988).[6] Until the mid-1960s, when other significant opposition parties came into play, the socialists presented a growing threat to conservative rule. During the general elections of 1952, 1953, and 1955, the left-wing Socialist Party increased its share in the House of Representatives from 11.6% to 15.5% to 19.1%, and the Right-wing Socialist Party from 12.2% to 14.2% to 14.3%. Furthermore, in the general election of 1955, the opposition parties gained more than one-third of the parliamentary seats for the first time, which enabled them to block any attempts by the LDP to amend the constitution. In the 1957 House of Councillors election, they also passed the one-third threshold. To counter the rising tide of socialism in political circles, the LDP formulated several social policies that became the basis of the welfare though work system. Although the LDP might appear to have conceded to leftist policy, the actual design of the social protection system was influenced by statism, productivism, and cooperatism.

Full Employment Policy

The LDP signaled its commitment to full employment as early as 1955. Full employment policy was one item on the agenda pursued by anti-Yoshida political forces and was a manifestation of productivism. Once Hatoyama Ichirō became prime minister in 1955, he promptly issued the Five-Year Economic Independence Plan. The official formulation of a long-term economic plan in itself marked a policy shift from Yoshida's Liberals. The plan articulated that the government would pursue economic independence and full employment as the two main goals of economic planning. The expansion of economic activities was a primary route to full employment, but the plan also emphasized the need to reduce underemployment (*fukanzen shūgyō*), or low-income unstable employment, which was found in small and medium-size enterprises.

Initially, the plan's major priority was economic independence. It was Prime Minister Ishibashi Tanzan (1956–1957), a well-known Keynesian, who shifted the policy priority to full employment and pursued active fiscal policies.[7] He shifted the focus from economic independence, which required fiscal austerity, to economic growth, which involved fiscal expansion.[8] In his first interview as prime minister, he stated: "I intend that the goal of economic policy should be the realization of full employment...The expansion of the economy—the realization of full employment—is my ideal. I will do my very best from now on to pursue this. As my political life resides in the achievement of this economic policy, I cannot change my belief no matter how I am criticized."[9] Endorsing the prime minister's commitment to full employment, the Ishibashi cabinet launched the so-called positive finance policy, which increased spending on public works such as roads and ports.[10]

Kishi continued this policy shift when he succeeded Ishibashi only two months later due to the latter's poor health. In 1957, the Kishi cabinet approved the New Long-Term Economic Plan (full title: the new economic plan to achieve full employment and double the national income), which revised Hatoyama's Five-Year Economic Independence Plan and endorsed the policy shift from economic independence to "maximum growth" (Sorai 1993). The policy shift became further institutionalized in the same year when the government created the Employment Advisory Council to formulate a comprehensive employment policy in order to achieve full employment. The naming of the council symbolizes the policy shift, as its predecessor was the Unemployment Measures Advisory Council. Whereas unemployment policy deals with the unemployed, employment policy aims to prevent unemployment. The emphasis of state activity, therefore, shifted from ex post relief of the unemployed to an ex ante policy of creating jobs.

By this time, the economic and social policy of the LDP was being shaped according to the rationale and goals of productivism. Although Kishi's successor, Prime Minister Ikeda Hayato, hailed from the Yoshida school, he further accelerated this policy orientation with his Income Doubling Plan.[11] The conservative government justified its commitment to the goal of full employment from the standpoint of national wealth. Maximization of available human resources was regarded as vital to Japan's economic development given the scarcity of capital and natural resources. Ishibashi, who was vocally committed to the goal of full employment—although often described as a "liberal"—also emphasized that workers had an obligation to produce (Ishibashi 1970, 351). Productivism had a strong affinity with statism, as production increase would contribute to national strength. Thus, productivism and statism were easily combined, further justifying state efforts to ensure full employment.

Employment Protection

While productivism and statism provided the ideational justification for the government's commitment to "full employment," cooperatism introduced "employment protection" to the social contract in the late 1950s and the early 1960s. I use the term "social contract" because both employers and workers accepted the norm of lifetime employment, which embodied a mutual commitment: employers do not discharge workers unless workers engage in wrongful conduct or their firm faces a managerial crisis, whereas employees continue to work in the same company and cooperate with their managers in terms of productivity increase. Employment protection was a key component of the social contract.

Full employment policy and employment protection, despite their apparent similarity, are two very different things. Full employment theoretically means a situation in which the entire able workforce is employed, whereas lifetime employment necessitates a dualized labor market in which the job security of insiders needs to be compensated for by flexible employment of outsiders, because providing job security for all workers is economically impossible. Full employment policy requires adequate social safety nets in the form of unemployment benefits, minimum wages, and social assistance to eliminate underemployment as well as to cope with cyclical economic downturns.

Labor movements in Japan burgeoned in the early years of the postwar period, assisted by the democratization policies pursued by the Supreme Commander for the Allied Powers. One of the main goals of the postwar labor movements was the retraction of dismissals. Following World War II, the two most intensive labor disputes were caused by national railways and seamen's unions fighting against mass dismissals. The deflation policy implemented in 1949 on the recommendation of Joseph Dodge pushed Japanese industries to crisis point, and this was accompanied by amendment of Labor Union Law, giving employers the right to unilaterally terminate labor contracts. Armed with this new weapon, employers implemented large-scale dismissals, which in turn gave rise to frequent and intensive labor disputes across the country, resulting in the characterization of the 1950s as "the decade of the knock-down-drag-out strikes" (Gordon 1998, 104).

At the macro-level, Sōhyō (Nihon Rōdō Kumiai Sōhyōgikai; the General Council of Trade Unions), which was initially expected to be a cooperative non-communist labor federation, came to support the left-wing socialists and aggressively pursued wage bargaining and shop-floor struggles. At the same time, Nikkeiren (Nihon Keieisha Dantai Renmei; the Japan Federation of Employers' Associations), the top employers' association primarily engaged with labor issues, took a hardline approach. Confrontation between these two leading organizations hardly provided a favorable platform for the construction of cooperative industrial relations. As a result of the growing influence of socialists and communists in the political and economic spheres, "the politics of productivity" came into being in Japan (Maier 1987). The idea behind the politics of productivity was that constructive industrial relations would enhance productive efficiency, which would lead to capital formation as well as economic growth. Although this idea may appear to be an apolitical solution, the underlying motive was certainly political. Its purpose was to deideologize the labor movement by securing labor's commitment to economic growth, and to contain the spread of communism. The politics of productivity was "the American organizing idea for the postwar economic world" and "depended upon superseding class conflict with economic growth" (Maier 1987, 146). The United States provided war-devastated Western Europe with the Marshall Plan, which facilitated the spread of the productivity movement in that part of the world (Carew 1987; Rupert 1995; Weathers and Ebizuka 2004). Similarly, it encouraged Japan to set up the Productivity Center as part of President Dwight D. Eisenhower's labor policy toward Japan (Nakakita 2006).

The politics of productivity melded together the concepts of productivism and cooperatism. In its essence, this idea was often called "pie theory" (Tsutsui 1998, 133–151). Overall increase of the pie would transcend class interests and enhance industrial accord, and fair distribution of gains among capital, labor, and consumers would reduce or eliminate class struggles, which would further increase production. Having been conceived of as a political project to counter socialism and communism, it was necessary to disseminate the idea to the masses by means of a national movement. The Japan Productivity Center (JPC), created in 1955, played a central role in disseminating the ideology of productivity in Japan. The key architect of this movement was the Keizai Dōyūkai (the Japan Association of Corporate Executives), a business association that adopted a more progressive stance as compared to the hardline approach of Nikkeiren, and whose director, Gōshi Kōhei, had a firm grasp of the movement's ideological foundation. Both labor and capital met this ideology with skepticism, making a cross-class coalition between moderate groups of managers and unions crucial to the success of the productivity movement. On the one hand, some unions regarded the concept simply as a disguised form of rationalization, whereby corporate profits were to be maximized at labor's expense. On the other hand, hardline managers objected to the possibility that unions might infringe on managerial autonomy.

The Three Guiding Principles of Productivity, proposed by Nakayama Ichirō, a prominent economist and an ideologue of the productivity movement, laid the ideational foundation for such a cross-class coalition by calling for mutual concessions from capital and labor. The principles stated:

1. Expansion of employment: In the long term, improved productivity should lead to expansion of employment. However, from the standpoint of the national economy, a public-private partnership is essential in formulating valid policies to prevent the unemployment of surplus personnel through job relocation or other measures.
2. Cooperation between labor and management: Labor and management must cooperate in researching and discussing specific methods to improve productivity in consideration of specific corporate circumstances.
3. Fair distribution of the fruits of productivity: The fruits of productivity should be distributed fairly among labor, management, and consumers in line with the state of the national economy.[12]

The guiding principles represented the social contract at the macro-level and embraced the core ideology of the Japanese management model, which required employers to refrain from firing redundant workers (Nitta 2003, 170–173). Such employment protection, it proposed, should be coupled with job relocation and supported by public policy. Although the first principle stated that productivity increase should lead to the expansion of employment, it did not oppose dismissal per se and advocated full employment from the perspective of the national economy. In view of the non-compromising approach of labor movements at the time in their struggle for job security and opposition to rationalization, the first principle did not live up to union demands. Managers also resisted this principle because it would require that they assume social responsibility in terms of contemplating alternatives to dismissal (Nitta 1998). The first principle thus implied mutual concessions by labor and capital.

Acceptance of the Three Guiding Principles by the relevant parties was not achieved overnight. Sōhyō was critical of the productivity movement from the beginning, claiming that it constituted an ideological assault as part of a "class harmonization campaign" to paralyze workers' class consciousness, thereby safeguarding the prerogative of capitalism to exploit workers.[13] It also viewed the US-led productivity movement as part of Japan's military cooperation with the United States. In contrast, right-wing unions offered only "token resistance and enrolled in the movement readily" (Tsutsui (1998, 145).[14] Represented largely by Zenrō (Zen Nihon Rōdō Kumiai Kaigi; the All-Japan Trade Union Conference) at the time and later by Dōmei, they were favorably disposed toward cooperatism, according to which union cooperation in production was considered to be mutually beneficial to employers and employees. Indeed, the right-wing unions have consistently sought an institutionalized role in governmental process, as the historical legacy of Sōdōmei (Carlile 2005, 218; Garon 1987, 243). This aspiration was compatible with the essence of the Three Guiding Principles of Productivity.

Despite Sōhyō's opposition, the ideological appeal of the productivity movement was so strong that left-wing resistance was soon overcome. As early as 1956, Sōhyō member unions began to participate in Productivity Center programs.[15] A decade later, even left-wing unions displayed tacit approval. William M. Tsutsui concludes that Japanese unions, like their British counterparts, "actually ended up among the movement's most dedicated participants, embracing business unionism and the technocratic, materialistic appeal of productivity in an environment where the scope for political activism was increasingly constrained" (1998, 146).

When the Three Guiding Principles were invented in 1955, the term "lifetime employment" (*shūshin koyō*) had not yet been coined. It was not until the late 1950s that this term was invented and began to be used widely.[16] Diffusion of lifetime employment to the extent that it became a norm occurred via the process of formation of the social contract at the micro-level. In contrast to the macro-level contract spelled out in the Three Guiding Principles, it is not easy to identify the precise chain of events that culminated in the formation of the micro-level contract. A rare example was the "modernization accord" concluded by Oji Paper and its union in 1961. After a fierce labor dispute over rationalization, both sides agreed on a trade-off between "protection of employee status" and "union cooperation in rationalization" (Takeda 1993, 73). The other symbolic case was the Mitsui Miike coal mine strike in 1960, the most intensive and longest labor dispute in postwar Japan. As a result of the government's new energy policy, which promoted a shift from coal to oil, the Mitsui Mining Company tried to dismiss 60,000 employees in an attempt to revitalize the company, including 2,210 coal miners from the Miike coal mine. The most controversial issue pertinent to the dispute was that the company specifically listed 1,278 employees, including union activists, as targets of personnel reduction. A year-long dispute eventually ended in defeat for the Miike union, which ultimately accepted the dismissals. However, the dispute taught employers the lesson that the dismissal of designated workers was extremely costly. An intensive labor dispute at the Muroran Plant of the Japan Steel Works, which had broken out the previous year, also demonstrated that company unions would vigorously resist dismissals. It was around 1960 that employers began to adopt a softer approach by, for example, inducing early retirement with the additional offer of a retirement lump-sum payment.[17]

The social contract at both the macro- and micro-levels was essentially formed by social actors who subscribed to productivism and cooperatism, but power struggle at the level of national politics also influenced and was reflected in the formation of cross-class alliances. Labor accommodation was championed by Kuraishi Tadao and Ishida Hirohide, the LDP's leading labor specialists.[18] Kuraishi was appointed labor minister under Hatoyama's third cabinet and Kishi's second cabinet, and Ishida served in this position six times for a total of about four years under Kishi, Ikeda, and Satō. The mass media often contrasted Kuraishi's hardline approach with Ishida's soft-line stance, but they shared the same fundamental views regarding the positive role and responsibility of unions in a modern capitalist economy.[19] Kuraishi once stated, "it is our view that workers' living standards cannot be improved without the assumption that the interests of managers and workers are eventually compatible" (Iijima 1987, 406) and Ishida also dismissed the dialectic of class-based antagonism and argued that it was necessary to treat wage earners as ends rather than means (Ishida 1986, 107).

Following Kuraishi's initiative, the LDP created the Special Research Commission for Labor Issues under its Policy Affairs Research Council in 1957. Three months later, the Commission drafted Kishi government's "New Labor Policy Outline," which stated that the LDP's first policy goal was the construction of a welfare state. The basic gist of the outline resonated with the politics of productivity. It separated ordinary workers from left-leaning, disruptive labor movements and proposed various measures aimed at the former, including welfare policy, full employment, and wage increases. For the latter, it proclaimed that legal measures including criminal punishment should be considered to deal with illegal labor disputes committed by public-sector employees.[20]

Later, Ishida further integrated the idea of cooperatism into the LDP's policy philosophy by drafting the LDP's "Labor Charter" in the mid-1960s. This document was progressive insofar as it declared that the LDP was committed to full employment, the improvement of working conditions, and the promotion of social security. Opposed by right-wingers, it took two-and-a-half years before the charter was officially approved and finally issued in 1966. Ishida was keenly aware of the electoral threat posed by leftist forces and warned in 1963 that the LDP would lose its parliamentary majority in six years due to rapid urbanization and industrialization, urging his party to appeal to wage earners to forestall such an outcome (Ishida 1963). The LDP approved the Labor Charter in this political context. Iwai Akira, Sōhyō's secretary general, unofficially commented on Ishida's draft, saying, "The LDP has put together something quite impressive. It seems that Ishida was in charge of it, but I heard there was opposition within the party. Either way, the LDP won't be able to implement it. If they do actually implement it, we'll just have to accept defeat, as will the JSP" (Tsuji 1978, 302).

It is possible to perceive something akin to a Japanese version of a postwar settlement in the LDP's concession to Ishida's social reformism. For instance, in Britain, the victory of the Labour Party allowed the implementation of mild social democratic reforms, under a policy often known as Butskellism, named after R. A. Butler and Hugh Gaitskell, the leading figures in the British politics of moderation. Interestingly, both Ishida and Kuraishi were influenced by the British politics of this period. Kuraishi had graduated from the University of London where he studied social policy under Harold Laski in the early 1930s (Iijima 1987, 396). Ishida was inspired by the postwar British Conservative Party, especially by Butler's approach to consensus-oriented conservatism (Tory modernizers) (Ishida 1986, 126). In the Japanese case, Ishida may be likened to Butler in terms of his social reformism. However, although the LDP formulated a policy of full employment and supported the productivity movement in response to the mounting electoral threat from the socialists, the actual design of social policy was compatible with conservative ideology and owed little to the socialist influence in conceptual terms.[21]

Social Safety Nets

Similar to its predecessor, the Japan Democratic Party, the LDP unequivocally pledged to construct a welfare state. What merits investigation here is to what extent and in what ways this promise was kept other than through the pursuit of full employment policy. Three important policy innovations took place during this period: (i) comprehensive coverage of pension and health-care insurance, (ii) legislation of the minimum wage law, and (iii) improvement of social assistance. Although these policies may have substantiated the LDP's promise to create a welfare state, statism and productivism infused these policies with a conservative bias, thereby putting a cap on numerical expansion of social expenditure.

Japan achieved comprehensive coverage of pensions and health insurance in 1961,[22] which was extraordinarily early by international standards,

coming fourth and twelfth in the world, respectively. During the prewar period, wage earners in large firms and civil servants were already covered by
social security. It was left to the postwar government, therefore, to extend
coverage to wage earners in small businesses, farmers, fishermen, and the
self-employed. The government created a new pension scheme and a new
health insurance system for these remaining sectors of the population. Thus,
although all citizens came to be covered in 1961, the social insurance system
continued to be highly segmented, and universal coverage, where all citizens
participate under the same terms and conditions, was not achieved.[23] The
conservative nature of Japan's social protection system was thus maintained.

Comprehensive coverage of pension and health-care insurance made it
onto the political agenda because of the insistence of the opposition parties.
The Ministry of Health and Welfare (MHW) recognized the direct impact
of party politics on the creation of the National Pension System, its official
history noting that "it is impossible to believe that the policy statements and
campaigns promises of the Japan Socialist Party concerning the establishment of National Pension System had no influence on the LDP" (Kōseishō
Nenkin-kyoku 1962, 16–17, [for English translation see Lewis 1980, 56];
Kōseishō 50nen Shi Henshū Iinkai, 1988, 941–948). In fact, it was the right-
wing Socialist Party that first proposed the extension of pension coverage
to farmers and fishermen and, after socialist party unification, the JSP continued to apply pressure on the government and the LDP by presenting a
concrete social security policy.

The realization of comprehensive coverage of pensions and health insurance was part of the LDP's statist agenda.[24] In particular, Kishi's initiative was
indispensable. Although usually viewed as a politician who was only interested in high politics, among the prime ministers who held office between
1955 and 1960, Kishi alone expressed any great interest in the development
of the social security system. In 1956 he mentioned that the LDP would pursue comprehensive coverage of health insurance and pensions in order to
stabilize people's livelihoods, which eventually led to the LDP's policy pledge
during the upper house election in the same year to provide health insurance to all citizens by 1960 as well as to prepare for the creation of old-age
pensions and widow-children pensions. Kishi's aspirations for the creation
of a welfare state were deep-rooted, as he had been inspired by state socialism as a prewar progressive bureaucrat (Amamiya 2007; Kishi 1953). In the
postwar period, pledging to construct a welfare state appeared to serve at
least three purposes. First, it was a means for encouraging the development
of party politics. Kishi was heavily involved in party realignments, especially
in the first half of the 1950s, and considered a two-party system of the moderate left and progressive conservatives appropriate to Japan (Watanabe
1994). Strategically, he saw the welfare state as a program to unite conservatives. Second, Kishi conceived of the welfare state as a means of promoting
national integration or national mobilization toward the goal of economic

development and independence. In other words, the nation's welfare was assigned a rather instrumental role in the achievement of his more pressing national goals and priorities such as rearmament, the revision of postwar democracy (most important of which was constitutional revision), and comprehensive planning for economic independence. Finally, the welfare state was also intended to counter the communist threat.[25] Social security was thus integrated into his agenda for home and international security. Accordingly, although the goal of comprehensive coverage was rather swiftly achieved, social spending did not significantly increase until the 1970s, suggesting that formal implementation of the program took precedence over substantive betterment of the people's welfare.

The enactment of the Minimum Wage Law in 1959 under the Kishi cabinet was similarly a statist project, but this time cooperatism also played an important role. The legislation was necessary for the government to fend off international criticism that Japan was conducting social dumping. The law legalized employer cartels on the minimum wage, which the Ministry of Labour (MOL) had already been encouraging through administrative guidance, and consultation with labor in setting the minimum wage was minimal (Milly 1999). It was thus not the minimum wage that would meet the standards set by the International Labour Organization. Moreover, the law stipulated that the minimum wage should be determined with reference to basic living costs, the wages of similar types of workers, and the capacity of ordinary enterprises to pay wages. All three principles were given equal weight. The minimum wage was thus not designed to guarantee wages sufficient to cover basic living costs. The government did not intend to raise the level of the minimum wage because such a policy would have triggered vigorous resistance from small businesses. Big business was not in favor of such a policy either. Though they could logically have supported an effective minimum wage as a measure to reduce unfair market competition based on cheap labor, Japanese big business opposed such a move relying on cheap supplies from small businesses (Fujimoto 1967).

Despite the deficiencies of the legislation, Zenrō, which heavily represented workers in small businesses, showed its willingness to compromise on the minimum wage but in return insisted on the creation of a mechanism through which workers would be represented. Ultimately, Zenrō prioritized making a slight modification to the government bill over maintaining a united front among workers together with Sōhyō (Milly 1999, 147–160). Labor Minister Ishida took the side of Zenrō, showing the LDP's willingness to compromise, which induced Zenrō's departure from the JSP. This rupture in the labor movement during the legislative process was one of the factors eventually leading to the formation in 1960 of the Japan Democratic Socialist Party (DSP), which was backed by Zenrō. The LDP's cooperativist policy thus had an impact on the party system as well, which transformed the dynamics of partisan competition.

In the realm of social assistance, substantial improvements were made only under the Ikeda cabinet. Interestingly, Hatoyama's Five-Year Economic Independence Plan proposed the expansion of social welfare policy as this would induce workers to exit the labor market: those who needed social welfare would not work once welfare became available, thereby reducing the burden on employment policy (Eshita 1957, 33–51). Pressed by the Ministry of Finance, which was eager to retrench social assistance expenditures, the MHW tightened the rules of eligibility for social assistance, which led to a steady decline in the relative level of social assistance allowances as well as in the percentage of recipients. It was under Ikeda's Income Doubling Plan that the level of social assistance was substantially raised. One of the five main agendas of the plan was the amelioration of the dual economic structure and the establishment of social stability. The plan focused on sectors that would not share in rapid economic growth and emphasized the need to reduce the size of low-income strata through the development of social security systems and social welfare programs (Economic Planning Agency 1961). At the same time, welfare bureaucrats began to play with the concept of relative poverty, rather than absolute poverty, and invented a new formula to calculate minimum living standards. They also advocated extending social assistance to all eligible persons, including the able-bodied, rather than simply to deserving persons like widows, the sick and disabled persons. Consequently, the levels of living assistance rose by 16% in 1961 and by 18% in 1962. The mass movement triggered by the *Asahi Shigeru vs. Minister of Health and Welfare* court case and Asahi's victory in 1960 may have influenced the government's policy change, but Ikeda's Income Doubling Plan was also a decisive factor.[26]

Although the Kishi cabinet was involved in initiating some social security policies aimed at low-income workers in small businesses and the agricultural sector, it was under the Ikeda cabinet that policy innovation occurred in the realm of anti-poverty measures and social assistance was used to compensate for ineffective minimum wages. However, this political sponsorship of social assistance did not last long, and in the following decades social assistance came under constant threat of retrenchment.

Fragmentation of Opposition: Selective State Intervention

The growing strength of socialist forces under the polarized party system was a driving force behind welfare through work formation. The following years were characterized by the fragmentation of the opposition parties and the decreasing popularity of the LDP. This tendency continued until the LDP resurgence in the 1980s. This section explores how changes in the dynamics of partisan competition affected policy development with respect to the social protection system.

From Retrenchment to Expansion

The differences in policy orientation between the Satō Eisaku cabinet (1964–1972) and the Tanaka Kakuei cabinet (1972–1974) could not have been starker. The Satō era was characterized by welfare retrenchment, whereas Tanaka launched various welfare programs accompanied by quantitative expansion of social spending. Satō was a staunch upholder of the conservative policy line, more loyal to Yoshida's policy orientation than Ikeda had been. Satō claimed to pursue a policy of social development and stressed the necessity of increasing social welfare, thus suggesting a departure from Ikeda's productivism. However, despite such statements, his cabinet reduced social assistance and the share of social expenditure in the national budget declined from 1966 and stagnated during his premiership.

In 1964, the MHW embarked on the second wave of its "adjustment" campaign and restricted the criteria for means test eligibility, making it extremely difficult for working households to receive assistance. The rate of recipients of social assistance began to decrease steadily from 1964 until 1974: from 18.1 persons per thousand (‰) in 1963 to 14.3‰ in 1968 to 11.9‰ in 1974. The decline in the rate of recipients is due in no small part to high economic growth, but is also attributed to the MHW's efforts. In fact, after the campaign ended in 1972 the rate of recipients stabilized and remained at the same level between 1974 and 1984. Moreover, the MHW's efforts to exclude able-bodied recipients from the social assistance program were reflected in the proportion of working households among the recipients, which declined drastically from 55.2% in 1960 to 33.6% in 1970 to 22.8% in 1975 (Yokoyama and Tada 1991, 241, 243).

Subsequent to Satō's premiership, the Tanaka Kakuei cabinet radically shifted the government's policy orientation. Despite Satō's ostensible emphases on "social development" and balanced development, his government continued to concentrate much of its resources in major industrial areas. Tanaka's initiatives spread regional development across the country, including rural areas under the slogan "remodeling the Japanese archipelago" (Kamo 1994). It was also under his initiatives that major welfare reforms were carried out, overriding resistance from the Ministry of Finance. Nineteen seventy-three is often referred to as "the first year of welfare" because of the implementation of free medical care for people over 70, an increase in the level of employee pensions and national pensions, indexation of pensions to the inflation rate, an increase in reimbursement provisions under the National Health Insurance, revision of the criteria for social assistance, and creation of the childcare allowance. These policy innovations, taken together, caused a massive quantitative increase in social spending. Figure 3.1 shows that social spending per GDP began to increase rapidly from 1973 until at least 1982. The share of social security expenditure in the national budget also soared from 16.5% in 1973 to 18.4% in 1974 to 21.7% in 1975.[27]

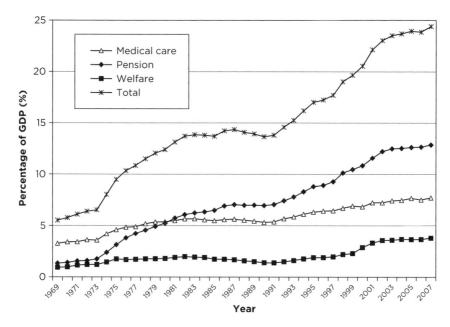

Figure 3.1. Social expenditure by item per GDP (%)
Source: National Institute of Population and Society Security Research (http://www.ipss.go.jp/ss-stat/j/toukeisiryou/toukeisiryou.html).

This share remained at around 20% until 2001. The increase between 1973 and 1975 was truly remarkable in this respect.

Why did this policy shift occur? Explanations based solely on the LDP's political vision and values are not convincing. Tanaka's decision was strategic in the context of the electoral environment at the time (Calder 1988; Campbell 1992). By the mid-1960s, the polarized state of partisan competition had been replaced by a new dynamic characterized by fragmentation of the opposition. Despite continuing urbanization and industrialization, the JSP failed to expand its support base among urban salaried workers. In the general election of 1969, it lost 50 seats, leaving only 90 seats, in contrast to the LDP's 288 seats. While the JSP began to experience long-term decline, the LDP also suffered from waning popularity (Figure 3.2). The share of LDP seats in the House of Representative did not exceed 60% between the general elections of 1967 and 2005, but the JSP's decline reduced the intensity of polarized partisan competition. The JSP was particularly weakened in urban areas where the Japan Communist Party (JCP) and Kōmeitō (founded in 1964) attracted people uprooted from their places of origin who were not sharing in the fruits of double-digit GDP growth.

The growing political clout of centrist parties meant that pressure to formulate accommodative policy had been relieved to some degree, despite

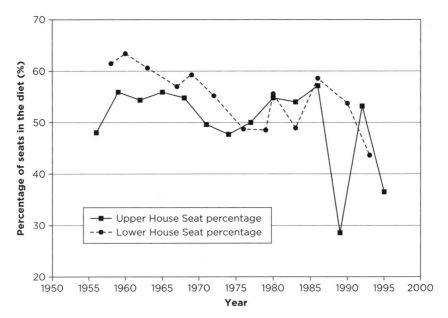

Figure 3.2. The LDP's share in the Diet
Source: Ministry of Internal Affairs and Communications (http://www.stat.go.jp/data/
chouki/27.htm). The LDP's share is based on the number of seats won by candidates officially
endorsed by the LDP, without including independent candidates who joined the party after the
election.

the LDP's waning popularity. From the mid-1960s, the government ceased to
make any effort to reduce underemployment or eliminate low-wage jobs. The
timing suggests that the fact that the alleviation of social tension was no longer
an urgent priority was not only a result of economic growth but also of the
new dynamics of partisan competition. The fragmentation of the opposition
was significant in this respect, but the radicalization of the JSP was also telling.
In 1964 the party adopted its de facto platform, "A Road toward Socialism in
Japan," which is generally seen as marking the JSP's refusal to become a social
democratic party. The increasing influence of left-wingers within the party
pushed it further left, while the center of the political spectrum was filled with
small parties like the DSP and Kōmeitō. In this political context, the LDP was
safely able to neglect the working class population as a constituency of any
great consequence.

   Although the JSP stagnated at the national level, leftist forces made great
leaps forward at the local level. Progressive governors and mayors supported
by the JSP and the JCP were elected throughout Japan. When Tanaka became
prime minister, nine out of forty-seven governors were from the JSP-JCP camp,
including those of major urban centers such as Tokyo, Osaka, and Kyoto.
Further, six out of the nine major cities were governed by the progressive

camp. Several local governments led by these officials initiated free medical care for the aged and childcare allowances starting in the late 1960s, thus effectively garnering votes. At the national level, the LDP won only 271 seats in the 1972 general election, which was its lowest haul since 1955. The LDP's policy shift was, therefore, triggered by this transformation of the political environment.

Since Tanaka's commitment to welfare reform was a result of electoral strategy, ideological justification for his policies was lacking. Indeed, a conservative backlash was in the offing. Welfare promises that would not further the interests of the ruling elite or facilitate production increase were ultimately doomed under conservative rule. However, the political opportunity to undertake welfare retrenchment did not arrive until the 1980s.

From Labor Transfer to Employment Stability

During the 1960s and 1970s, a significant policy shift also took place in the realm of employment policy. As already discussed, full employment policy was formulated by the conservative government to counter socialist forces in the face of intense competition in the ideologically polarized party system of the 1950s. Conversely, employment protection was created as a cornerstone of the social contract based on a cross-class social coalition. The diffusion of the norm and practices of lifetime employment substantiated the social contract. These two policy ideas resulted from the same political, social, and economic conflicts, but differed in a fundamental way. Full employment policy requires adequate social safety nets and the elimination of underemployment; however, employment protection at the individual company level entails a dual labor market. These two routes to a secure employment environment coexisted in the 1960s, but by the late 1970s, the government had shifted the paradigm of employment policy away from full employment in favor of employment protection.

Under the policy paradigm of full employment, the government encouraged labor transfer in order to achieve its goal. In the immediate postwar period, the Unemployment Relief Project, a program of government-subsidized public works jobs, was the main policy instrument aimed at the unemployed. The program soon became burdensome to the government. This was partly because MOL officials did not favor the idea of public works programs through which the government directly provided jobs, and partly because street-level officials were constantly confronted by recipients of the programs, who were mostly organized by an aggressive labor union—Zennichi Jichirō—closely linked to the JCP (Campbell 1992, 256–257). High-speed economic growth after 1955 then changed the conditions of the labor market, absorbing much of the labor force. After that labor shortages rather than unemployment became the issue of concern. In the manufacturing sector, the number of temporaries (*rinjikō*) rapidly declined during the first half of the 1960s. The proportion of temporaries relative to full-time regular workers decreased from 7.9% in 1961 to 4.5% in 1965 (Ministry of Labour, 1966, 99). Many temporaries became regular workers, which also alleviated social tensions. However, the new energy policy resulted in a large number of unemployed coal miners. These were mainly employed by the Unemployment Relief Project, yet also received social assistance due to the low level of wages provided by jobs under the project. Further, the Labor Minister stated in 1962 that the Unemployment Relief Project should eventually be abolished. As it became harder to qualify for social assistance, unemployed workers were compelled to take jobs in the labor market.

In this context, in 1963, the MOL amended several laws in order to encourage middle-age and elderly workers to find jobs in the construction sector. This approach was referred to as "active employment policy." The MOL aimed to create a modern labor market that would enable the smooth transfer of labor. In addition, the enactment of the Employment Measures Law in 1966 provided comprehensive legal support for the implementation of active employment policy. Labor bureaucrats perceived Japanese industrial relations as premodern in character, depriving old-age workers of employment opportunities because Japanese firms mistakenly prioritized long-term employment. The MOL promoted active employment policy that intended to encourage labor transfer in the external labor market.

Although the Employment Measures Law stipulated that the goal of the law was to achieve full employment, its intended aim was to facilitate smooth labor transfer in order to address disequilibrium in labor force supply and demand. The original draft of the Employment Measures Law did not mention the term "full employment" as the law's goal. Sōhyō criticized the draft, arguing that it would only serve to facilitate short-term economic goals beneficial to employers such as securing sufficient labor to the detriment of workers' welfare (Arima 1966, 26–42). In response to this protest, the term "full employment" was included in the final text to be introduced at the Diet. Interestingly, Japanese unions have used the term to mean employment protection at the level of individual firms. It is unclear as to why and how the term "full employment" was transformed from one associated with macro-level economic policy to a micro-level banner in the struggle against dismissals. According to Nitta Michio's (2008) study, such terminology was seen as early as during the labor disputes of the national railways and seamen's unions in 1946. By the early 1960s, policies based on cooperatism had engendered the social contract according to which employers were expected to commit to employment protection, yet policy makers undervalued the social contract and aimed to achieve full employment through unimpeded labor transfer. In contrast, unions accepted and even supported employment protection at the firm level under the slogan of "full employment."

The fundamental contradiction between full employment and employment protection was resolved after the first oil crisis due to the paradigm shift from full employment to employment protection. The Employment Insurance Law enacted in 1974 enshrined a fundamental policy change from active employment policy to employment stability policy, or from labor transfer in the external labor market to employment protection in the internal labor market (Hagamuchi 2004, 104, 133). The main instrument of labor stability policy was the Employment Adjustment Allowance, which subsidizes wage payments to temporarily laid-off workers in designated industries.[28] The government further amended the Employment Insurance Law in 1977, whereby the prevention of unemployment officially became one of the purposes of employment insurance. As a result, the Employment Stability Fund was created, which allowed the MOL to expand its resources for rescuing workers and employers in depressed industries during the following decades.[29]

How, then, did this paradigm shift occur? It was in some ways an unintended consequence of the Employment Insurance Law in the sense that a minor section of the bill ultimately served as a rallying point around which a cross-class coalition in the private sector, and the manufacturing sector in particular, was formed. One of the most controversial issues in reforming unemployment insurance was the status of seasonal and young female workers. MOL officials viewed these workers as abusing the unemployment insurance system, as they received about 70% of the total unemployment benefits paid out by the government.[30] However, the government's announcement of its intention to reduce benefits to these workers provoked opposition from the JSP and the JCP, who blocked the passage of the bill. However, the outbreak of the first oil shock transformed the attitude of unions as well as of the opposition parties, and the Employment Adjustment Allowance played an important role in the construction of a new alliance.[31] Employers and workers facing the possibility of restructuring welcomed the allowance bill, with both business and Dōmei calling for the prompt passage of the bill. Even private-sector unions in Sōhyō began to demand its swift enactment, which eventually resulted in Sōhyō changing its official position. Sōhyō's conversion then affected the JSP's stance, which resulted in the issue of benefit cutbacks being sidelined. Consequently, all opposition parties except the JCP supported the bill's passage.

The paradigm shift occurred not only within the rather narrow policy community dedicated to employment issues, but also took the broader form of social consensus. The judiciary also played an important role by providing legal authority and substance to the social contract established during the previous decade. The doctrine of abusive dismissal and the four requirements for dismissal for economic reasons endorsed the social norms that dismissals should be the very last resort; that employers are obligated to retain their employees for as long as possible; and that the government should provide financial and legal assistance to employers who are willing to retain and rehire workers (for more on this, see chapter 1). The 1975 Supreme Court's decision in the case of Nihon Salt Manufacturing established the doctrine of abusive dismissal and the Tokyo High Court's decision the same year in the case of Tōyō Sanso is widely referred to as providing the case law for the four requirements for dismissal for economic reasons.

Japan's approach to unemployment as developed in the mid- to late 1970s was distinctive. At the time, most advanced industrialized countries explored explicit links between employment adjustment and social safety nets in order to deal with the first massive industrial reorganization following the 1970s oil crises. In Continental Europe, redundant elderly workers were induced to exit the labor market, which was a feasible solution as a system of generous welfare benefits had already been developed. However, as this option was not available in Japan, the problem of redundant workers needed to be addressed in a different way. Employment protection was fortified and the government expanded various programs to assist employers who provided jobs. The links between work and welfare are thus quite contrasting in Continental Europe and Japan. The underdevelopment of the welfare state in Japan provided the backdrop for the government to formulate various employment maintenance policies.

The de facto paradigm shift in employment policy took place as an emergent response to the first oil crisis. However, the paradigm shift remained in accord with conservative ideology. Employment stability policy was a logical extension of cooperatism, which had been embodied in employment protection at the firm level. The difference here resided in the role of the state. Whereas the state directly assumed the responsibility to achieve full employment under the old policy paradigm, the state essentially outsourced the task to the private sector under the new policy paradigm. It was now employers who directly bore the responsibility to protect employment. The state's role was limited to managing the Employment Adjustment Allowance.

Does this mean that statism receded under the new paradigm? Statism justifies welfare programs from the standpoint of the governing apparatus. That the state's responsibility to full employment was reduced was consistent with statism. A direct challenge to statism was Tanaka's overcommitment to welfare expansion, which could only be justified in view of the exigencies of LDP survival. Consequently, an ideological backlash began to swell as early as 1975 and political backlash followed once the LDP had regrouped.

Conservative Resurgence: Redefining the State's Responsibility

The LDP did not immediately recover its popularity even after the implementation of supposedly popular welfare policies. The governing party lost its majority in the Lower House between 1976 and 1980 and again between 1983 and 1986 as well as in the Upper House between 1974 and 1980 (see Figure 3.2). Rather, a conservative resurgence first took place at the local level. Influential progressive governors and mayors began to retire around 1978. The electoral alliance of the JSP and the JCP was replaced by that of the JSP, Kōmeitō, and the DSP. In the meantime, the LDP sought an alliance with Kōmeitō and the DSP in order to break up the Center-Left coalition, which then resulted in the grand coalition (*ainori*) of all the parties other than the JCP at numerous governor and mayoral elections. At the national level, the LDP regained a majority in 1980 securing 284 seats out of 511. Although it lost the majority again in 1983, it recovered it in 1986. From the perspective of the share of seats held in the Diet, the LDP faced a more serious threat from the opposition parties in the late 1970s and mid-1980s than ever before. In fact, this period is referred to as one of parity between conservatives and progressives (*hokaku hakuchū*). The opposition camp became even more fragmented than in the previous decade, as centrist parties secured and maintained a certain degree of presence.

Although a full-fledged conservative resurgence did not occur until 1986, a conservative backlash against the welfare state was not long in coming. Repudiating the welfare expansion precipitated by the LDP's electoral strategy, conservatives denounced the welfare state by discrediting its productive element. For instance, conservative intellectuals began to propagate the discourse that the welfare state was the primary cause of Europe's decline.[32] An anonymous group named Group 1984 published a provocative article in 1975 titled "The Suicide of Japan," arguing that postwar (pseudo-)democracy taught Japanese rights, but made them oblivious to social responsibility and the spirit of self-help (Gurūpu 1984, 1975). Resonating with this line of argument, the term the "British Disease" (*igirisu byō* or *eikoku byō*) became a buzzword in the mass media in the latter half of the 1970s and early 1980s. Several books were published incorporating the term in their titles, not to mention numerous articles using this sensationalist terminology.[33] English-language books analyzing British economic problems were translated into Japanese with the "British Disease" featured in the titles, despite the fact that none of the original books used such language.[34] The argument went that Britain's long-term decline and stagnation were due to the strong trade unions, the large public sector, Keynesian economic policy, and the welfare state. Although Japan did not share any of these traits, conservative ideologues urged the Japanese government to change direction in order to preempt Japan's infection by the British disease. This type of discourse aimed to praise Japan's achievements in the light of British failings and ring alarm bells about the possibility that Japan would be contaminated by the same disease unless social spending was reduced and the labor unions emasculated. Absent from this causal and normative framework were positive linkage between the welfare state and economic growth. Welfare programs represented charity rather than social rights, and were thus burdensome, rather than beneficial, to the state.

Assisted by various conservative intellectuals, Prime Minister Ōhira Masayoshi (1978–1980) presented a conservative vision of the welfare state, which was fully articulated by the LDP's document titled "The Japanese Type of Welfare Society" (Jiyū Minshutō 1979). It advocated the concept of welfare society instead of the welfare state, in which self-reliance was prized and traditional families and communities were considered to bear the primary responsibility for welfare. It also argued that the big government would create the "Keynesian disease" and the "welfare state disease" and, therefore, that small government should be preserved to lessen the social burden on families and firms (see also Takahashi 1997).

Reliance on families and communities instead of the state is nothing new in the conservative thought. Japan's statism was based on the idea that the interests of the state should be prioritized over those of the people; families and communities should bear the primary responsibility to take care of their infirm and aged. The principle of subsidiarity—where the state intervenes only after families and communities can no longer cope—is a universal conservative idea that European conservative welfare states also subscribe to, but statism in Japan went so far as to presume that people and their families should not become a burden to the state. Self-help was a very important component of this concept. It should be noted that the concept of self-help in the Japanese context differs from the concept as found in liberal thought. In the latter, self-help is advocated as a bulwark against state encroachment into the private domain. In Japan, conversely, the state and ruling elites promote self-help in order to reduce the state's burden.

A new development during this period was that neoliberal discourse emphasizing individual choice and personal responsibility began to discredit productivism and, moreover, appeared to resonate with statism. This affinity between statism and neoliberalism is not as odd as it might initially seem. David Harvey succinctly defines neoliberalism as "a theory of political economic practices that proposes individual entrepreneurial freedoms and skills within an institutional framework characterized by strong private property rights, free markets, and free trade. The role of the state is to create and preserve an institutional framework appropriate to such practices" (2005, 2).[35] As Karl Polanyi's classic rendition reminds us, "while laissez-faire economy was the product of deliberate state action, subsequent restrictions on laissez-faire started in a spontaneous way. Laissez-faire was planned; planning was not" (1944, 141). The state is indispensable to the creation of the market. Although neoliberals understand the importance of the state's role in creating a free market, they deny that the state is responsible for protecting people's welfare. The legacy of statism in Japan is thus compatible with neoliberalism, which increases the impetus for welfare retrenchment.

Rinchō's Lasting Influence

Within the government, the Ministry of Finance began to stress the principle of beneficiary burden, according to which recipients of welfare programs would need to bear equivalent costs in order to receive benefits. The MHW also embraced this principle, supporting an economic framework that prioritized efficiency and self-help over redistribution and social rights (Shinkawa 1993, 142–145).

Moreover, the Second Rinchō (the Second Provisional Council for Administrative Reform, 1981–1983, hereafter "Second Rinchō" and "Rinchō" refer to the same organization in this book.) paved the way for welfare retrenchment in subsequent decades (Ōtake 1994). Prime Minister Suzuki Zenkō set up Rinchō, an ad hoc panel under the auspices of the prime minister's office with a mandate to realize fiscal reconstruction without increasing taxes. It was led by the charismatic Dokō Toshio, former president of Keidanren, who had reportedly been inspired by the Group 1984 article. The council laid a blueprint for neoliberal administrative reform including the privatization of Japan National Railways and the Nippon Telegraphs and Telephone undertaken by the cabinet of Nakasone Yasuhiro.

Rinchō also vocally supported welfare retrenchment. Its final proposal published in March 1983 stated in no uncertain terms that the role of the administration in the new era should be minimized in order to guarantee sufficient freedom for the private sector to operate. A dynamic welfare society, it was argued, can exist based on people's energy and creativity emerging from the principles of independence and self-help (Rinji Gyōsei Chōsakai 1993). Further, Rinchō left its mark on the debate regarding welfare retrenchment by creating a new concept, the "public burden rate" or "people's burden rate" (*kokumin futan ritsu*). The people's burden rate is the proportion of total tax revenue (combining tax and social security contributions) to national income. Rinchō's third proposal issued in 1982 stated that the people's burden rate would inevitably increase from the then-level of 35%, but should be kept much lower than the European level of 50%. (In fact, the 50% ceiling has been maintained by successive LDP cabinets.) Further, there seems to have been deliberate political intent behind the use of the people's burden rate as a gauge of the government's performance. The very terminology of "the people" (*kokumin*) and "burden" tends to give the impression that it is only the people that bear the costs. The word *kokumin* obscures the fact that corporations also pay taxes and social contributions. The word "burden" further creates the impression that the people bear the costs without receiving any of the benefits, thus having the effect of making public opinion sympathetic to welfare retrenchment. The government has used the percentage of the people's burden as a yardstick to measure the vitality of the Japanese economy. High people's burden rates have been constantly and explicitly associated with slow economic growth, with the ulterior motive of forging or maintaining a national consensus in support of a small state.[36]

The people's burden rate has repeatedly appeared in government documents since the creation of the concept, especially those written by fiscal and economic bureaucrats. Furthermore, a new concept of the "potential" people's burden rate came into use in the mid-1990s. In 1996, the Fiscal

System Council recommended the adoption of the concept of the potential people's burden rate, which includes fiscal deficits in the people's burden. The people's burden rate at the time was only 37.2%, much lower than the official ceiling of 50%. Because this low figure would not justify fiscal retrenchment, the government needed to inflate the figure by calculating a potential burden, which could be done by including fiscal deficits in their calculations. Prime Minister Hashimoto Ryūtarō declared in his general speech at the Diet in 1997 that necessary reforms needed to be swiftly conducted in order to keep the potential people's burden rate below 50%, a pledge that has been reiterated by subsequent cabinets. The high profile of the discourse of the people's burden rate in government documents and LDP speeches illustrates the decline of productivism in conservative thinking.

It was in the 1980s that the LDP actually initiated welfare retrenchment. Once public opinion accepted the importance of fiscal austerity and deficit-cutting policies, the LDP was the only party that publicly committed to cutting down governmental waste, which allowed it to gain new electoral strength (Curtis 1988, 72). Free medical care for the aged was abolished in 1982; copayment for national health-care insurance increased in 1984; and pension reform, which reduced the benefit level, was introduced in 1985. In terms of social assistance, the MHW initiated a third wave of its "adjustment" campaign in 1981, issuing "Notification No. 123." This required local welfare offices that received applications for social assistance to ask applicants to sign an agreement authorizing them to inquire at any relevant financial institutions in order to determine an applicant's means and income. If an applicant refused to sign, the notification ordered the welfare offices to reject the application and to file a criminal complaint if illegal recipients were discovered. The effect of the strict new means test is clear. The proportion of recipients began to decrease again from 1985: 11.8‰ in 1985, 8.2‰ in 1990, and 7.0‰ in 1995.[37] In 1987, the death from starvation of a thirty-nine-year-old mother and her three children who were refused an application for social assistance sent shockwaves through Japanese society, but it took another decade for the MHW to revise the requirements stipulated by the notification.

Figure 3.1 shows that social spending in relation to GDP stagnated in the 1980s. The trend reversed and began to climb in 1992, but overall welfare retrenchment continued in the 1990s and 2000s, as the rapid increase in relation to GDP resulted from economic recessions and weak recovery after the burst of the bubble economy as well as from the rapidly aging population. The average rate of increase in social expenditure in the 1970s was 22.9%, but was only 5.3% in the 1990s. Slow economic growth during this period, often called "the lost decade" or even the "lost twenty years" put further pressure on the government to reduce benefits and restrict eligibility.

An infusion of neoliberalism refashioned the concept of statism, thereby justifying the reduction of state responsibility for people's well-being. However, cooperatism remained the basis of employment policy throughout the 1980s. The MOL expanded the coverage of employment maintenance programs funded by the Employment Stability Fund in the 1980s and 1990s. With the basic menu for retaining, retraining, and rehiring already established, over a hundred such programs existed as of 1981, with differing qualification criteria for recipients. The precise extent to which the Employment Adjustment Allowance had a positive effect on actual employment security is unclear, yet experts believe that it at least contributed to the formation of social consensus with regard to employment protection.[38]

Cooperatism also continued to uphold the social contract based on employment protection at the firm level. As I have already noted, the policy paradigm of employment protection requires a dualized labor market in which a flexible workforce plays the role of shock absorber and enables economic adjustment. Male temporaries all but disappeared due to high-speed economic growth in the 1960s, but slow economic growth after the oil crisis once again created the need for a flexible workforce. Both employers and the government encouraged the employment of female workers, especially housewives, as a principal source of flexibility. Approximately 350 million female *pāto* were already in existence in the mid-1980s, making up 8.5% of the workforce (this share would increase to 10.6% in 1990 and 14% in 2005). Housewives/part-timers are a convenient labor force for employers who have to provide lifetime employment to their male regular workers. Most housewives take part-time jobs in order to supplement the family income. Because they are not the main breadwinners, policymakers have not considered their low wages and unstable working conditions as a social problem. Because male temporaries were often a source of labor disputes in the past, the gendered dual system was convenient from the standpoint of cooperative industrial relations. In other words, the persistence of cooperatism well into the 1980s was very much facilitated by the gendered division of labor (for more on this, see chapter 4).

At the time, the Japanese management system was almost universally praised as a major factor behind the competitiveness of the Japanese manufacturing sector. There was no suggestion of any attempt to dismantle the social contract based on employment protection during this period. It can even be said that the impact of cooperatism peaked in the 1980s, as the influence of the left-wing labor movement—which was mainly active in the public sector and was opposed to cooperatism—was irrevocably eroded during this period. In retrospect, the passage of the 1974 Employment Insurance Law can be seen to have put a significant dent in the predominance of public-sector unions in the Japanese labor movement. The rupture between the public-sector unions that were already protected and the private-sector unions that were eager to gain government support for employment protection became increasingly evident in the legislative process. Moreover, the privatization of the national railways, authorized by Rinchō, undercut the strength of the public-sector unions and, therefore, of the left-wing labor movement, as had been intended by conservative politicians. This shift in the power balance eventually led to the unification of the four top labor confederations under the leadership of the private-sector unions, and the formation of Rengō in 1989. The birth of Rengō heralded the triumph of cooperatism within the labor movement.

The impact of neoliberalism in the 1980s was thus limited to administrative reform and welfare retrenchment.[39] Interestingly, private-sector unions were zealous supporters of privatization which, they expected, would stave off tax increases (both corporate and personal) and weaken their rival unions. However, in the 1990s, neoliberalism gained currency even in the realm of labor market institutions. Employment stability was targeted by neoliberal reformers, and the labor market ultimately became more flexible. Was this because cooperatism withered under the rising influence of neoliberalism? If so, how has the replacement of cooperatism with neoliberalism affected the welfare through work system? Does Japan still rely on the welfare through work system or has a new social protection system emerged in line with the ascendance of neoliberalism? The following chapters examine the process of diffusion of neoliberalism, and explore how Japan's welfare through work has changed since the 1990s.

4

Reforming the Labor Markets

Since the late 1990s, the Japanese labor market has undergone a major transformation. The once-feted system of lifetime employment has been replaced by flexible employment and more than a third of the workforce has been relegated to the status of non-regular worker, receiving lower wages, fewer benefits, and fewer opportunities for promotion, all at greater risk of dismissal. Conversely, regular workers are now granted enhanced employment security, at least with respect to legal protection. These changes beg the following questions. What sort of labor market reform has been implemented and how has it changed Japan's labor markets? To what extent has Japan's employment system been transformed? Most pertinently to the main concern of this book, can the Japanese system of welfare through work be sustained by flexible employment?

This chapter reveals that although legal employment protection for regular workers was maintained, further internal and external flexibilities were necessarily created in an effort to preserve the status quo. The coexistence of strong employment protection and high employment rates in Japan has been possible because a number of flexibilities have been embedded in the labor markets (for more on this, see chapter 1). Labor market reform since the 1990s has preserved this trade-off, thereby degrading working conditions across the board. I show that it is misleading to regard male regular workers as winners benefiting from vested interests at the expense of other workers. Japan's experience refutes the conventional insider-outsider theories.

This chapter also examines the impact of gender equality and work-family balance measures that could potentially have provided sufficient legal protection to redress the balance between flexibility and security. I show that the absence of any principle of equal treatment of regular and non-regular workers precludes any meaningful attempt to realize de facto gender equality, resulting instead in the pauperization of women.

As a result of the above-mentioned changes, the limits of welfare through work as a social protection system began to become evident in the 2000s. Rather than this simply being a case of the welfare through work system unable to deal with new social risks that have emerged in a globalizing market economy, I contend that these risks have been created by welfare through work. It is the policy framework of welfare through work that has allowed the expansion in numbers of non-regular workers as a politically acceptable alternative to mass unemployment. At the same time, strong employment protection has been accompanied by the creation of further internal flexibilities, which have reinforced the gendered dual system by making work and family responsibilities incompatible. Moreover, the weak social safety nets that were justified under welfare though work system have detrimentally affected the living conditions of low-income workers. Therefore, incremental adaptation to new market realities under the welfare through work system has resulted in the dysfunction of the system itself.

Asymmetrical Deregulation: Regular Workers vs. Non-Regular Workers

Labor market reform is generally conducted in order to increase flexibility in the labor market, but sometimes also to enhance protection and security for workers. All countries engage in both these aspects of labor market reform, albeit to varying degrees and at different speeds. In Japan, the temporary labor market has been made increasingly flexible while, at the same time, employment protection for regular workers has been strengthened. Asymmetrical deregulation of this kind is an international trend and Japan is not unique in this regard. Given the political difficulties inherent in curtailing the protection of regular workers, it should not be surprising that employers and governments would seek greater flexibility elsewhere, such as in the temporary labor market. We might expect deregulatory pressure to be high in countries that have higher levels of employment security for regular workers.

Figure 4.1 illustrates recent regulatory changes in selected countries measured by the Organization for Economic Co-operation and Development (OECD). The chart traces changes between the late 1980s and 2003 with respect to the overall strictness of protection against dismissals and the overall strictness of regulation on temporary employment, and confirms our expectation that deregulation of temporary employment has been implemented in many countries while the level of protection against dismissals remains almost unchanged. Sweden, Germany, Denmark, Italy, and Belgium provide the most drastic examples of asymmetrical deregulation; Japan, the

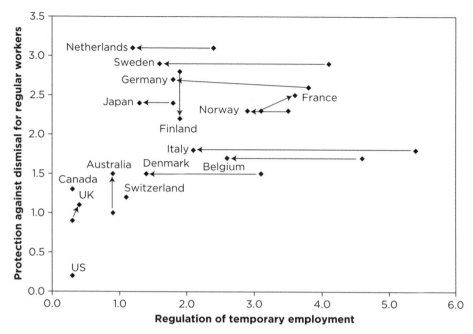

Figure 4.1. Changes in employment protection indexes for regular and temporary workers (late 1980s to 2003)
Source: OECD 2004, table 2.A.2.1.and table 2.A2.2.

Netherlands, and Norway also conform to this pattern. Several studies reveal that a "two-tier" approach has been pursued in most European countries, with the exception of the United Kingdom (Bertola et al. 2001; Lodovici 2000).

Japan's score on the overall strictness of regulation of temporary employment moved from 1.8 in 1990 to 1.3 in 2003, whereas the overall level of protection against dismissals remains the same during this period (2.4). This reduction may appear rather moderate by international standards as many European countries underwent more drastic deregulation, but the distributional consequences of asymmetrical deregulation are more severe in Japan due to large pay differentials between regular workers and temporary workers as well as the inequality of these two groups in terms of social rights. As suggested by the term "flexicurity," a balanced combination of flexibility and security is an achievable aim. As long as security measures are integrated, flexibility in the labor market does not inevitably engender precarious working conditions, or "precarity." Japan's labor market reform did not include adequate security measures for those workers who are vulnerable to flexible circumstances. Although the degree of labor market deregulation was modest by international comparison, one-sided reform caused distributional

TABLE 4.1
Labor market reforms, 1986–2007

Strengthened protection		Major changes
1985	Equal Employment Opportunity Law	Partial ban on discriminatory conduct against women
1991	Childcare Leave Law	Creation of childcare leave
1994	Employment Stability Law for Elderly Workers	Mandatory retirement under age 60 became illegal
1995	Childcare Family Care Leave Law	Creation of family care leave
1997	Equal Employment Opportunity Law	Strengthening of anti-discrimination regulations
2003	Labor Standards Law	Legalization of dismissal law
	Employment Stability Law for Elderly Workers	Mandatory retirement under age 65 officially discouraged
2006	Equal Employment Opportunity Law	Prohibition of indirect discrimination
2007	Part-time Labor Law	Equal and balanced treatment of regular and part-time workers
	Minimum Wage Law	Strengthening of the function of regional-level minimum wages

Deregulation		Major changes
1985	Temporary Work Agency Law	Legalization of TWAs under a positive list
1997	Labor Standards Law	Abolition of protective measures for women
1998	Labor Standards Law	Expansion of discretionary working hour rules
1999	Temporary Work Agency Law	Shift from a positive list to a negative list method
	Job Security Law	Liberalization of job replacement services
	Labor Standards Law	Extension of the fixed-term contract to three years for special workers
2003	Temporary Work Agency Law	Removal of the manufacturing sector from the negative list
	Labor Standards Law	Extension of the fixed-term contract to three years for general workers
		Expansion of discretionary working hour rules

inequality. In essence, Japan's labor market reform has reinforced, rather than modified or dismantled, the gendered dual system, thereby both creating and aggravating new social risks. (See Table 4.1 for a summary of labor market reforms.)

Employment Protection for Regular Workers

A prominent feature of labor market reform since the 1990s is that employment protection for regular workers has been strengthened. In 1998, mandatory retirement before the age of 60 became illegal when the 1994 Employment Stability Law for Elderly Workers became effective. Although the term "lifetime employment" is conventionally used to describe Japan's long-term employment practice, mandatory retirement was often set as early as at the age 55 or even before. This practice of de facto "early" retirement was embedded in Japanese employment practice. Japanese firms tended to more generously remunerate employees who had worked in the same company for a longer period, which made long-term employees financially burdensome to their employers. Early mandatory retirement was thus necessary in order to alleviate the financial burden. The government, however, intervened in this corporate practice, pushing for an increase in the mandatory retirement age, because the gradually aging and shrinking population of Japan was having a deleterious impact on the financial foundation of the pension system, which compelled the government to extend the pensionable age from the age of 60 to 65 in 1994.[1] This change in the pension system necessitated reform of the mandatory retirement system in order to prevent the creation of an income vacuum between working life and pensioned retirement. In 2004, the government further amended the law in order to encourage employers to extend the mandatory retirement age to 65 (effective since 2006). It is likely that mandatory retirement under 65 will eventually become illegal.

The other aspect of enhanced employment protection was the legislation of dismissal rules by amendment of the Labor Standards Law in 2003. The doctrine of abuse of the right of dismissal as well as the application of the four requirements for dismissal for economic reasons had made dismissals both costly and troublesome. The enactment of the 2003 law made the doctrine statutory through the restatement of case law. Most labor law experts believed that the dismissal law would ensure that the existing level of employment protection was maintained. Interestingly, however, the government did not initially commit to protecting the existing level of employment protection. The trend toward neoliberal policy under the Koizumi cabinet (2001–2006) lent greater weight to the voices of those who wished to expedite easier dismissals. The Ministry of Health, Labour, and Welfare (MHLW) first drafted a business-friendly bill, stipulating the right of employers to dismiss workers. In the Diet, however, the Democratic Party of Japan (DPJ) and the unions succeeded in modifying the law by erasing the very phrase stating that employers have the right to dismiss workers. Consequently, the doctrine of abuse of the right of dismissal was restated in the law. Unlike in the case of the extension of the mandatory retirement age, it was not the intention of the government to preserve employment protection. Rather, the outcome of this bill was the result of partisan politics.

Although the restatement of the doctrine of abuse of the right of dismissal in the Labor Standards Law is generally interpreted to mean that workers in Japan enjoy the same level of employment protection as previously, some critics have voiced concerns that the four requirements for dismissal for economic reasons were not actually restated in the law and that the courts have recently loosened the application of the four requirements. The Tokyo District Court took the position that the "four requirements" are merely "four factors," meaning that an economic dismissal can be found legally valid even if one of the factors is not met.[2] This new approach has prevailed in subsequent decisions by the courts. The unions and labor lawyers worry that Japan's employment protection became weaker de facto, whereas mainstream legal scholars consider the protection level to remain higher than that in the United States and Germany, even with looser application of the four requirements.[3]

The general perception among the policy community that Japan has a high level of employment protection affected the way in which the Labor Contract Law was formulated. This law applies to all aspects of employment contracts from hiring to retirement, secondment to related firms, or transfer of a worker's contract to another firm.[4] Rengō demanded the enactment of such law and the MHLW also saw that contractual rules between company and worker were necessary to deal with the increasing number of disputes between individual workers and employers. All the parties agreed on the necessity of enacting a labor contract law, but disagreed on the specific content thereof. Legal experts commissioned by the MHLW to draft the basic design of the law proposed a comprehensive framework.[5] However, due to major disagreements between the unions and employers, all the controversial portions were ultimately removed from the government bill except for the section related to "work rules."[6]

"Work rules" (*shūgyō kisoku*) is a company document that determines the rights and obligations of workers with respect to working hours, allowances, transfers, sanctions, dress codes, and so on. The Labor Standards Law requires companies employing more than ten people to establish work rules. Employers are required to consult a trade union organized by a majority of the workers regarding the work rules, but are not obligated to obtain the consent of the union, and the contents are essentially determined at their discretion. Employers are theoretically able to reduce wages and alter working conditions to the detriment of their employees by unilaterally revising the work rules. The Supreme Court has established the doctrine that disadvantageous changes to work rules legally bind workers, including those opposing the changes, as long as reasonableness can be established.[7] It is generally held that the doctrine of abuse of the right of dismissal and the doctrine of unfavorable changes to work rules work in tandem in that the former doctrine limits managerial discretion while the latter grants employers flexibility in managing the employment relationship. Therefore, the legal restatement of the dismissal rules necessitated the restatement of the doctrine of unfavorable changes to work rules.

In the final version passed at the Diet in November 2007, the Labor Contract Law stipulates the principle that an employer shall not unfavorably alter working conditions by revising work rules without the consent of workers (Art. 9). It then sets forth the conditions under which Art. 9 shall not be applied (Art. 10); that is, when an employer informs workers of the changes in the work rules and when the changes in the work rules are reasonable in view of (1) the degree of disadvantage to workers, (2) the necessity of changes in working conditions, (3) the appropriateness of the revised work rules, and (4) the state of negotiations with a labor union or the like. Critics contended that the enactment of the law would send a message to employers that they are free to degrade working conditions by changing the work rules at will.[8] Some legal scholars criticized the aspect of the law whereby the unilateral setting of working conditions by the employer becomes part of the employment contract as long as the work rules are reasonable, even for those who oppose disadvantageous changes to working conditions. In contrast, Rengō, the DPJ, and mainstream labor law experts took the position that the law indeed clarified the principle that changes in work rules should be reasonable, thereby contributing to the prevention of disputes between individual workers and their employer.

What was manifested in the policy debate on work rules was the existence of a trade-off between strong employment protection and extensive managerial discretion. The perception in the policy community that Japanese employment protection is strong, and perhaps even too strong, created support for policy changes that would facilitate greater functional flexibility. The combination of strong employment protection for regular workers and a high degree of internal flexibility continues to define Japanese employment practice, and is more concretely embodied in the law because of labor market reform. Consequently, one aspect of the gendered dual system, a trade-off between employment protection of male regular workers and functional flexibility, was reinforced.

Expanding and Diversifying Non-Regular Workers

The other aspect of the gendered dual system, a trade-off between employment protection and external flexibility, was also reinforced, as labor market reform has proceeded more drastically in the realm of non-regular workers. As non-regular workers are a necessary and integral part of the gendered dual system guaranteeing employment protection for regular workers, the history of deregulation of the temporary labor market goes back a long way in Japan. The Job Security Law, which originally prohibited labor supply businesses, was amended in 1952 to allow labor-contracting businesses to operate.[9] Large companies began to use external laborers (*shagaikō*) to cope with the economic boom after the Korean War, which compelled the government to introduce the 1952 amendment to the Job Security Law to legalize this practice. The use of external laborers became a common method for large manufacturing companies to retain flexibility, but high economic growth limited the role of this practice. Instead, after the economic recovery following the oil crisis, women began to enter the labor market, usually as part-time or temporary workers.[10] The 1985 Temporary Work Agency

Law legalized staffing businesses that were already illegally operating at the time. The law had previously allowed temporary work agencies to fill jobs only in certain specialized areas on a "positive list."[11] As temporary agency workers, or dispatched workers, are likely to be placed in a relatively weak position with respect to employment protection, the restrictions enforced by the positive list method aimed to allow staffing businesses to operate only in areas where dispatched workers possessed specialized skills. The other, perhaps more important, aim of the restrictions on staffing businesses was the protection of regular workers in client companies. Unfettered expansion of staffing businesses, policymakers feared, might undermine lifetime employment in companies using temporary agency workers (Hamaguchi 2004, 69).

The 1999 revision of the Temporary Work Agency Law introduced the "negative list method" according to which only jobs where staffing agencies are not allowed to fill slots are specified; that is, construction work, port transport services, and security services.[12] This kind of liberalization could have flung the door wide open to the creation of a low-cost and flexible labor force. Among the numerous controversial issues raised by the 1999 revision, the unions most vehemently opposed the introduction of dispatched workers to the manufacturing sector. The government proposal was altered in order to obtain union approval, with the addition of an exception clause that allowed the manufacturing sector to be exempted for a certain period (see chapter 6 for more detail). Moreover, a one-year term limit was introduced in order to prevent the replacement of regular workers by temporary agency workers.[13] In other words, the role of the staffing business was defined as facilitating the temporary adjustment of supply and demand in the labor market. The idea of setting a limited term period essentially aimed to protect regular workers rather than dispatched workers. Although some protective measures aimed toward the latter group were added to the bill during deliberation at the Diet, the level of protection remained weak (Weathers 2004).

The introduction of the negative list was part of an international trend. In 1997, the ILO revised the Fee-Charging Employment Agencies Convention (No. 96) and adopted the Private Employment Agencies Convention (No. 181), thereby allowing fee-charging employment agencies to operate under the negative list. Japan implemented the deregulation according to this international framework.[14] However, the principle of equal treatment of agency workers received scant attention in Japan, despite the fact that equal treatment and other protective measures were an essential part of the ILO Convention and recommendations.

Further deregulation in Japan was implemented by amendment to the Temporary Work Agency Law in 2003. In this instance, the legislation abolished the exemption measure applied to manufacturing jobs, thereby opening up this sector to staffing agencies. At the same time, the one-year term limit was expanded to three years. With respect to the manufacturing sector, the term limit was set at one year until 2006. Because the term limit was originally designed to protect regular workers, the expansion of the term period would inevitably threaten their job security. As a compromise, the amended law required an employer to solicit the opinion of an employee representing the majority of workers (*kahansū daihyō*) with regard to the time period for which the employer would accept temporary agency workers. In terms of protection of agency workers, the amended law encouraged the direct employment of such workers, as employers utilizing an agency worker for longer than the term limit became obligated to offer that person a direct employment contract.

The protective measure formulated in exchange for deregulation—the obligation to offer direct employment—did not function as expected. It was burdensome to employers, who regarded dispatched workers as cheap labor, and created an environment in which employers began to seek loopholes in the law and sometimes even engage in illegal conduct. Employers are able to evade this obligation as long as they employ contracted workers (*ukeoi*) instead of dispatched workers (*haken*). The differences between contracted and dispatched workers are sometimes blurred. The latter are under the control of and subject to orders from the firm they are dispatched to, whereas it is illegal for a boss in a client company to give direct order to contracted workers. Partly due to the impracticability of these regulations and partly due to the lack of compliance, use of "disguised contractors" (*gisō ukeoi*) became extremely widespread. In 2004, the MHLW began to strengthen its organizational resources with a goal to detect disguised contractors. In the same year, there were 974 cases in which Prefectural Labor Bureaus advised employers to correct their employment practice, meaning that they identified wrongful conduct in one-third of the firms and agencies they inspected. The manufacturing sector, and high technology factories in particular, have been particularly prone to exposure of illegal conduct. The fact that Canon, whose president was the chairman of Nippon Keidanren at the time, was found to have employed disguised contractors in its factories became a minor scandal, forcing the corporation to hire an increased number of regular full-time workers. Some employers, however, blamed the current labor laws, which, they argued, did not reflect the realities of the manufacturing sector, and advocated the legalization of illegal conduct in this area.

The lack of regulation of fixed-term contracts is another loophole in Japanese labor law that allows abusive treatment by employers.[15] The Labor Standards Law had stipulated that a fixed-term contract could be made for up to one year. The 1999 amendment allowed workers who possess highly specialized knowledge and those over the age of 60 to conclude a contract for up to three years. Furthermore, the 2003 amendment expanded the term limit to three years for general workers and five years for the special case workers. There are no other restrictions on the conditions under which fixed-term contracts can be made. Employers are able to use fixed-term contracts for any reason and to renew contracts as many times as they wish.

Therefore, employers are effectively able to fire fixed-term workers simply by not renewing contracts. Moreover, by employers determined to evade protective measures for workers often use repeated renewal of very short-term contracts (Nakano 2006). In 2001, 44.3% of part-time workers worked under the terms of fixed-term contracts.[16] Numbers of those who work as-and-when required, so-called on-call workers, are also on the rise. Among this kind of worker, those enrolled in staffing agencies receive job information on their mobile phones and take jobs as day laborers. Approximately 53,000 people were "on call" each day in 2007.[17] In 2008 the MHLW raised concerns regarding the necessity to regulate fixed-term contracts, creating a study group to formulate new guidelines.[18] It also created another study group the following year to prepare for legislation and introduced the bill to the Diet in 2012. Although the courts have established a legal precedent according to which repeated renewal of a fixed-term contract is considered to constitute an open-ended contract, insufficient attention was paid to the vulnerability of fixed-term contract workers and thus the idea of regulating fixed-term contracts did not gain currency among the policy community until the late 2000s.[19]

The series of measures aimed at deregulation of the temporary labor market discussed above resulted in the diversification and proliferation of non-regular workers. The share of non-regular workers in the total labor force increased from 20.2% in 1990 to 26.0% in 2000 to 34.4% in 2010.[20] Although 80% of male workers are still regular employees, over half of female workers are non-regular workers (Figure 4.2). The share of non-regular workers among young people (ages 15–24, excluding those attending school) is also high, surpassing the 30% level in 2003. Labor market reform essentially caused the gendered dual system to become even more deeply entrenched.

Toward Equality?

Deregulation of the temporary labor market per se does not automatically result in unilateral deterioration of the working conditions of temporary workers as long as, for example, sufficient protective measures are provided. However, the Japanese approach to deregulation resulted in exacerbation of the precarious situation of non-regular workers due to lack of an effective enforcement mechanism for equal treatment of regular and non-regular workers. This section examines policy development and debates on legislation aimed at the establishment of equality between full-time and part-time workers as well as between the two sexes. Although some protective measures have been advanced, overall protection for non-regular workers remains insufficient because the principle of equal treatment directly contradicts the mechanisms of the gendered dual system.

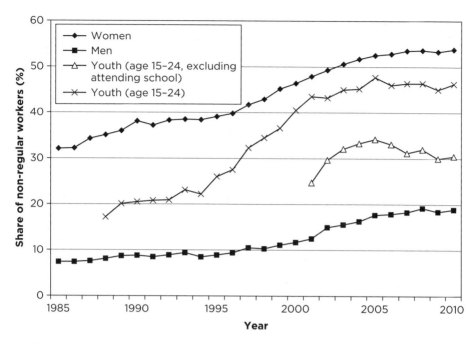

Figure 4.2. Share of non-regular workers (1985–2010)
Source: Ministry of Internal Affairs and Communications, *Labour Force Survey* (http://www.stat.
go.jp/data/roudou/).

Balanced Treatment: The Rationality of Discrimination

The Part-Time Labor Law is the main legal protective measure for part-time
workers. The legislative process that led to its enactment shows how the gendered dual system framed deliberations, making elimination of discrimination against non-regular workers extremely difficult in Japan. The Part-Time
Labor Law was first enacted in 1993 in response to persistent pressure from
socialists, yet it was not until the 2007 amendment to the law that a certain
degree of protection for part-time workers was finally secured.[21] The most
controversial question was how to redress the unequal status of full-time and
part-time workers. Because the existence of this inequality is the very reason
that employers hire part-time workers, employer opposition to equalization
of status proved intransigent. The Japanese government had abstained from
approval of the ILO's Part-Time Work Convention (C175) in 1994 due to
such employer opposition. During the negotiation process for the original
law, the Japan Socialist Party pushed hard to legislate "equal treatment"
(*kintō taigū*) of full-time and part-time workers. The Ministry of Labour
(MOL) steadfastly refused to use the term, but instead accepted the concept
of "balanced treatment" (*kinkō taigū*). The law consequently stipulated that

employers shall endeavor to maintain balance between regular and non-regular workers.[22] This negotiation sparked a conflict, which continues to the present day, between advocates of equal treatment and those who will go no further than reluctant acceptance of balanced treatment.[23]

The creation of the concept of balanced treatment prompted the MOL to begin theorizing about the meaning of balance. In 1998, the Ministry established a study group on part-time labor, often called the Measurement Study Group (*monosashi ken*), because it was commissioned to invent a measurement to gauge balance.[24] The final report of the Study Group published in 2000 stated that part-time workers who have the same job assignments as regular workers, classified by the report as Type A workers, should be treated in the same way as their regular counterparts, or that the working conditions of the respective groups should be more closely approximated. At the same time, the report argued that rational discrimination can be implemented when Type A workers are exempt from overtime work, working on holidays, transfers, or relocation. The grounds for rational discrimination advanced by the report were to be considered in terms of the degree to which workers are obligated to follow their employers' orders—in other words, the degree of "constraint" (*kōsokusei*) imposed on workers. As regular workers are not able to reject employers' orders regarding overtime work, working on holidays, transfers and relocation, the report considered it to be reasonable that they receive higher wages than part-time workers who are not obligated in the same manner.

It is noteworthy that policy experts stressed the degree of constraint to justify discrimination. Theoretically, the rationalization behind wage inequality between full-time workers and part-time workers should be found in types of job assignments, levels of skills, or degrees of responsibility. However, as some part-time workers engage in the same job assignments, acquire the same skill levels and assume the same responsibilities as regular workers, these conventional differences became inappropriate for justifying pay inequality. It was constraint, or "unlimited duties" to companies that continued to characterize the working style of regular workers and thus was used to justify the more favorable treatment they received. The reason why part-time workers were subject to a low degree of constraint was that these workers were mostly housewives—the working style of regular workers obviously clashed with family responsibilities. The argument formulated by the Measurement Study Group thus accentuated the conventional division of labor between men and women by taking male breadwinner families for granted.

The idea of highly obligated and constrained full-time regular workers was further advanced by the Study Group on Part-Time Workers that the MHLW set up in 2001–2002.[25] This group proposed to establish new rules of Japanese-type balanced treatment for part-time workers by diversifying work styles, breaking away from the dichotomy between regular workers who are highly obligated and part-time workers who only engage in supplementary job assignments, and recommended creating a third type of work style, less constrained than regular workers but better paid than part-time workers. Although the study group aimed to design a fairer employment system, it did not question differentiated treatment based on degrees of constraint. The proposition invited criticism from those who, dissatisfied with the concept of balanced treatment, considered equal treatment indispensable to the advancement of part-time workers' rights. However, under the conservative rule of the Liberal Democratic Party, even the MHLW's definition of balanced treatment was politically unacceptable. Due to strong opposition from employers, the MHLW gave up on making a new law in March 2003, and amended its ministerial guidelines instead.

It was not until 2006 that a window of opportunity opened up for the legislation. When the Equal Employment Opportunity Law was passed at the Diet in June 2006, a supplementary resolution was added, stipulating that the government should proceed to ensure balanced treatment of full-time and part-time workers so that the latter would be able to "fulfill their capabilities with positive feelings." At the same time, the then Abe cabinet (2006–2007) advanced the re-challenge (*sai charenji*) policy under which it attempted to support those who had suffered as a result of the structural reforms implemented by the Koizumi cabinet. The prospect of the Upper House election scheduled for the following year stimulated the Abe cabinet to address the negative consequences of the Koizumi reforms. In this new political climate, amendment of the Part-Time Labor Law suddenly appeared on the agenda in 2006 (see chapter 7 for more detail).

Now certain of political backing for the amendment, the MHLW quickly concluded deliberations at the advisory council despite employer opposition, passing the government bill in April 2007. The new law stipulated prohibition of discriminatory treatment of part-time workers who are equivalent to regular workers. This was a notable advancement from the previous law; however, the coverage of equal treatment under this provision is tremendously limited. Part-time workers equivalent to ordinary workers are those who (i) assume the same job assignments and responsibilities, (ii) conclude indefinite work contracts, and (iii) are subject to changes in job descriptions and assignments to the same extent as ordinary workers. It should be noted that the third criterion stipulates the degree of constraint as an important factor in differentiating part-time workers who benefit from equal treatment from those who do not. Family responsibility continues to be used to justify discrimination under Japan's principle of equal treatment. Labor bureaucrats had expected that 4–5% of part-time workers would fulfill these conditions.[26] According to a survey conducted after the implementation of the law, only 0.1% of part-time workers were regarded as equivalent to ordinary workers.[27]

The 2007 amendment was a significant step forward in the sense that the term "equal treatment" is included in the law. However, the fact that its coverage is extremely limited illustrates the difficulty of universal application of this principle. The establishment of equal treatment will entail the overhauling of the gendered dual system, under which attempts to redress discrimination can go no further than pursuit of balanced treatment and under which it will always be possible to rationalize discrimination.

Gender Equality and Work-Family Balance

Approximately 70% of non-regular workers are women. Accordingly, it is pertinent to examine the extent to which gender equality policies have, or have not, improved the unequal status of non-regular workers. Since the mid-1980s, successive amendments have gradually steered labor law toward embodiment of gender equality. The Japanese government signed the Convention on the Elimination of All Forms of Discrimination against Women in 1980, which necessitated the enactment of equal opportunity law. A controversial issue in this respect was the conflict between equality and protection. Feminists divided into two camps on this issue—those who prioritized equality over protective measures for women and those who opposed elimination of protective measures. Businesses vehemently opposed gender equality yet also welcomed and pursued the elimination of protection of women. In contrast, Sōhyō claimed that a new law should include penalties for employers who discriminate against women and that the existing protective measures should not be amended. The Equal Employment Opportunity Law (EEOL) was enacted in 1985, born as a compromise between these different positions. It prohibited discrimination against women in terms of training, fringe benefits, mandatory retirement, and dismissal but not in recruitment, hiring, assignment, and promotion. Further, employers were obligated only to endeavor to eliminate discriminatory conduct in these areas. At the same time, protective measures were relaxed for only a certain portion of white-collar women and maternity protection was strengthened.[28]

The EEOL's most conspicuous effect was that two-track, or multiple-track, employment management systems began to proliferate.[29] Most women were hired on a second, or lower, track with severely limited possibilities of promotion and wage raises. As long as a few elite women were hired on the general course (*sōgō shoku*) or managerial track, this discriminatory employment system was not considered to violate the law.[30] The MOL issued a guideline stating that it would consider discrimination illegal only against women within the same category of recruitment and hiring, and not across different categories. The MOL's stance has not essentially changed to date, although its theories and arguments have become more sophisticated. The 1997 amendment to the EEOL prohibited discrimination against women in all areas including recruitment, hiring, assignment, and promotion, but the new guidelines accompanying the revision introduced the concept of "employment management categories" (*koyō kanri kubun*) and indicated that discrimination was only illegal within the same employment management category. Acceptance of transfers accompanied by residential relocation was often used as a condition for hiring on the managerial track. This condition often discourages those women who bear greater family responsibilities from applying for managerial track positions. In 2000, the MOL issued a new document to clarify that employment management categories should be objective and rational.[31] The MOL began to implement more robust administrative guidance based on this document, scrutinizing inappropriate application of employment management categories. Despite the legal changes and administrative intervention, in reality employment management categories—originally created to conceal gender discrimination—continue to justify different treatment of the two sexes by emphasizing the traditional role of women as primary caregivers. Among the companies that operate course-based employment management, 94.4% used acceptance of relocation as a condition for the managerial track as of 2000–2001 and 83.4% in 2005–2006.[32]

With respect to protective measures for women, the 1997 amendment put an end to the debate over equality and protection, eliminating the remaining protective measures for women. The Labor Standards Law was then amended to enable women to work night shifts. The upper limit on overtime work for women was raised from 150 hours to 360 hours per year, the same level as for male workers. Given the notoriously long working hours of Japanese workers, the labor unions were divided regarding the elimination of protective measures for women. Communists opposed to this deregulation argued that the upper limit should be set at 150 hours for both men and women. Some unions affiliated with Rengō made the same demand, but Rengō itself decided to prioritize equality over protection and thus agreed to the abolition of all the protective measures for women with regard to working hours.

Deregulation of working hour restrictions often clashes with family responsibilities. The Childcare Leave Law, which was first enacted in 1991, has been steadily amended since then to strengthen the rights of workers who bear responsibilities for childcare and family care.[33] Demographic concerns have prompted conservative governments to improve the childcare environment for working women, albeit without any tangible results to date. The 1995 amendment granted both mothers and fathers of preschool-age children the right to claim exemption from night shifts.[34] Furthermore, the 2001 amendment granted these workers the right to refuse to work more than 150 hours of overtime per year or more than 24 hours of overtime in a given month, and prohibited unfavorable treatment of employees who take childcare and family care leave. These protective measures were granted not only to mothers but also to fathers with family care responsibilities. Protective measures for women, except for maternity protection, were replaced by protection of those responsible for family care, essentially implementing a gender-neutral policy of work-family balance.

The most recent amendment to the EEOL in 2006 embodied the ideal of gender equality. The amendment prohibits discrimination not only against

women but also against men. It also prohibits indirect discrimination, a provision that feminists have longed for since the 1997 amendment. Indirect
discrimination occurs when a company places unnecessary conditions and
requirements on a particular job description in order to prevent a certain
group from applying. Feminists expected that the prohibition of indirect discrimination would expose various company practices that constitute de facto
discrimination against women. However, during parliamentary deliberation
the MHLW made it clear that it would issue an ordinance for enforcement
that would specify, rather than merely exemplify, the nature of indirect discrimination. Much to the disappointment of many interested parties, the
eventual ordinance stipulated that only three scenarios are to be viewed as
virtual discrimination based on gender.[35] The state's definition of indirect
discrimination significantly limits the potential usefulness of the concept of
indirect discrimination to women.[36] One of the factors pertinent to the three
cases of indirect discrimination stipulated by the ordinance is a worker's availability for relocation. The ordinance specifies that the EEOL prohibits the
corporate practice of recruiting and hiring workers for the managerial track
based on their availability for reassignments that would necessitate residential relocation, despite the fact that such relocations are entirely superfluous
to the realities of personnel management in that company. The application
of indirect discrimination to course-based human resource management is
a major step forward, although its actual impact remains to be seen.[37] When
the United Nation's Committee on the Elimination of Discrimination against
Women (CEDAW) examined the sixth periodical report submitted by the
Japanese government in 2009, it expressed concern that employment management categories "may provide leeway to employers to introduce a track-
based system which discriminates against women."[38] In fact, as of 2008, the
practice of employment management categories continues to be highly gen-
derized, and the share of women employed in the managerial track positions
remains low: 6.0% of the total number of employees on the managerial track
and 16.9% of those who were scheduled to be hired on the managerial track.[39]

How did these reforms aimed at increased realization of gender equality
affect wage inequalities between regular workers and non-regular workers?
The wage gap between male regular workers and female regular workers has
been steadily reduced, albeit to a limited degree overall. As of 1985, when the
EEOL was enacted, general female workers (including fixed-term full-time
workers but excluding part-time workers) earned 59.6% of the wages earned
by their male counterparts, which rose to 65.5% in 2000, and 69.3% in 2010.
For regular workers, women earned 68.7% of male wages in 2005, which rose
to 72.1% in 2010. In contrast, the wage gap between general female workers
and female part-time workers has increased: the ratio of the latter group's
wage to that of the former was 73.0% in 1985, 70.4% in 1995, and 65.7% in
2004, which was the lowest point in recent history. Since then, the ratio has
remained at around 69–70%.[40] Given that the share of non-regular workers

among female workers increased from 32.1% in 1985 to 52.5% in 2005, the reality would appear to be that the majority of women do not benefit from enhanced rights. Rather, it appears that the working conditions of women have been steadily stratified.[41]

One of the reasons for the low-wage levels of non-regular workers is the nature of the tax system, which encourages housewives to take part-time jobs. People whose annual income is less than ¥1,030,000 are exempted from income-tax liabilities. Moreover, when dependent spouses earn less than ¥1,030,000, their partners can deduct ¥380,000 of their own earnings as a tax exemption for spouses (*haigūsha kōjo*), which means that households consisting of a primary breadwinner and a part-time worker receive double tax deductions. Tax exemptions for spouses were created in 1961 to achieve greater parity between the financial circumstances of wage earners and the self-employed, and have resulted in housewives working part-time being treated more favorably than married women working full time. Both the amount of the tax deduction and the earning limit for spouses have been steadily raised so that the increasing numbers of housewife-*pāto* would be able to benefit from tax deductions. This tax system, feminists argue, discourages married women from earning over the tax threshold of ¥1,030,000, thereby perpetuating the low-wage structure for non-regular workers. In 1987, the special exemption for spouses (*haigūsha tokubetsu kōjo*) was created in addition to the tax exemption for spouses, which enabled those whose spouses earned ¥700,000 or less a year to receive the full spousal deduction of ¥760,000 (in contrast to the previous deduction of ¥360,000). For dependent spouses that made over ¥700,000, the amount of the deduction was incrementally reduced to a minimum of ¥380,000, commensurate with the previous tax threshold of ¥1,030,000. When dependent spouses made more than ¥1,030,000, the spousal deduction was incrementally reduced until a tax threshold of ¥1,410,000, at which there was no spousal deduction. This system of special exemption for spouses gave generous deductions to wealthy breadwinners—usually the husbands—whose wives did not need to work, while also providing tax incentives for housewives in lower middle class families to take up part-time jobs that would earn them up to ¥1,410,000 rather than ¥1,030,000.

The timing of the institution of this new tax system coincided with the conservative backlash of the 1980s. The new system was also consistent with business interests that relied on the housewife labor force (Shiota 2000; Sugii 1990). As Ōsawa (1993) has pointed out, the male breadwinner model was in fact fortified in the 1980s as a result of the above tax reform as well as by the establishment of pension rights for non-working housewives. These reforms institutionally endorsed the status of housewives within the family, thus providing preferential treatment to male breadwinner families over other types of families. The special exemption for spouses was finally abolished in 2002 (effective 2004) for workers whose spouses earn less than ¥1,030,000. The decision was made in order to increase tax revenues rather than in response to feminists' demands. The Democratic Party of Japan (DPJ) has pledged to abolish the tax exemption for spouses in order to make the tax system more gender neutral and to finance a new comprehensive child allowance program. The DPJ's victory in the general election in 2009, however, did not bring about the promised abolishment owing largely to opposition from conservative forces within the party.

Another aspect of the gap between regular workers and non-regular workers relates to the unequal coverage of legal protection. Although recent legal amendments have strengthened protective measures for working parents, non-regular workers rarely benefit from these measures. The Childcare Family Care Leave Law was not applied to fixed-term contract workers until its amendment in 2004.[42] The 2006 amendment to the EEOL prohibited unfavorable treatment of pregnant women, including those who are employed under fixed-term contracts. In reality, complaints from workers who have been treated unfavorably due to pregnancy, childbirth, or maternity/childcare leave, are increasing. The number of cases in which workers have consulted regional labor offices regarding unfavorable treatment after returning from childcare leave increased from 521 in 2004 to 1,262 in 2008. Cases of unfavorable treatment due to pregnancy and childbirth jumped from 875 to 2,030 during the same period.[43] Though the MHLW does not provide data that breaks these cases down between regular and non-regular workers, it is likely that many non-regular workers have suffered the unfortunate experience of being fired while on childcare leave (*ikukyū kiri*) as they are not protected by employment protection measures in general.

In sum, labor market reform aimed at gender equality and work-family balance has proceeded to an extent, but their beneficiaries have largely been limited to regular female workers. Even for these workers, the wage gap between men and women remains substantial. Employment management categories that justify occupational sex segregation and the continued practice of indirect discrimination in the workplace make it difficult for women to enter the domain of traditionally male jobs. Affirmative action has never been seriously considered. As a result, the share of female managers is only 11% in private sector firms (as of 2010) and 5.7% in the public sector (as of 2009).[44] The elimination of protective measures for women in 1997 has made it difficult for many women with family care responsibilities to maintain regular jobs, prompting them to take up part-time jobs. The enactment of Temporary Work Agency Law was deliberately designed to provide temporary jobs for women who were unable to accept overtime work and nightshifts under the equal opportunity framework.[45] The absence of any legislated principle of equal treatment of regular and non-regular workers largely offsets any gains made by the EEOL toward the realization of gender equality. The fact that over half of Japanese women are non-regular workers and over one-third of full-time *pāto* subsist on their own earnings indicates that gender equality measures have not prevented the pauperization of women.

From Function to Dysfunction

Welfare through work acts as a social protection system as long as jobs are constantly created and the work is of sufficiently high quality. However, what has taken place since the late 1990s has essentially amounted to degradation of employment conditions across-the-board. The asymmetrical deregulation described above might appear to suggest that regular workers retained previously acquired social rights at the expense of non-regular workers. This view, which emphasizes the gap between regular workers and non-regular workers and is represented by a body of work often referred to as the insider-outsider theories, does not adequately capture either the realities or the consequences of Japan's gendered dual system (Fukui 2006; Lindbeck and Snower 1988, 2002; Ōtake and Okudaira 2006; Saint-Paul 1996, 2000).[46] Insiders are not necessarily always the winners, as regular workers often have to endure long working hours and sometimes even unpaid overtime. Conversely, the increase in numbers of contingent workers reveals a fundamental deficiency in the welfare axis of the welfare through work system, as many non-regular workers are excluded from social safety nets. When only undesirable jobs are available, the Japanese social protection system becomes a problem rather than a solution.

Further Flexibility in the Internal Labor Market

Evidence of enhanced flexibilization in the internal labor market can be found by closer inspection of working hours and of the various methods that have been used in an attempt to avoid overtime payment. The length of working hours in Japan is well known and often portrayed in a negative light in international society. In 1988, the Japanese government made an international commitment to reducing working hours to 1,800 hours annually. As of 2006, according to the Monthly Labour Survey, Japanese annual labor hours had been reduced to 1,880 hours excluding overtime, and 2,041 hours including overtime. Though this would seem to suggest that the government had almost achieved its goal, these numbers were based on employers' reports on paid working hours. According to the Labour Force Survey, which documents the actual hours worked by workers, Japanese annual labor hours were 2, 288 hours in the same year. The gap between the two sets of data is essentially explained by unpaid overtime work, often called "service overtime work" (*sābisu zangyō*).

Long working hours are a phenomenal feature of not only the Japanese economy but also of the Anglo-American economies in general. According to an ILO study, in 2004 the proportion of male employees working long hours was 24.7% in Japan, 23.5% in the United States, 33.5% in the United Kingdom, 26.1% in Australia, and 24.9% in New Zealand. In contrast, in Continental Europe, the proportion was only 11.9% in France, 8.0% in Spain, 5.4% in

Norway, and 2.2% in Netherlands (Lee, McCann, and Messenger, 2007). "Long hours" here is defined as more than 49 hours per week (except in Australia, which uses a 50-hour threshold). The uniqueness of the Japanese case becomes evident when we compare the ratios of male workers working longer than 60 hours per week: 17.8% in Japan, 10.9% in Australia, 9.9% in the United States, 8.3% in New Zealand, and 7.0% in the United Kingdom. Over 20% of male workers between the ages of 25 and 44 worked longer than 60 hours a week in 2004.[47] Between 1993 and 2003, the percentage of workers who work over 60 hours per week increased from 13% to 16%, whereas that of those who work less than 35 hours from 18% to 24% (Morioka 2005, 129).

Long working hours make it difficult for these workers to assume domestic and caring responsibilities and can cause various health problems and sometimes even *karōshi,* death from overwork. In 2001, the MHLW expanded the criteria according to which overtime work of longer than 100 hours in the month prior to a death or that of longer than 80 hours a month during two to six months prior to a death are taken into consideration to determine if the death qualifies as *karōshi.* Over 60 work hours a week means overtime work of at least 80 hours a month. It is extraordinary that almost one-fourth of prime age male workers are thus threatened by the risk of *karōshi* according to the MHLW criteria. Around 200 cases a year are recognized as *karōshi,* receiving industrial accident compensation.[48] Moreover, applications for industrial accident compensation for mental disorders increased by twenty times in ten years, from 42 in 1998 to 952 in 2007, superseding the number of applications for compensation for physical illness.[49] The officially recognized *karōshi* and health problems may only be the tip of the iceberg. The Osaka Karōshi Mondai Renrakukai, a civil group working to prevent *karōshi* and assist victim families, estimates that several tens of thousands die from *karōshi* a year, which amounts to more deaths than caused by car accidents (Osaka Karōshi Mondai Renrakukai 2003).[50]

Long working hours are problematic not only from the viewpoint of health but also from that of remuneration. The widespread practice of "service overtime" prompted the government to bolster the enforcement of working hour regulations. In 2001, the MHLW began to take steps to expose the illegal practice of unpaid overtime more systematically by increasing numbers of inspectors and issuing the so-called 4.6 ordinance, which set a new standard for employers to adhere to and reminded them that they are responsible for appropriately managing working hours. As a result of boosted levels of inspections between April 2001 and March 2005, 5,161 firms were required to pay over ¥1 million as compensation for unpaid wages in individual cases of infringement, which resulted in their paying 666,917 workers a total of ¥85.1 billion. When local labor standards offices conduct regular inspections, they discover some kind of illegal conduct in about two-thirds of firms inspected. Further, a quarter of the illegal conduct discovered in 2005 related to the practice of unpaid overtime work.

Employers also attempt to avoid paying overtime premiums by shifting employees to "managerial" positions. Managers (*kanrishoku*) are not entitled to overtime pay under the law, but the managerial position is not clearly defined by the law. The existence of the "managerial position in name only" (*nabakari kanrishoku*) became known following a lawsuit against McDonald's, which, in 2008, was ordered by the court to pay ¥7.55 million in overtime compensation to a store manager who had sued the firm for failing to remunerate overtime accordingly. Managerial positions in name only are widespread in the restaurant business. According to a survey by the Nikkei Marketing Journal, close to 70% of restaurant operators classify store managers as a managerial position, and only 20% of restaurants firms provide overtime payment to store managers.[51]

These cases show that the insider-outsider theories are inadequate for explaining the degradation of the insiders' working conditions. Employers are able to compensate partially for the high labor costs associated with strong employment protection by increasing functional and wage flexibilities in the internal labor market. In practice, long working hours including service overtime serve to lower wages, as does the extended application of managerial positions. The availability of such functional and wage flexibilities shows that the idea of a clash of interests between insiders and outsiders is misleading. Moreover, several reports have indicated the emergence of "regular workers on the periphery" (*shūhenteki seishain*) or "regular workers in name only" (*nabakari seishain*), which suggests that some regular workers are treated like non-regular workers in the sense that they do not receive adequate training, regular raises, bonuses, or fringe benefits (Konno and Honda 2008). Although a significant gap continues to exist between regular and non-regular workers in terms of wages, working conditions, career opportunities, and workers' rights, further stratification among regular workers makes the boundary between the two types of workers less distinct than the insider-outsider theories assume.

The Emergence of Poverty

As long as *pāto* were mostly housewives who "preferred" to keep their earnings below the relevant tax thresholds, the precarity of non-regular workers was not immediately apparent. However, as of 2001, 27.7% of non-regular workers were breadwinners, making a living mainly from their own earnings, as were 34.3% of female full-time non-regular workers.[52] As of 2007, 25.1% of all workers earned less than ¥1.5 million per year and 26.2% earned between ¥1.5 and ¥2.9 million.[53] Given that a standard three-person household receives around ¥1.8 million of social assistance per year, the fact that a quarter of workers earn less than ¥1.5 million suggests that there are substantial numbers of working poor in Japan.

Several data sources indeed point to growing poverty in Japan, which had previously established a reputation as an egalitarian society. For instance, the number of recipients of social assistance decreased from 17 million in 1985 to 10 million in 1995. Accordingly, the rate of recipients of social assistance also decreased: 11.8 persons per 1,000 persons in 1985, 8.2 in 1990, and 7.0 in 1995. This downward trend began to reverse in 1995. In 2005, over 17 million people received social assistance and the rate of recipients had reached 11.6 persons per 1,000, fundamentally having returned to the level of two decades previously. Then, in 2010, over 23 million received social assistance at a recipient rate of 15.2‰, which is an equivalent level to that seen in 1967.[54]

Japanese academia was not blind to signs of growing inequalities and scholarly debate on this topic has been active since the late 1990s. Experts agree that the extent of social inequality has grown since the 1980s and even more so in the 2000s, yet they disagree on the degree of inequality as well as on its causes. Tachibanaki Toshiaki's book titled *The Economic Gap in Japan* (*Kakusa Shakai*) published in 1998 was one of the earliest publications casting doubt on the then widely accepted myth that Japan was an equal society (see also Tachibanaki 2009). The book showed that the Gini coefficient, commonly used as a measurement of inequality of income distribution, has risen in Japan since the 1980s and surpassed the level of the United States in the late 1980s. His findings and arguments triggered a widespread debate among economists and sociologists regarding the degree of inequality in Japanese society. For instance, Ōtake Fumio (2000, 2005) was critical of Tachibanaki's statistical analysis, arguing that inequality in the 1980s was largely caused by the aging population rather than by globalization, technological advancement or labor market reform.[55] Ōtake's findings lent support to the Koizumi government's argument that structural reform was not the cause of growing inequality. Prime Minister Koizumi Jun'ichirō repeatedly denied the existence of growing inequality, and at the same time contended that a widening gap is not necessarily a bad thing and that Japan should aim to create a society that gives losers a second chance.

Multiple surveys exist that can be used to measure the Gini coefficient. Tachibanaki's figures are among the highest because he used income data taken before redistribution through taxation and social security. Moreover, the Income Redistribution Survey, used by Tachibanaki (1998), has a tendency to yield a higher level of inequality because it includes data for single households. Figure 4.3 illustrates trends in the Gini coefficient in selected countries using data provided by the Luxembourg Income Studies (LIS). The Japanese government does not provide comparable data to the LIS, thus I use the National Consumption Survey, which is generally considered to be the closest to the LIS in terms of method used.[56] It should be noted that the Gini coefficient based on the National Consumption Survey tends to be lower than that based on the Income Redistribution Survey, as the former survey tends to exclude low-income households that often lack the wherewithal to respond to lengthy and complex survey questions. By using such "conservative" data, Figure 4.3 shows that the level of inequality in Japan is

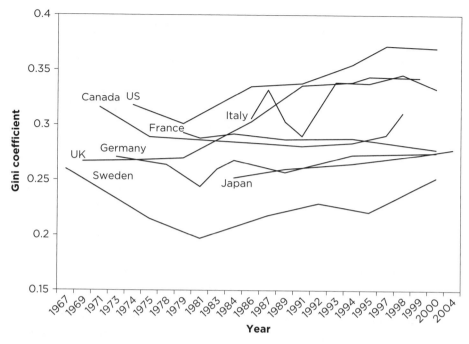

Figure 4.3. Gini coefficient transition (1967–2004)
Source: Luxembourg Income Study Database (http://www.lisdatacenter.org); Japan: Ministry of Internal Affairs and Communications, *National Consumption Survey* (http://www.stat.go.jp/data/index.htm).

similar to that seen in Germany and France and remains relatively modest compared to the United States and the United Kingdom.

The other indicator of inequality is the proportion of the population living in relative poverty, which is defined as having less than half of the median household disposable income. An OECD report issued in 2005 indicated that Japan's poverty rate was 15.3% as of 2000, the second highest among developed countries after 17.1% in the United States (Förster and d'Ercole 2005). Moreover, the same report showed that more than half of single parents were in relative poverty, far surpassing the OECD average of around 20%. Further, significant poverty among single parents is a factor raising the child poverty rate to 14.3%, well above the OECD average of 12.3% (Förster and d'Ercole 2005). Both the general public and policymakers in Japan received these results with shock because they were in stark contrast to conventional understanding of the egalitarian nature of Japanese society. In response, the government attempted to downplay the degree of poverty in Japan and refused to calculate relative poverty rates. It was the DPJ's election to government in 2009 that pressured the MHLW to publish these rates. A month after the election, the welfare minister announced that the relative poverty rate was 15.7%, that of children was 14.2%, and that of single-parent households was 54.3% as of 2006, confirming the OECD data. Moreover, in 2011, the MHLW disclosed trends in relative poverty rates over the past several decades, showing that the rate increased from 12.0% in 1985 to 15.3% in 2000 to 16.0% in 2009. Children's poverty rates also increased from 10.9% in 1985 to 14.5% in 2000 to 15.7% in 2009. Ironically, the relative poverty rate for single parent households declined from 54.3% in 2006 to 50.8% in 2009 because overall poverty increased during this time period.[57]

What is indicative with regard to the poverty rates is not only the fact that Japan has come to experience a high degree of relative poverty in the 2000s, but the fact that this phenomenon is not recent.[58] Table 4.2 compares the OECD's relative poverty rates before and after taxes and transfers at two time points, the mid-1980s and around 2000. It is clear from the table that Japan's poverty rate was already internationally high in the mid-1980s, marking 12.0%, after the United States, Turkey, Belgium, Spain, and Greece. Though Japan might have had similar levels of equality to Germany or France in terms of Gini coefficient, it has experienced a higher degree of relative poverty.[59]

What is all the more striking is the fact that Japan has failed to combat poverty by utilizing its social security system. The gap in poverty rates before and after taxes and transfers signifies the degree of redistribution. It was 5 points in the 1980s and 8.6 points in 2000. In contrast, the gap was 25.8 in France, 21.9 in Germany, 21.7 in Sweden, 17.6 in the United Kingdom, and 8.3 in the United States (as of 2000). Japan's low degree of redistribution is outstanding. For child poverty, the poverty rate actually increases after taxes and transfers from 12.9% to 14.3% (2000) (Whiteford and Adema 2007). In fact, Japan is the only OECD country in which the rate of child poverty has been consistently higher after redistribution since the 1980s. Furthermore, child poverty is concentrated in working families: only 2% of child poverty is found in households with no earners, in contrast to the OECD average of 32% (OECD 2006, 113). In other words, Japan's system of welfare through work induces single mothers to enter the labor market, but does little or nothing to address child poverty. The gendered dual system in the labor market lays an extremely heavy burden on single mothers and their children.

New Social Risks

Growing evidence of poverty in Japanese society points to the deficiencies of welfare through work as a social protection system. Labor market reform resulted in diversification of employment types, thereby providing increased opportunities for employers to find cheaper labor. However, comparatively speaking, the degree of deregulation in Japan has been modest by international standards. In fact, the proportion of temporary agency workers, a new category of worker that was the direct outcome of the labor market reform,

TABLE 4.2
Dysfunction in social protection systems

	Poverty rate before and after taxes and transfers				Minimum wages	Collective bargaining coverage	Product market regulation	
	Before		After					
	mid-1980s	2000	mid-1980s	2000	2000	2000	1998	2008
Welfare with work								
Denmark	20.1	23.2	6.0	5.1	-	80	1.6	1.1
Norway	18.7	22.6	6.4	6.3	-	70	1.9	1.2
Sweden	26.1	27.0	3.3	5.3	-	90	1.9	1.3
Average	**21.6**	**24.3**	**5.2**	**5.6**	-	**80**	**1.8**	**1.2**
Welfare without work								
Austria	-	-	6.1	9.3	-	95	2.3	1.3
Belgium	-	35.6	14.6	10.4	0.53	90	2.2	1.4
Finland	15.1	18.0	5.1	6.4	-	90	2.1	1.2
France	35.8	33.0	8.3	7.2	0.59	90	2.5	1.5
Germany	26.9	31.1	6.3	9.2	-	68	2.9	-
Netherlands	-	23.6	-	6.8	0.47	80	1.7	1.0
Italy	21.1	31.1	10.3	11.8	-	80	2.6	1.4
Average	**24.7**	**28.7**	**8.5**	**9.1**	**0.53**	**85**	**2.3**	**1.3**
Workfare								
Australia	-	29.8	-	12.2	0.58	80	1.5	1.2
Ireland	-	25.7	10.6	15.4	0.52	-	1.6	-
United Kingdom	-	27.8	-	10.2	0.34	30	1.1	0.8
United States	25.6	25.4	17.9	17.1	0.36	14	1.3	0.8
Canada	21.5	21.6	10.7	10.3	0.41	32	1.3	1.0
New Zealand	20.2	26.9	6.2	9.8	0.50	25	1.4	1.3
Average	**22.4**	**25.9**	**11.4**	**13.0**	**0.45**	**36**	**1.4**	**1.0**
Welfare through work								
Japan	12.5	23.9	12.0	15.3	0.32	15	2.2	1.1
Switzerland	-	16.5	-	7.5	-	40	2.5	1.3
Average	**12.5**	**20.2**	**12.0**	**11.4**	**0.32**	**28**	**2.3**	**1.2**

Source: OECD Stat (http://stats.oecd.org).
*Minimum wages are calculated as a proportion relative to the median of full-time workers' wages. The poverty rate is the ratio of those who earn less than 50% of median household earnings. The year 2000 indicates statistics compiled around that year.

remained relatively small. In the Japanese labor market, *pāto* constitute a large share of non-regular workers at 48.2% while the share of temporary agency workers is only 5.5% (as of 2010).[60] The category of *pāto* had existed well before the labor market reform without any legal prohibition of their use. Why, then, has modest labor market reform coincided with growing evidence of poverty, and to what extent were labor market reforms responsible for growing inequality? I argue that the welfare through work system was responsible for the creation of new social risks.

First, the government's reliance on the availability of jobs to maintain the social protection system justified the creation of low-paid jobs as preferable to the alternative of mass unemployment. As will be discussed in chapter 6, the threat of mass employment was a factor behind the government's decision to deregulate the temporary labor market. As it happened, prolonged and recurrent recessions since the burst of the bubble economy in 1991 did not generate mass unemployment. The highest unemployment rate was recorded in 2002, at 5.4%. Although this figure was high in light of Japan's previous experience, it is nonetheless remarkable that Japan was able to contain unemployment rates at such a low level. However, the reliance on non-regular jobs to prevent mass unemployment created another problem: the emergence of the working poor. The lack of enforcement mechanisms for equal treatment of regular and non-regular workers has meant that the fact of becoming a non-regular worker in itself is a new social risk.

Second, under a system of welfare through work social assistance and minimum wage levels play a marginal role. The inadequacy of social safety nets exacerbates the problem of the working poor in circumstances of high unemployment or underemployment. Some economists estimate that only 16–20% of those in need receive social assistance (Komamura 2002; see also chapter 2). The low level of regulation against low wage structures also aggravates the problem of poverty. As Table 4.2 shows, the proportion of the minimum wage relative to the median wage of full-time workers was 32% in Japan, well behind the proportion of 59% in France, 41% in the United Kingdom, and 38% in the United States (as of 2000). As a result, those who are paid at the minimum wage level are compelled to work for long hours in order to match the level of social assistance. (The inconsistency between the minimum wage and the social assistance program was finally rectified by the passage of the 2007 Minimum Wage Law, which states that the minimum wage must be determined in accordance with social assistance.) The other feature of wage regulation pertinent to this discussion is the low coverage of collective bargaining: only 15% of workers are covered in Japan. Wage regulation in Japan, both in terms of the minimum wage and collective bargaining, does not provide an adequate safety net.

Table 4.2 also includes data on "product market regulation."[61] These numbers indicate that Japan's relatively high level of product market regulation in the 1990s may have served as the "functional equivalent" of a social protection system, but subsequent deregulation greatly reduced any such function. The low level of wage regulation facilitated the proliferation of low-paid jobs, which has led to a rapid rise in poverty rates due to the absence of adequate income support mechanisms.

With regard to "production market regulation," it should be also noted that Japan's level of regulation was equivalent to those of the welfare without work countries throughout both the 1990s and 2000s. Despite the same level of market regulation, Continental European countries were unable to create as much employment as Japan, but succeeded in reducing poverty. As consistently asserted in this book, the labor market–welfare nexus is the key to understanding the differences between the respective models.

Finally, the increase in numbers of non-regular workers highlighted the inadequacy of conventional social safety nets, which were not expanded in accordance with the altered demographic, thereby producing large numbers of workers neither subject to the standard regulations on working time nor covered by the social security system. Conventional social safety nets are created on the premise of typical workers having full-time jobs with open-ended contracts. As a result, those who work under short-hour contracts and/or fixed-term contracts are excluded from coverage. Firms are not legally required to provide healthcare insurance or employee pensions to those who work for less than three-quarters of full-time working hours. Moreover, unemployment insurance only covers those who are expected to work for longer than 20 hours a week for more than one year. Until 2001, part-time workers who earned less than ¥900,000 a year were not able to enroll in unemployment insurance. The government distinguished between general workers and short-hour workers (who work for 20–30 hours), requiring a work record of 6 months from the former, but a 12-month work record from the latter, in order to be eligible for unemployment insurance. In 2007, the government abolished this distinction, requiring a 12-month work record from those who voluntarily quit their jobs and a 6-month work record from those who are fired. In 2009, the government further relaxed the criteria, applying a 6-month work record to all workers, as a result of which 1.5 million workers are estimated to have been newly covered.[62] Although the government has expanded the scope of coverage, the gap between the number of the unemployed (2,750,000) and the number of recipients of unemployment insurance (530,000) remains large: less than 20% of the unemployed receive unemployment benefits (as of 2006).[63] According to a 2009 ILO study, Japan's low coverage is outstanding: 77% of the unemployed do not receive unemployment benefits, whereas the share is 57% in the United States and Canada, 40% in the United Kingdom, 18% in France, and 13% in Germany.

In the Japanese labor market, the significant risks associated with non-regular jobs stem not only from the fact that non-regular workers are poorly paid but also from the fact that they face significant challenges in gaining adequate training to increase their employability as regular workers. Although they are a high-risk group with respect to dismissal, they are often excluded from unemployment insurance. Even a moderate level of labor market reform, therefore, has increased the risk level of non-regular workers, which, coupled with the low degree of redistribution, has aggravated poverty levels in Japanese society.

In essence, the system of welfare through work, which worked to underwrite previous social risks such as the unemployment, sickness, and retirement of regular workers, became unable to cope with new circumstances engendered by changes in the labor market. What merits attention here is the fact that welfare through work is not simply dysfunctional in the context of new market realities but has actually created new social risks. It was the very policy framework of welfare through work that justified the creation of further flexibility in the labor markets, which resulted in degradation of working conditions across the board. Regular workers continue to have strong employment protection but have to endure long working hours and de facto wage reductions. The poor working conditions of non-regular workers are well known, but the government has been slow to address this issue because non-regular workers are an integral part of the welfare through work system. It is also this system's policy framework that has justified the inadequacy of the social safety net, detrimentally affecting the working and living conditions of low-income workers. Gender equality policy and work–family balance policy remain ineffective in transforming the gendered dual system on which welfare through work is built, because it has been the logic of constraint based on male breadwinner-female part-timer families that has justified differential treatment of regular workers and non-regular workers. The fact that non-regular workers are predominantly women and young people ages 15–24 also deterred the conservative government from modernizing the social protection system, as conservative thinking, which stresses family responsibility for taking care of dependents, renders public policy unnecessary in this regard. The inadequacy of work-family balance policy, in turn, aggravates Japan's low birth rates, which makes social security system unsustainable (Schoppa 2006a). Without a complete overhaul of the gendered dual system, cosmetic attempts to patch the inherent flaws of welfare through work will only ultimately expose further limits and shortcomings of the system.

5

Who Wants What Reform?

The previous chapter showed that given the significant disparities between regular and non-regular workers in terms of wages, career opportunities, employment protection, and social security, the increase in numbers of non-regular workers has resulted in rising levels of poverty in Japanese society. As the replacement of regular workers by non-regular workers proceeded unchecked, the myth of lifetime employment was finally debunked. (The truth has always been that bona fide "lifetime" employment had been granted only to male workers in large companies and that actual job security of this group of workers was more fluid that the term implied.) The Japanese employment system based on long-term mutual trust and cooperative industrial relations was supposed to be the basis of the competitiveness of Japanese firms. Even if downgrading of employment conditions is a natural response in liberal market economies in order to cope with the globalization of, and fluctuations in, the world economy, this strategy is not necessarily natural or rational in Japan where competition had been primarily based on quality rather than price. Why, then, have Japanese firms increased the proportion of non-regular workers in the workforce, and why did they advocate deregulation of the labor market? Did an ideational shift from cooperatism to neoliberalism occur in the realm of employment policy? Was globalization, the usual suspect behind deregulation, the cause of the ideational shift, if such, indeed, occurred? Further, what shaped employers' policy preferences? This chapter examines in detail the policy demands pursued by Japanese businesses and analyzes the formation of their policy preferences.

The Quest for Flexibility

Research in the field of comparative politics often specifies common challenges and then attempts to account for different national responses by investigating different national-level institutions. Rather than looking in detail at the sources and degree of pressure to change, I focus on the policy demands made by employers and identify the challenges that Japanese employers attempted to address. There is no reason to assume that Japan faced similar types or degrees of policy challenges, in view of the country's rather unique economic experiences (i.e., steady economic growth and low inflation in the 1980s, decade-long economic stagnation and a deflationary economy in the 1990s, the slow pace of deindustrialization due to the world-class competitiveness of manufacturing, and a relatively low level of exposure to globalization). The question to be asked here is "who wants what reforms?" Instead of theoretically deducing actors' preferences, I reveal them empirically through analysis of documents and policy demands put forward by employers.[1] The empirical analysis presented in this chapter demonstrates that neither capital nor labor is a single actor embracing preferences that can be deduced simply from their socioeconomic position. Individual actors within the respective groups have their own, varying views and ideas about how the labor market should be organized and these ideas are shaped over time by subjective political experience.

In 1995, Nikkeiren released a position paper titled "Japanese-style Management in a New Era," proposing the grouping of employees into three categories.[2] Employers should offer lifetime employment and in-house training only to their "long-term skill formation-type" employees, whereas both "professional-type" workers and "flexible-type" workers would be supplied from the external labor market. The latter types of workers were expected to invest in their own skill formation as necessary, and were perceived to have a high degree of mobility in the labor market. Just as fund managers select an investment portfolio to maximize profits, employers would be expected to design an optimal employment portfolio by adjusting the relative share of the three types of workers.

Though Nikkeiren's proposal declared an explicit intention to create different layers of employees, the stratification of the workforce in itself is nothing new in Japanese management (Crump 2003). Workers in small and medium-size enterprises and female workers were already excluded from job security and wage protection prior to this proposal. What was new about the 1995 proposal was that its implementation would mean that even the permanent male workforce in large companies would not be able to automatically secure lifetime employment with a range of benefits. Nikkeiren anticipated that the proportion of "long-term skill formation-type" workers would decrease from the then level of 80% of the total workforce to 70% in the near future. In order to facilitate downsizing by 10 percentage points, Nikkeiren launched a call for labor market reform to increase external flexibility.

Although Nikkeiren began to emphasize the necessity of higher labor mobility, it also took pains to mention the merits of long-term employment and the disadvantages of the American way of corporate restructuring.

In 1997, Nikkeiren proposed the "Bluebird Plan," proclaiming that Japan should explore the possibility of a "Third Way."[3] In the European context, the term refers to social democracy with a market economy, as was first intellectually proposed by Anthony Giddens and politically crystallized by Tony Blair. Although the term itself was most probably imported from Britain, Japanese employers used it very differently. Japan's Third Way, Nikkeiren argues, differs from the Anglo-Saxon market economies where unemployment rates do not skyrocket but wage dispersion is unacceptably large and social stability is sacrificed. Japan's Third Way also differs from the European market economies where welfare programs are highly developed but where society suffers from high unemployment rates, economic stagnation, and high social security and tax burdens. According to Nikkeiren, Japan should pursue a Third Way under which structural reform could be carried out without generating high unemployment. It predicted that Japan would face a serious unemployment problem in the near future due to industrial restructuring, deregulation, and administrative reform. In order to restore Japan's international competitiveness, structural reform of industry and government was inevitable, but Nikkeiren warned that such reforms would raise unemployment rates to as high as 6 or 7%. In order to avoid economic stagnation with high unemployment, Nikkeiren's "Bluebird Plan" proposed further structural reforms, containment of wages and non-wage labor costs, and deregulation.

On the one hand, Japan's Third Way anticipated structural reform or, to put it more bluntly, a departure from "convoy capitalism." Through industrial restructuring, deregulation, and administrative reform, companies were expected to swiftly shut down unprofitable factories and branches. On the other hand, it aimed to avoid mass unemployment, which inevitably follows industrial restructuring. How did Nikkeiren propose that Japan achieve such conflicting goals? It did not propose any specific employment policy other than the deregulation of private placement services. Instead, it simply expected structural reform to create new jobs, thereby reducing unemployment rates. It also contended that the containment of labor costs constituted an important part of the Third Way strategy in order to avoid high unemployment. Because labor cost reduction was intended as an integral part of this approach, it is unclear as to the extent to which Japan's Third Way would differ from the approach of the Anglo-Saxon market economies. As it happened, within ten years, labor cost reduction measures pursued by employers had produced a vast number of working poor in Japan.

If we look at the aspect of employment protection, the differences between Japan and the Anglo-Saxon model could not be clearer, at least insofar as employment protection remained a fundamental principle of Japanese management. Okuda Hiroshi (chairman of Toyota Motor Corporation), who succeeded to the Nikkeiren presidency in 1999, declared this position even more explicitly than his predecessor. Okuda claimed that Japanese employers should aim for "a market economy with a human face," by which he meant to imply that employment protection is indeed an employer's responsibility. In his own words: "recently the opinion has been voiced that employers should dismiss excess employees in order to strengthen competitiveness. However, the employer's role is to consider how to use excess employees in new business opportunities. Employers who do not have such entrepreneurship should resign first."[4] On numerous occasions when giving speeches, he reiterated his philosophy of the market economy with a human face. Nikkeiren even sent a petition letter to its member companies in 1999, calling for further efforts toward employment stability.

These efforts on the part of Nikkeiren culminated in the "Employment Stability Declaration" jointly released by Nikkeiren and Rengō in 1999, which proclaimed that employers should refrain from relying on expedient employment adjustments as their default reaction to economic difficulties. Even if the number of employees in a company became a financial burden, they demanded that employers should be socially responsible, considering employment protection first and exploring ways to use redundant employees in new business endeavors. They also requested that when downsizing was unavoidable, employers should minimize the scale of dismissals and consider the impact on related companies and regional economies.[5] Further, prolonged recession prompted them to release another joint "Declaration of Promoting 'Social Agreement on Employment'" in 2001. This time the government was also involved, making the declaration the first top-level tripartite pact in Japan.

While Nikkeiren showed its concern for employment protection and emphasized the merits of long-term employment, other business associations called for more drastic reforms of the labor market. In the 1990s, Keidanren was vocal about the necessity of labor market deregulation, a topic previously monopolized by Nikkeiren, with a view to restoring the Japanese economy as well as corporate profits. The first case of such action was the Hiraiwa Report published in 1993. This was a collection of policy recommendations written by the Economic Reform Study Group created by Prime Minister Hosokawa Morihiro and chaired by Hiraiwa Gaishi (ex-chairman of Tokyo Electric Power Company), the then president of Keidanren. Although, the Hiraiwa Report was not technically Keidanren's official position paper, it clearly represented the preferences of big business. The report touched on the issue of labor market reform, arguing that a flexible labor market, in which workers are able to easily find and switch jobs, should be established in order to deal with restructuring, deregulation, and globalization.

Keidanren advanced its position further in 1996 in a policy statement titled "An Attractive Japan: Keidanren's Vision for 2020," often called the "Toyoda Vision" after the name of the then president of Keidanren, Toyoda Shōichirō (chairman of Toyota Motor Corporation). The document stated that a paradigm shift was necessary in the realm of employment policy from employment stability within same-group companies to the guarantee of employment opportunities at the level of the whole of society. For this goal to be realized, it argued, smooth job transfers based on a worker's own volition should be encouraged through far-reaching reforms of labor-related regulations and the transformation of the current enterprise pension system, which inhibits job transfers. By using the term "paradigm shift," Keidanren signaled its adoption of a much more extreme stance than Nikkeiren, according to which employers would be released from any responsibility to protect employment. Nikkeiren's preference for cooperative industrial relations naturally prevented the articulation of such a drastic vision.

Keizai Dōyūkai was also an enthusiastic supporter of the flexible labor market. It is both ironical and indicative that Keizai Dōyūkai, which contributed to the establishment of the "politics of productivity" in the 1950s, radically changed course in the 1990s. In 1992, Keizai Dōyūkai created a study group to explore new corporate governance models based on an assessment that the "reformed capitalism," which it had propagated since its birth in 1946, was no longer a viable model for Japan. In 1997, it published a report titled the "Market-ism Manifesto," advocating structural reform of the Japanese economy and the establishment of individual autonomy as a basis for small government. In fact, Keizai Dōyūkai championed the market-oriented neoliberal stance much earlier and more enthusiastically than Nikkeiren and Keidanren.[6] It had already released policy statements advocating the creation of a flexible labor market in the early 1990s.[7] This may be explained by the fact that the membership of Keizai Dōyūkai consists of individual business leaders, rather than entire companies, encouraging the expression of personal opinions generally more extreme than the opinions officially endorsed by business associations.

Keizai Dōyūkai's study group on corporate governance was an arena where the differing views of Japanese businessmen were openly aired. The debate between Imai Takashi and Miyauchi Yoshihiko symbolically illustrates the divisions among Japanese businesses with regard to employer responsibility for employment protection. Imai was the president of the Nippon Steel Corporation (1993–1998) and chairman of Keidanren (1998–2002), and represented the interests of assembling manufacturers, whereas Miyauchi had served as the president and CEO of Orix Corporation since 1980, thus representing the interests of global finance. Orix is an integrated financial services group that started as a leasing company. Imai and Miyauchi debated the appropriate form of corporate governance for Japan when Keizai Dōyūkai organized a conference in Maihama in 1994. Reflecting on the debate, Imai later commented that "it is natural that companies which sustain Japanese assembling manufacturing differ from companies that operate globally. It comes as no surprise that managers of global companies prioritize a return on equity (ROE) and consider employment security to be the government's responsibility.... I understand that ROE is important, but employment is also important and I have not changed my view" (Shinagawa and Ushio 2000,

126; translated by the author). Later, Imai reaffirmed his position stating: "in my view, treatment of employees is the most important matter.... Even in the case of excessive employment, I believe that a company cannot get rid of employees once it has hired them."[8]

Imai's comments implicitly suggest the emergence of a new management philosophy, distinct from his own, which maximizes the interests of stockholders instead of satisfying all the stakeholders including employees.[9] The two schools of management philosophy continue to coexist, their relative degree of influence on government policy dictated by changes in the political environment. Imai's prioritization of domestic employment over structural reform-cum-stockholders became the dominant paradigm after he was appointed Keidanren president in 1998. The financial crisis at the time also strengthened his position. Business community pressure on the government to help ailing companies eventually brought about the legislation of the Industrial Revitalization Law (1999). This included tax breaks and low-interest loans to support companies that submitted restructuring plans aimed at reducing capacity and shifting focus to growth areas (Tiberghien 2007; Vogel 2006, 85–88).[10] Likewise, in 1998, the then Hashimoto cabinet was compelled to loosen the strictures imposed by the Fiscal Structural Reform Law, which had been passed the previous year in order to expedite fiscal retrenchment, but the Obuchi cabinet eventually abolished it. Imai's successor, Okuda Hiroshi, as the first chairman of Nippon Keidanren, created in 2002 by the amalgamation of Keidanren and Nikkeiren, continued to espouse the idea of a market economy with a human face. The paradigm shift proposed by the Toyoda Vision seems to have disappeared from business leaders' discourse by around the turn of the century.

Keidanren/Nippon Keidanren's continuous emphasis on employment does not mean that there were no longer any neoliberal reformers active among representatives of business. Under the new process that emerged in the late 1990s, neoliberal business leaders were directly involved in policymaking. Safe from dilution by intra-organizational coordination, their radical opinions found avenue for expression and could be reflected in policy outcomes.[11] Although Japanese business was split on the issues of corporate governance and government intervention to save companies from bankruptcy, they agreed on the issues of public corporation reform, retrenchment of social spending, increasing the consumption tax, and most important to the concerns of this book, labor market reform.

Cooperatism in Decline?

Japanese employers, having persistently advocated the benefits of lifetime employment, now accept the necessity and advantages of the flexible labor market. This transformation has steadily progressed since the 1990s. The "flexible labor market" here refers to the expansion of the temporary labor market, which was expected to supplement the system of long-term employment for regular workers. In other words, employers were eager to reduce labor costs as far as possible by various means without disturbing the norm of lifetime employment.

What specific reforms did employers advocate? Their policy preferences can be discerned from various position papers and demands that were officially submitted to the government. They can be summarized as follows.[12] The list is not exhaustive, yet illustrates general orientations.

Wages

- Abolition of industry-level minimum wages.
- Increases in the share of performance-based payments and bonuses.*
- Decreases in the share of age-based and seniority payments.*
- Introduction of the yearly salary system.*

(*These items do not represent official demands made by employers' associations to the government but, rather, represent demands that are subject to firm-level collective bargaining and that can be realized through collective bargaining without amending the law.)

Employment and the Labor Market

- Deregulation of temporary work agencies.
- Liberalization of free-of-charge job placement agencies.
- Liberalization of private job placement agencies.
- Liberalization of fixed-term contracts.
- Extension of discretionary working hour rules.
- Deregulation of irregular working hour rules.
- Abolition of breaks taken by all employees.
- Deregulation of overtime, holiday, and late-night labor for female workers.
- Abolition of penalties encoded by the Labor Standards Law.
- Deregulation of rules regarding the recruitment of high-school graduates.

Others

- Simplification of notifications to Local Labor Standards Offices regarding changes in work rules and collective agreements on overtime and holiday work.
- Lowering the interest rate of corporate savings for employees.

- Simplification of applications for employment adjustment subsidies.
- Establishment of programs that assist individuals' investment in training and education.
- Reforms of social insurance systems and corporate allowances in facilitating labor mobility and female labor market participation.
- Easing of regulation on foreign workers.

This list of policy proposals does not show the order of priority given to respective policies, which changed depending on the economic situation, the feasibility of reforms, and the government's reaction. The list shows what employers perceived as institutional obstacles in Japan. Employers called for the reform of regulations on the temporary labor market, working hour rules, and minimum wages as well as for collective agreements on wage determination systems. It was thought that these reforms taken together would bring about reductions in labor costs.

The Transformation of Shuntō

There are many ways to reduce labor costs. Labor market reform is one possible approach and changing the system of collective bargaining is another. The former is a political process in which the range of actors is not necessarily predetermined, thereby containing a high level of uncertainty; the latter can be accomplished by a limited number of actors thus offering a higher level of predictability. Moreover, collective bargaining reform has a much more direct impact on overall labor costs than labor market reform. Nikkeiren simultaneously pursued both approaches, but maintained a firm and uncompromising stance throughout the process of transformation of the collective bargaining system, which is known as the spring offensive (*shuntō*). *Shuntō* is a system of concerted collective bargaining within and across industries, conceived by Sōhyō in 1955 in order to compensate for the structural weakness of Japanese unions organized at the enterprise level. Nikkeiren launched "the structural reform of the spring offensive" in 1995 and since then has aggressively challenged the established pattern of wage determination.[13]

Shuntō had contributed to the achievement of a certain degree of wage equalization (Sako 1997). Indeed, the most important function of the spring offensive was to level wages across companies and industries rather than to secure wage increases. One of the strategies unions had employed to realize wage solidarity was to call for an increase in the basic wage rate, known as "base-up", which provided all relevant workers with a share in the fruits of wage increases.[14] However, in 1998, Rengō was compelled to agree to a freeze of the basic wage rate. Given the role played by base-up demands in the spring offensive, this decision was significant. As a result, between 1998 and 2006, the wage level negotiated at the spring offensive declined.[15] Moreover, after 1998, wage disparities began to widen, manifesting the end of the "spring offensive level" (Nakamura 2006, 16). In 2002, Rengō finally gave up on calling for a unified basic wage rate raise. To make things worse, the same year Toyota Motor Corporation refused the basic wage rate raise of 1,000 yen demanded by its union. Although the Japanese economy as a whole had not yet recovered at the time, Toyota generated record high profits of over ¥1 trillion in 2002. The fact that Okuda, as the president of Nikkeiren/Nippon Keidanren, was orchestrating wage restraint in all industrial sectors encouraged Toyota executives to stand their ground. The following year the Toyota union gave up on demanding a basic wage rate raise. The effect of this decision was enormous as the Toyota union had been a leading wage setter. Consequently, Nippon Keidanren confidently declared in 2003 that "the spring offensive, in terms of unions calling for wage increases and using forceful means in their 'struggle' to achieve social leveling, has ended" (Nippon Keidanren 2003, 61).

The collapse of *shuntō* as it was meant the end of "politics of productivity." The productivity movement aimed to transcend class conflicts by promising wage increases in accordance with improved productivity. The parallel increase of wages and productivity was achieved at least until 1975, as shown in Figure 5.1, which indicates the increases in labor productivity and real wages by calibrating the 1975 rates as 100. Until the mid-1970s, labor productivity

Figure 5.1. Labor productivity and real wage indexes (manufacturing)
Source: Shakai Keizai Seisansei Honbu, *Shinban Rōshi Kankei Hakusho* (Tokyo: Shakai Keizai Seisansei Honbu, Seisansei Jōhō Sentā, 2006), 202–203.

and real wages had increased constantly and in tandem. However, the politics of productivity began to fall into decline after 1975 when private-sector unions began to curb wage increases in exchange for employment protection. In fact, Figure 5.1 shows that the gap between the increase in labor productivity and the increase in real wages has diverged ever since. The final blow was Nikkeiren's sustained assault on the collective bargaining practice beginning in 1995. As wage increases have stagnated and even gone into the negative since 1998, the gap has widened further.

How did employers succeed in transforming *shuntō*? Why did unions not defend their position more strongly and more effectively? It might be argued that the unyielding commitment of employers to transforming the wage determination system extinguished the unions' will to fight. In fact, unions have demanded only modest wage increases since the 1990s, thereby reducing the gap between the wage increases demanded by unions and those agreed upon. Between 2003 and 2005, the gap was almost zero.[16] Indeed, the unions' tacit support of wage restraint has a long history. Since 1975, the leadership of shuntō shifted to unions belonging to the IMF-JC (Japan Council of Metalworkers' Unions), which advocated wage increases within the bounds of economic growth, or "rational economism" (Kume 1998; Shinkawa 1984). The financial crisis in 1998 and subsequent economic stagnation lent further support to rational economism and induced unions to accept whatever employers offered. Decreasing numbers of collective labor disputes also reflected the unions' loss of the willingness to fight. Hardly any strikes occurred despite increasing cases of personnel reduction and cost cutting. Collective labor disputes accompanied by strikes lasting more than half a day peaked in 1974, at 5,197 cases, but have steadily declined: 1,128 cases in 1980, 283 cases in 1990, 117 cases in 2000, and just 38 cases in 2010.[17] The number of cases heard by local courts regarding labor-related civil litigations was 647 in 1990, 1,552 in 1995, 2,063 in 2000, and 3,127 in 2010.[18] The rapid increase in numbers of individual labor disputes suggests that individual workers have perceived limitations in the capacity of unions to solve the problems they face in their workplaces.

Legislating Dismissal Law: Reform or Status Quo?

One issue that is conspicuously absent from the above list of employers' policy demands is the easing of restrictions on firing. Does this mean that employers still embrace cooperatism? As has been discussed earlier, Japanese employment protection was comparatively stringent due to the accumulation of case law. Nonetheless, employers did not openly call for measures to expedite the termination of employment. The dismissal law was finally enacted in 2003; it preserved the same level of employment protection that case law had provided, perhaps even strengthening it. The legislation of dismissal law made it onto the agenda not because Nikkeiren or other major business associations had lobbied for it, but because the deregulation panels, which were the strongholds of the neoliberal reformers, recommended the passage of the legislation. In 1999, the Regulatory Reform Committee (RRC) urged the government to examine legislation for a dismissal law, which was listed as one of the issues to be discussed in a public forum that the RRC would organize the following year.[19] The Ministry of Labour (MOL) responded that it would be difficult to enact dismissal law. Professor Kojima Noriaki, a member of the RRC and a leading writer of the RRC's recommendations regarding labor market reform, recalled that the MOL repeatedly asked him why the RRC pushed for such legislation despite the fact that no organizations were calling for it.[20] The RRC proceeded to argue that employment policy should shift from employment maintenance at the enterprise level to employment security at the societal level.[21] The advent of the Koizumi government in 2001 strengthened the position of the neoliberal reformers. It is reported that Prime Minister Koizumi told the MOL that facilitating dismissals would induce companies to hire more people.[22] Koizumi's support resulted in cabinet endorsement of the enactment of dismissal law in March 2002.[23]

The enactment of dismissal law was politically driven in the sense that employers were not demanding it. The then president of Nikkeiren Okuda Hiroshi expressed a rather negative view of such legislation.[24] Nikkeiren feared that the law's enactment would fortify employment protection because the Labor Standards Law, under which dismissal law would be codified, includes penal provisions. At the same time, Nikkeiren claimed that relaxation of the rules governing dismissals would generate moral hazards for employers who might be tempted to abuse any such deregulation. By the fall of 2002 Nikkeiren had changed its stance due to a perception that the enactment of the law could not be avoided. It instead began to demand the institution of a new process by which employers would be able to settle legal disputes on unfair dismissals by paying compensation even when a court judges that a dismissal is invalid.[25] In Japan, when a court judges a dismissal unfair, it orders the employer to return the dismissed worker to their previous workplace. Monetary resolution is not an option for employers. Employers demanded a new resolution system according to which, when a court judges a dismissal invalid, an employer would be able to offer monetary compensation in order to terminate employment. The introduction of this kind of monetary resolution system had already been discussed within the Ministry of Health, Labour, and Welfare (MHLW). Shortly before Nikkeiren changed its position, the MHLW proposed the examination of a monetary resolution system. It is possible that the ministry introduced this idea as a quid pro quo for dismissal law in order to elicit concessions from the business community. Issue linkage is a conventional method used by the MOL/MHLW to forge consensus among conflicting parties. However, this time the issue linkage did not bring about compromise. Rengō chose not to oppose the legislation of dismissal rules in the hope that it would guarantee the existing level of employment protection by consolidating existing case law, but vehemently opposed the monetary resolution system.[26] Along with other critics, Rengō contended that such a system would allow employers to freely fire workers, thereby undercutting the doctrine of abuse of the right of dismissal.

The MHLW included the dismissal rules in its draft bill, but, faced with union resistance, dropped the idea of monetary resolution system. At the same time, it changed the wording of the dismissal rules to differ from what unions and employers had agreed on at the advisory council. Rengō complained that the new wording of the bill would give the impression that workers, rather than employers, bear the burden of responsibility to demonstrate unfair dismissal.[27] Because it was employers that bore the burden of proof under the existing case law, Rengō and the Democratic Party of Japan (DPJ) were opposed to what they viewed as an underhand attempt to transform the balance of power by manipulation of wording. At the Diet, Jōjima Masamitsu (DPJ) aggressively questioned a MHLW official as to whether the bill would indeed transform the doctrine of abuse of the right of dismissal or not. Because such a transformation would receive support from neither unions nor employers, the MHLW was compelled to change its position during parliamentary deliberation. The Liberal Democratic Party (LDP), the DPJ, and the Liberal Party agreed to modify the bill, erasing the actual phrase stipulating that "employers are able to dismiss workers." The final law passed at the Diet essentially did not change the existing level of employment protection, neither expediting dismissals as had been hoped for by the neoliberals nor significantly increasing the level of employee protection.

Broken Promise: Still Protecting Employment?

Why were employers so reluctant to diminish the level of employment protection for regular workers and why did they refrain from openly calling for a US-style "employment at will"? Although employers had come to support the legislation of dismissal rules by the end of the process, it is, nonetheless, noteworthy that they refrained from publicly advocating the reduction of employment protection. During the parliamentary deliberations on the dismissal law, a representative of Nippon Keidanren, Kiriku Takashi, repeatedly emphasized that "employment protection is the employer's responsibility."

Economists tend to emphasize the importance of skill formation as a yardstick for gauging an employer's commitment to lifetime employment. Human capital formation theory, based on Gary Becker's (1993) work, gives the most popular account of seniority wage and long-term employment practices (see also Arai 1996; Koike 1999). Firms that invest in human capital formation by offering in-house training avoid dismissals for economic reasons in order to collect the returns on the sunk costs of skill formation. Wage increases correspond to seniority because workers supposedly acquire asset-specific skills by experiencing a wide range of jobs over the years spent in a company. Thus, the theory posits, a tacit agreement exists between employers and employees. Workers avoid the risk of dismissals by agreeing on a long-term trade-off between asset-specific skill formation and long-term employment. Only with the guarantee of lifetime employment are workers able to invest safely in asset-specific skills that are not highly valued in the external labor market. Moreover, incomplete contract theory also explains the combination of lifetime employment and the seniority wage as well as the rationality of dismissal law. A labor contract can be considered incomplete between a worker's commitment to human capital formation and an employer's promise to pay adequate rewards and guarantee long-term employment. It is incomplete because the contract does not guarantee the prevention of employer opportunism. It is only when employment protection legislation limits opportunistic behavior by a firm that workers are able to safely accumulate human capital (Chūma 1998).

My own reading of Japanese employers' intentions in committing to employment protection differs from the economic accounts. There is no evidence that employers are staunch supporters of seniority-based wages. The truth is that they have actually endeavored to reduce the weight of seniority-based wages by increasing merit-based wages from as early as the 1960s.[28] Meritocratic employment practice, especially in terms of personnel assessment (*satei*), has been an important component of the Japanese approach to human resource management. The presence and importance of personnel assessment runs counter to explanations based solely on seniority-based wages. Moreover, there is disagreement as to the extent to which legal employment protection has actually reduced opportunistic behavior by employers. The actual practice of lifetime employment has been rather flexible. Despite the norm of lifetime employment, in reality companies have tended to resort to dismissals after they have produced deficits for two consecutive years (Koike 1999). Consequently, as of 1992, the ratio of employees who had not switched companies among those ages 50–54 employed in large firms (over 1,000 employees) was only 27.1%, while the ratio was 38.4% among those ages 45–49 (Kameyama 1994).

Historically, employment protection at the firm level emerged as a result of the social contract between employers and unions, thereby inducing workers' support of the goal of increasing productivity (see chapter 3). Employment protection for regular workers has been accompanied by functional flexibility in the internal labor market. While their employment is protected, workers are expected to accept company decisions on job relocations. This exchange is articulated in the First Guiding Principle of Productivity. Likewise, at the micro-level, a document written by the Yawata Steel Company union in 1966 confirmed that the union would continue to accept job relocation from the standpoint of lifetime employment (Nitta 2003, 20). As a legal norm, the trade-off between employment protection and relocation has been established since the 1980s.[29]

Although these written documents testify to the establishment of the social contract, it is misleading to say that workers have been convinced that they could not refuse job relocation because their employment was protected. Rationalization, which has often accompanied relocations, has continually provoked conflict. As a result, managers have been compelled to foster and rely on "informal groups" in their companies to induce worker cooperation with their rationalization plans.[30] The micro-level social contract is thus in no way clear-cut. Employees who do not agree to the social exchange have always existed and the terms of compromise are not always evident.[31] What is important for the purpose of my argument is that employment protection, which was otherwise costly and restrictive, afforded employers ample flexibility in terms of personnel deployment. It is this embedded flexibility that has offered employers an incentive to commit to employment protection.

If employers prefer employment protection in order to secure functional flexibility, why have they also called for a monetary compensation system for settling labor disputes regarding unfair dismissals? This demand suggests that employers are in search of a new way to dismiss employees. How are we to understand this apparent double standard on the part of employers? The tacit support given by cooperative unions to downsizing provides a clue. I have already mentioned that personnel reduction is more likely to take place when a firm experiences deficits for two consecutive years. Once employers have decided to cut personnel, company unions often collaborated, as Andrew Gordon (1998) vividly showed. Even though company unions tend to cooperate with employers in this respect, there are always people who refuse to accept a company's decision. These types of workers often join community-based general unions (*yunion*) because company unions are not useful to them. Japanese law compels employers to negotiate with any union regardless of the share of employees it represents. Whereas company unions tend to accept a company's restructuring plans, community unions tend to fight in order to protect the interests of individual workers. From the perspective of employers, the cooperation of company unions alone is insufficient to enable them to smoothly implement personnel reductions. A monetary resolution system would thus provide employers with new ammunition to deal with non-cooperative workers and unions. The seeming double standards of employers in this respect can be understood when we take into consideration the simple fact that, beneath the surface of cooperative industrial relations, Japanese workers are not homogenous and workplaces inherently harbor the seeds of contention.

Although employers naturally seek alternative avenues through which to further their interests, it is clear that they continue to emphasize their commitment to lifetime employment. However, whether or not unions and workers fully believe their employers' assurances is a different question. For instance, Sasamori Kiyoshi, who was president of Rengō from 2001 to

2005, denounced employers that unilaterally annulled the Three Guiding Principles of Productivity which, he asserted, had sustained the competitiveness of Japanese firms.[32] He referred to the reduction of regular workers as a sign of employers' breach of the principles. The rapid increase in numbers of non-regular workers reveals that companies implemented downsizing even while professing their commitment to lifetime employment. Between 2000 and 2002, 27.2% of large firms employing over 5,000 workers solicited "voluntary retirement" (*kibō taishoku*).[33] Between 1997 and 2008, a total of over 4 million regular jobs were lost.[34]

The contradiction between employers' words and deeds potentially yields different interpretations on the continuity of cooperatism. At the level of discourse expressed by employers, cooperatism seems to persist to the present day. Likewise, a number of studies reveal that actual cooperation between employers and company unions remains in evidence (see Inagami and Whittaker 2005). In contrast, I take the position that the politics of productivity has ended and that cooperatism as an ideology has lost its raison d'être. Although cooperative industrial relations still exist at the company level, the territory protected by this kind of institutional continuity is steadily shrinking as the number of workers protected by company unions decreases. The decline in wage levels in general and the widening gap between wage increases and productivity increases shown in Figure 5.1 are quite telling with respect to the collapse of the politics of productivity. Furthermore, increased instances of individual labor disputes and corporate misconduct also imply that employer commitment to the productivity movement has all but evaporated.[35]

Paradoxically, the presence of cooperative unions and the lack of threat from leftist labor movements has diluted the very raison d'être of cooperatism. As was discussed in chapter 3, the politics of productivity originated as a political program to counter leftist forces. With this threat having all but disappeared, it comes as no surprise that the ideological appeal of cooperatism has vanished. Employers now enjoy a relatively free hand in their decisions on wage levels, employment portfolios, and personnel reductions. The triumph of cooperatism in the 1980s was, ironically, the cause of its downfall in the following decade.

Hollowing-Out the Nation State: Globalization, Privatization, and Marketization

It is often argued that globalization and deindustrialization prompt employers to reduce labor costs, including both wages and non-wage costs. As this book provides a predominantly political account of policy change, let us now explore the impacts of these two factors to assess the extent to which economic changes directly influence policy changes. First, we must look at the extent to which Japanese firms have been globalized. In 1996, the overseas profits of Japanese firms surpassed the value of Japanese exports for the first time.[36] As of 2005, Japanese companies operating overseas employed 3,820,000 workers abroad, amounting to 35% of their domestic employees. This ratio has more than doubled since 1995.[37] In companies to which Keidanren's executives belong, the degree of globalization is more apparent. Among these companies, the ratio of overseas profits to total profits increased from 18.7% in 1970 to 24.6% in 1980, 27.5% in 1990, 38.6% in 2000, and 40.9% in 2005.[38] For companies to which the presidents and vice-presidents of Keidanren belong, the ratio was 50.1% in 2005 (Sasaki 2007, 40).

Another aspect of globalization is the increasing presence of foreign stockholders. Because foreign stockholders are sensitive to short-term profits, their increasing influence is likely to subject Japanese firms to the mandate of the capital market. The rapid rise of foreign shareholders since the 1990s has been truly phenomenal. Foreign investors owned only 4.7% of the total stock market value in 1990, but their share jumped to 18.8% in 2000 and 28.0% in 2006, surpassing the share of business corporations in 2003.[39] Their share among companies to which Keidanren's executives belong steadily increased from 2.2% in 1980 to 8.3% in 1990, 21.4% in 2000, and 29.2% in 2005 (Sasaki 2007, 53). How has this drastic increase in foreign stockholdings affected Japanese management? A number of studies indicate that foreign ownership encourages downsizing. For instance, Ahmadjian and Robbins (2005) discovered that foreign ownership significantly increased the likelihood of downsizing between 1991 and 2000. Steven K. Vogel (2006) conducted a thorough statistical analysis for the 1990–2002 period to provide consistent evidence that companies with higher levels of foreign ownership downsize their workforces more aggressively. Interestingly, his analysis shows that manufacturers and exporters were less likely to downsize (Vogel 2006, 201–204). According to analysis by the Bank of Japan, the real wage gap, which is the rate of deviation of real wages from labor productivity, has become more negative in industries that have higher ratios of foreign stockholdings or exports.[40] These studies, taken together, suggest that the significant presence of foreign ownership in the Japanese capital market has applied further pressure to Japanese firms to reduce labor costs across the board, but that this pressure has been translated into wage restraint rather than downsizing in the export sector.

How have Japanese employers perceived the impact of globalization? Employers have repeatedly claimed that Japan's labor costs are high by international comparison, a point that has been raised in Nikkeiren's annual position papers on management-labor policy. Every year since 1995, Nikkeiren/Nippon Keidanren has emphasized the necessity of restricting total labor costs in order for Japanese firms to compete in the midst of intensified global competition. According to Nikkeiren, as of 1993, the level of Japanese labor costs in the manufacturing sector was the highest among the advanced industrialized countries, twice as high as in the United Kingdom and France, and 1.4 times higher than in the United States. Nikkeiren has remained alarmed that the Japanese level has consistently stayed among the highest, only being surpassed in 2003 by the United Kingdom as the country with the most expensive labor costs, 10% higher than Japan.[41] However, according to the estimation of the Japan Institute of Labour Policy and Training (JILPT; a think tank under the MHLW), a different picture emerges. When the Japanese manufacturing sector's labor costs are set at a constant of 100, the US cost was 185 in 1985 but dropped sharply to 71 in 1995. Due to the aggressive cost cuts pursued by Japanese managers, the level of labor costs has converged between the United States and Japan since 2001.[42]

The different estimations of Nikkeiren and the JILPT indicate how aggressively Nikkeiren pursued labor cost reductions and sought to justify their position from the viewpoint of international competitiveness. Nikkeiren also calls attention to the fact that China is now Japan's largest trading partner. Though comparative studies focusing solely on advanced industrialized countries might yield different conclusions, it is beyond dispute that Japanese wages are much higher than those in low-wage countries like China. In 2002 Japanese imports from China outnumbered those from the United States and doubled in 2005.[43] Most imported items from China are consumer goods such as textiles and home electronics, which has impacted Japanese industries and jobs. Nikkeiren's wage policy shows that Japanese wages now set not only with consideration of domestic factors such as productivity and inflation but also from the viewpoint of international competitiveness, especially vis-à-vis low-wage countries.

If globalization compelled employers to reduce labor costs, one might then reasonably ask whether or not this indicates that Japan had embarked on "the race to the bottom." According to the race to the bottom thesis, capital seeks the location where it will gain the highest rate of return. Because high rates of corporate tax and strict labor standards diminish rates of return, capital naturally gravitates toward countries with the lowest regulatory standards. The fickle behavior of capital encourages governments to lower taxes and regulatory standards if they are eager to attract foreign capital and/or afraid that domestic capital will depart elsewhere. The result of these processes is convergence at the lowest common denominator (Frieden 2006; Goodman and Pauly 1993; Huber and Stephens 1998; Kurzer 1993; McKenzie and Lee 1991; Mishra 1999; Moses 1994).[44] Despite the popularity of this model in the commentaries, academic works have consistently refuted it with an extensive array of evidence (Castles 2004; Drezner 2007; Flanagan 2006; Garret 1998; Pierson 2001; Rodrik 1997; Swank 2001; Sykes, Palier, and Prior 2001; Thelen and Kume 1999; Thelen and Van Wijnbergen 2003). It is often noted that the concept of globalization has been rather used as a frame to justify neoliberal policies (Krugman 1994; Piven 1995; Steger 2002).

The same can be said of Japanese employers who have used the concept in an attempt to convince policymakers and unions to accept their preferred policy options, propagating the discourse of the race to the bottom in order to justify their position. In particular, the growing importance of China as a trading partner played a role in fortifying their view that the race to the bottom was inevitable in order for Japanese companies to survive. If it was pressure resulting from globalization that forced them to undertake labor market reform, why did they not dismantle employment security for regular workers, who are the principal source of high labor costs? It should be emphasized that employers did not publicly advocate the dismantling of employment protection. Although the pressures of globalization could not be ignored, there were a number of options available to them for reducing labor costs and their policy priorities were generally determined by their historical experiences.

First, employment protection is the manifestation of the cross-class coalition and employers have benefited from cooperative industrial relations by guaranteeing employment protection. As long as organized labor continues to prioritize employment protection, employers will continue to publicly commit to employment protection as an obligatory responsibility for employers. Second, it should be recalled that the flip side of strong employment protection is the significant degree of internal and external flexibilities in the labor market that is sustained by the gendered dual system. Due to the beneficial nature of this arrangement, employers continue to commit to employment protection for regular workers while seeking to enhance flexibility through neoliberal labor market reform. Employer preferences, therefore, cannot be deduced from their economic standing. Their historical experiences of contention with the labor movement and with employees shape their ideas about how the labor market and the social protection system should be organized.

Commercializing the State

What about the impact of deindustrialization? Another significant driving force behind labor market reform has been political pressure from labor market businesses. Development of the external labor market creates various new service businesses related to job placement such as staffing services, private placement services, outplacement services, and job information publications. These "human resource businesses" are the first beneficiaries of labor market reform. In this sense, deindustrialization was one of the factors leading to labor market reform, but the way in which human resource businesses were able to influence the policy-making process presents a highly politicized story.

Human resource businesses grew rapidly thanks to deregulation of the labor market. The total sales of temporary work agencies jumped from ¥1.57 trillion in 2000 to ¥5.42 trillion in 2006. The contribution of the 2003 amendment of the Temporary Work Agency Law, revoking the exemption of the manufacturing sector, was enormous; in 2004 sales increased by 21.2% compared to the previous year, by 41.0% in 2005, and by 34.3% in 2006. For private placement services, total fee incomes increased from ¥86.7 billion in 2000 to ¥232.6 billion in 2006.[45]

Theoretically, deregulation is considered a difficult goal to achieve. According to the seminal work by J. Q. Wilson (1980), when costs are concentrated but benefits diffused, change cannot be realized without the presence of political entrepreneurs. Deregulation is a quintessential case of this political pattern. Industries protected by regulation use their political clout to oppose deregulation, whereas consumers who are likely to benefit from deregulation are not able to overcome the challenges inhibiting collective action. It is only when political entrepreneurs are active that the voices of diffuse interests can be heard.

Deregulation of the labor market does not follow this political pattern. Although job seekers may benefit from the expansion of the external labor market, the first beneficiaries of deregulation are staffing and placement service businesses whose interests are well concentrated. Those who bear the costs of deregulation are regular workers who may be replaced by cheaper non-regular workers and non-regular workers who are no longer able to find regular jobs. The interests of these groups are partially represented by labor unions, but this is not always the case. Without active labor unionism, the costs of labor market reforms are very much diffused. Thus, the politics of labor market reform match the "client politics" described in Wilson's framework where benefits are concentrated but costs widely distributed. Wilson categorized this pattern as a case of producer-dominant regulatory legislation. Client politics result not only from regulatory legislation to control entry to the market but also from deregulatory legislation to allow market entry, because deregulation commercializes state activities thereby bringing about new opportunities for profit making.

What policies do human resource businesses advocate? The demands of this group have included further liberalization of labor market regulations, especially the lifting of the remaining restrictions on the staffing business such as the term limit, the obligation of client companies to offer a regular employment contract after the term limit, and the prohibition on client companies interviewing and hiring their preferred choice of dispatched worker. They have also lobbied for privatization of public placement services. Currently, public placement organizations, known as Hello Work, handle approximately 20% of job placements. Private placement companies naturally expect that the privatization of Hello Work would provide huge business opportunities. As it became clear that total privatization of public placement services was unrealistic, the introduction of "market testing" to the activities performed by Hello Work became a goal for human resource businesses. Market testing is a method of exposing public services to competition from external bidders. If the results of market testing show that for-profit companies achieve the same goal with greater efficiency than public organizations, privatization and outsourcing would be justified.

The idea of market testing first appeared in the final recommendation of the Council for Comprehensive Regulatory Reform (CCRR) published in December 2003. This document claimed that market testing was an effective means to open public services to the private sector across the board. Half a year later, in accordance with the recommendation, the Koizumi cabinet decided to experimentally introduce market testing in 2005. Nippon Keidanren expected market testing to streamline public services and create new business opportunities for the private sector. In 2004, the Council for the Promotion of Regulatory Reform (CPRR), reorganized to succeed the CCRR, solicited proposals from the private sector for which public services they would like to make a bid. Seventy-five companies made propositions on 119 operations, including 18 companies that showed an interest in contracting out public placement services. The CPRR then chose four operations, including services offered by Hello Work and the Social Insurance Agency, as the first model cases of market testing. In addition to providing free-of-charge job placement services for the unemployed, Hello Work organizes various activities such as assistance for re-employment and vocational training programs. Because the MHLW resisted any hint of commercialization in the core job placement service activities of Hello Work, only peripheral programs were chosen for contracting out.

In the meantime, the government proceeded with the legislation of the Market Testing Law (officially called the Public Services Reform Law), which was passed in May 2006. The enactment prompted the ministries to expose some of their activities to market testing. The MHLW chose three areas for market testing: career exchange plazas, human resource banks, and discovering job vacancies. It continued to oppose the introduction of market testing in job placement services, but the power balance finally shifted under the Abe Shinzō cabinet (2006–2007). Abe nominated Yashiro Naohiro, a professor of economics widely known as a sincere believer in market mechanisms, to the Council on Economic and Fiscal Policy (CEFP), the decision arena for government fiscal and economic policy. Yashiro proposed a "Labor Big Bang," calling for fundamental reforms of labor market regulation. He also made a proposition at the CEFP that some of Hello Work's offices in Tokyo should be subjected to market testing. The CEFP was a much more powerful and higher ranking organization than the CPRR, with the prime minister chairing its meetings. Eventually, the MHLW conceded, allowing two Hello Work offices in the Tokyo metropolis to be contracted out for two–three years starting from 2008.

It has been surmised that the Hello Work services contracted out under the market testing scheme would create ¥150 billion in sales for the private sector.[46] However, it is merely a stepping stone to further commercialization of public placement services. The major lobbying organizations of staffing and placement companies assert that the role of the public sector should be limited to managing the safety net as a last resort and that even the safety net should be partially contracted out. The lobbyists claim that private companies should be able to selectively deal with job seekers in order to take advantage of market mechanisms.[47] Their proposals, neoliberal in tenor, pose a fundamental challenge to the idea of free-of-charge job placement. If the private sector were to be allowed to "cherry pick" services that would produce profits, the remaining public services would be "residualized." Only those having difficulty finding employment would use the public services, making them less efficient, more costly, and thus more susceptible to further rationalization.

The political influence of the human resource businesses did not last long. Unlike Koizumi, neither Prime Minister Abe nor his successors were enthusiastic about the neoliberal agenda. Although Abe nominated Yashiro to the CEFP, he did not side with him, but instead gradually altered the policy orientation of the council toward reregulation. The government submitted an amendment bill to the Public Services Reform Law to enable the application of market testing to free-of-charge placement services in March 2008, but the bill did not proceed to the Diet floor and was aborted in December that year. Lacking strong political sponsorship, the bill, which was not welcomed by the bureaucracy, was shelved and then aborted. When the Asō Tarō cabinet endorsed a new basic policy for public services in July 2009, it did not mention free-of-charge placement services, which suggests that political will to pursue this agenda had disappeared.[48]

Although client politics with respect to human resource businesses is a relatively recent phenomenon, its political influence has already been significant. This influence first became noticeable when the Recruit scandal broke out in 1988. The Recruit Corporation, a job information conglomerate, bribed MOL high officials in order to evade legal controls on the job-seeking advertisement business, which was criticized at the time for publishing prostitution advertisements. Recruit also widely distributed pre-flotation shares of a Recruit company to over 90 politicians, elite bureaucrats, and executives of Nippon Telegraph and Telecommunications (NTT) in an attempt to curry political favor. Twelve people were convicted, including the administrative vice minister of labor and the chief cabinet secretary. Financial Minister Miyazawa Kiichi and later Prime Minister Takeshita Noboru were compelled to resign as they had also received the pre-flotation shares. The Recruit scandal was one of the biggest and most consequential scandals in postwar Japan, generating intense dissatisfaction with LDP rule among voters and paving the way to the party's fall from power in 1993. That Recruit turned to illegal means to seek access to power in the 1980s is indicative of its lack of political clout. By the 1990s and 2000s, however, staffing and placement businesses had secured a legitimate voice in the government process, obviating the need for any such illegal maneuvers. Analysis of the transformation of the policy-making process is thus essential in order to understand the legitimization of the human resource business, which will be the task of the next chapter.

The Neoliberal Agenda and the Diet Veto

The transformation of the Japanese business community accounts for the origin and persistent momentum of neoliberal labor market reform. However, politics does not merely reflect the policy preferences of powerful actors. It also has its own logic and dynamics. Although there were occasions when more radical ideas than those proposed by employers made it onto the policy agenda, the actual content of reform was usually much more modest than the initial proposals. The struggle for power between political actors greatly affected the way in which policy agendas were set and deals made. This chapter reveals the nature of the political dynamics since 1993 that resulted in the transformation of the welfare through work system.

Japan has experienced various labor market reforms characterized by an overall deregulatory tendency since the 1990s. The actual extent of deregulation has been modest by international standards. Nevertheless, in the absence of concurrent development and upgrading of protective measures for workers, even relatively modest neoliberal labor market reform resulted in increased numbers of workers in precarious circumstances and rising levels of poverty. These developments raise several questions. How did neoliberal reform make it onto the political agenda in the first place? Why did reformers fail to achieve their initial goals? Why did the Japanese government not upgrade the social protection system to cope with the new social risks that resulted from new labor market conditions?

Similar to my analysis of party politics under the 1955 system (see chapter 3), I emphasize the ideologies and visions of the ruling parties as well as the strategic behavior of political parties as a whole. The Liberal Democratic Party (LDP) was ousted in 1993 for less than a year, following which they enjoyed a sustained period of rule until 2009. During this period, the ruling parties, whether in the non-LDP coalition or the LDP-led coalition, almost consistently pursued neoliberal reform. The role of key political leaders during this period, such as Hosokawa Morihiro, Hashimoto Ryūtarō, and Koizumi Jun'ichirō, was decisive in setting policy agendas. The personal convictions of these leaders affected their decisions, but strategic calculations governed by the constraints of partisan competition were also important. I argue that the decline of the Left created a political environment in which the new political parties were able to place a neoliberal policy agenda at the center of their political platforms in order to effectively counter the LDP's long-term rule.

In addition to ideas, institutions played an important role. Prime ministers Hosokawa and Hashimoto created new institutions that allowed the proponents of neoliberal reform to effectively influence the decision-making process. More specifically, two institutions played a critical role in accelerating and realizing neoliberal reform: the deregulation panels and the Council on Economic and Fiscal Policy (CEFP). These were the two principal vehicles of neoliberal reform, without which reform would have been much slower and more modest. This chapter pays due attention to the role of these institutions in transforming the policy-making process with respect to labor market regulations, thereby exploiting the shift in the balance of power between employers and workers that had already occurred.

The New Agenda for Power Struggle

Why did neoliberal reform make it onto the political agenda in the 1990s? I argue that patterns of partisan competition significantly influence the type of issue that appears on the agenda. The major difference in partisan competition between the 1955 system and the post-1955 system resides in the substance of issue cleavage. The Left-Right cleavage that characterized the 1955 system was replaced by issue cleavage between what the LDP came to represent and the opposition thereto. The essence of what the LDP came to represent is the collusive relationship between *zoku* politicians,[1] bureaucrats, and business (especially non-competitive industries). As a result of staying in power for such a long period, the LDP became entangled with various vested interests, which made it difficult to undertake neoliberal reform, and deregulation in particular. The LDP had already embarked on certain neoliberal projects in the 1980s, but deregulation was not a pertinent issue at the time. Advocates and supporters of deregulation, such as global companies, the US government, and urban wealthy voters, were frustrated with the LDP and longed for a political alternative. In this context, new parties emerged in 1992–1993 to fill this vacuum in the political landscape. These parties all diagnosed the cause of Japan's ills to be LDP rule as supported by bureaucratic power, which led them to call for both political and administrative reform. Accordingly, neoliberalism provided a consistent and cogent political formula to those who positioned themselves as anti-LDP reformers.

The creation of the Hosokawa cabinet was a critical juncture in the rise to preeminence of the neoliberal agenda. The LDP failed to secure a majority in the general election of July 18, 1993, which resulted in the birth of the Hosokawa cabinet formed by eight parties including both neoliberal reformers and socialists: the Japan New Party, the New Party Sakigake, the Japan Renewal Party, the Japan Socialist Party, the Democratic Socialist Party, Kōmeitō, the Social Democratic Federation, and the Democratic Reform League. The termination of one-party dominance was the lowest common denominator in the Hosokawa coalition. In particular, the coalition denounced the collusive relationship among the LDP, bureaucracy, and business. This "iron triangle" epitomized the lack of accountability and democratic control under LDP governance, but was also viewed as the cause of inefficient allocation of resources, which neoliberal reformers aimed to rectify. In other words, the iron triangle symbolized both the lack of democratic accountability and economic inefficiency. Sakigake and the Social Democratic Federation emphasized the former, whereas the Japan New Party and the Japan Renewal Party were keener on the latter (Nakano 1998). Thus, political liberalism and economic neoliberalism coexisted in the Hosokawa coalition as both causes shared the common goal of dismantling the LDP-bureaucracy amalgam.

Hosokawa's cabinet undertook two critical institutional reforms, which had an enduring effect on policymaking in Japan. The central agenda of the Hosokawa coalition was political reform, and particularly the overhaul of the single non-transferable vote system in order to reduce campaign financing and personal voting and thus enhance policy-centered partisan competition. The Hosokawa cabinet passed a series of political reform bills in March 1994, as a result of which the electoral system for the House of Representatives was transformed into a combination of single-member districts and proportional representation (see Christensen 1996). The introduction of the first-past-the-post system led to the eventual consolidation of the opposition parties, leading in turn to the emergence and development of the Democratic Party of Japan (DPJ) in subsequent years, which grew to become a viable competitor to the LDP and, indeed, ousted the LDP from power in 2009.

The other important institutional reform that the Hosokawa cabinet embarked on, and of greater interest to the concerns of this book, was the creation of the Administrative Reform Committee, which had an enduring impact on the deregulatory process. The creation of a strong third-party organization to promote administrative reform and deregulation was part of Prime Minister Hosokawa's agenda. When Hosokawa was governor of Kumamoto, he chaired the Full Life (*yutakana kurashi*) section of the Third Provisional Council for the Promotion of Administrative Reform to promote deregulation and decentralization. Encountering stubborn resistance from bureaucrats and *zoku* politicians, he eventually resigned from the council to establish the Japan New Party (Hosokawa 1992). The end of bureaucracy-led politics, the precondition for deregulation, was the founding objective of his party. In accordance with Hosokawa's policy preferences, in September 1993, his cabinet introduced ninety-four deregulatory items as part of its emergent economic recovery plan, signaling a strong commitment to deregulation. In December, the government decided to partially open the Japanese market to rice imports. In the meantime, Hosokawa established the Economic Reform Study Group and nominated Hiraiwa Gaishi, the then chairman of Keidanren, as its chair. The group issued its final report in December, recommending that "economic regulation should be abolished and social regulation should be minimal." This principle has been repeatedly endorsed by subsequent governments to justify comprehensive deregulation. The report also went on to recommend the establishment of a new administrative body that would promote deregulation with a strong monitoring function. The creation of such an organization already had been recommended by the Third Provisional Council for the Promotion of Administrative Reform that Hosokawa had previously been involved with. In its final report issued in October 1993, the council proposed the establishment of Administrative Reform Headquarters attached to the cabinet as well as a third-party organization in order to supervise the actual implementation of reforms and deregulation. At the time, the US government was also making forceful demands for economic deregulation in order to redress the US-Japan trade imbalance.

Responding to these recommendations, in March 1994, the Hosokawa cabinet proposed the establishment of an Administrative Reform Committee that would deliberate on the legislation of information disclosure, supervise the implementation of deregulation, and advise the government on these matters. This was approved by the Diet in November under the Murayama cabinet. The following year, the Administrative Reform Committee created the Deregulation Subcommittee to guide the deregulation process for the next three years.

Toward Structural Reform under LDP Rule

The Hosokawa cabinet's achievements in setting up a framework for the deregulation of subsequent years were largely in accord with Hosokawa's personal convictions. However, the collapse of the Hosokawa cabinet did not slow the momentum of deregulation. First, the institutionalization of deregulation procedure led by the Deregulation Subcommittee prolonged the life of the deregulation movement beyond the demise of the Hosokawa cabinet. Second, administrative reform under the Hashimoto cabinet and structural reform under the Koizumi cabinet became the focal points of the political contest, which ensured that the issue of deregulation continued to receive political support.

The Hosokawa coalition lasted for less than nine months and collapsed in April 1994 due to Hosokawa's embroilment in a financial scandal and general internal strife. After a short-lived coalitional government under Hata Tsutomu, the LDP returned to power in alliance with its longstanding rival the Japan Socialist Party (JSP) and the New Party Sakigake in June 1994. Murayama Tomiichi, the JSP's president, led the LDP-JSP-Sakigake coalition until Hashimoto Ryūtarō succeeded him in January 1996. The Murayama cabinet did not actively push the neoliberal agenda, as none of the coalition partners were its proponents. In the meantime, the opposition parties went through several breakups and mergers. Ozawa Ichirō, who had ended the 1955 system by splitting from the LDP, disbanded the Japan Renewal Party and created the New Frontier Party (NFP) in 1994, which included members of the Japan New Party, Kōmeitō, and the Democratic Socialist Party. Some of the Sakigake affiliated politicians, such as Hatoyama Yukio and Kan Naoto, as well as several socialists, such as Yokomichi Takahiro founded the DPJ in 1996. Partisan competition among the LDP, the NFP, and the DPJ pushed the issue of administrative reform to the center of the political agenda.

Prime Minister Hashimoto called a general election in October 1996, the first one under the new electoral system. Most parties pledged to promote administrative reform and showed a great degree of convergence on major issues. In particular, parties competed over the ideal number of central ministries and the electoral campaign came to resemble something like a bargain sale of central administration. Hosokawa, who had joined the NFP, published his personal proposals, including reforms such as the scrapping and merger of the central ministries, reduction in the number of public servants to the half the contemporary level, abolition of all economic regulations, and privatization of postal services. The NFP adopted most of his proposals as its electoral pledges.[2] Similarly, the LDP also pledged that it would reduce the number of the central ministries to eleven from twenty-two and consolidate the major advisory councils by establishing a new council attached to the prime minister in order to shift the real locus of budget-making power from the Ministry of Finance to the prime minister and his cabinet. The DPJ was no mere bystander at the bargaining sale, either. Having been committed to administrative reform since its formation under the banner of "the party of administrative reform," the DPJ promised reorganization of the central ministries into eight areas.

Several factors can account for the sudden willingness of all the parties to address the issue of administrative reform. First, politicians decided that bureaucracy bashing would be electorally rewarding, as several scandals involving high-ranking bureaucrats had broken out, and they aggressively probed the responsibility of bureaucrats with respect to the failed *jūsen* housing-loan companies and the HIV-tainted blood-product scandal. In both cases, politicians and the public identified the collusive relationship between supervisory ministries and banks/pharmaceutical companies maintained by the practice of *amakudari* (descent from heaven) as a root cause of the scandals. The *jūsen* scandal fueled the debate over the necessity of dismembering the almighty Ministry of Finance, separating supervision of the financial industry from control of fiscal policy. The idea of reforming the Financial Ministry spilled over to across-the-board reform of central administration. Second, administrative reform frequently has been employed as an incentive to convince voters to accept an increase in the consumption tax. Creating a shared perception of waste elimination through administrative reform was a prerequisite to tax reform. As the Murayama cabinet decided to increase the consumption tax from 3% to 5% in September 1994, which was expected to come into effect in April 1997, the governing coalition must have felt this imperative much more keenly than the opposition. Third, the presence of the NFP and, to a lesser extent at the time the DPJ, had intensified partisan competition. The LDP is known for habitually stealing policy ideas from opposition parties in order to retain power (Calder 1988). As the NFP and DPJ challenged the LDP on the grounds of administrative reform, advocating the same policy idea presumably appeared to be a winning strategy.

Although all the political parties pledged to implement administrative reform of some kind, they did differ in terms of sincerity and aim. Not surprisingly, the LDP did not actually intend to dismantle the iron triangle that had kept it in power for so long. The result of the election influenced the actual content of the reform. The LDP won the election by gaining 239 out of 500 seats.[3] The major loser in the election was the SDP (Social Democratic Party, renamed after the JSP), which suffered a drastic reduction in the number of its representatives from 70 to 15. The NFP gained 156 seats and the DPJ 52. The LDP's victory delivered a clear popular mandate to Hashimoto's policies. He set up the Administrative Reform Conference to discuss the function of the state in the twenty-first century and draw a blueprint for his reorganization project. As the chairman of the conference, he made it clear from the beginning that the realization of simple and effective government was the ultimate objective of his administrative reform. As Koichi Nakano argues, Hashimoto's emphasis on effectiveness departed from the nature of administrative reform pursued by the previous coalition governments. Sakigake, and later the DPJ, had pledged administrative reform in order to break up the LDP-bureaucracy amalgam, which they perceived as a hotbed of political corruption.[4] In contrast, for Hashimoto, the problem resided not in the lack of accountability but of effectiveness. In essence, "Hashimoto shifted the nature of reform away from the pursuit of accountability through confronting the bureaucracy toward the search for simple and effective government in cooperation with bureaucrats" (Nakano 1998, 307).

Hashimoto not only aimed to strengthen the function of the state through administrative reform but also embarked on structural reforms in order to revitalize the Japanese economy, such as fiscal structural reform and the

financial "Big Bang." Statism and neoliberalism were well blended in his reform vision. Hashimoto's aspiration for strong government gave birth to the
CEFP, which became a major engine of neoliberal reform under the Koizumi
cabinet. When the Administrative Reform Conference proposed the creation
of the CEFP in its final report issued in December 1997, the function and
authority of the proposed council remained rather vague. It was Obuchi
Keizō's cabinet (1998–2000) that designed the CEFP to comprise less than
eleven members, including the prime minister as chairman, the chief cabinet
secretary, the minister of state for economic and fiscal policy, and at least
four representatives from the private sector.[5] The fact that the prime minister
chaired the council was expected to give it political weight, and the inclusion of private sector members in the CEFP was designed to supply different
policy ideas from those held by the Ministry of Finance.[6]

Although the CEFP was intended to reinforce *Kantei* (prime minister's
office) functions, institutional design by itself does not determine the modus
operandi of the institution. The CEFP was scheduled for set-up in January
2001 and Mori Yoshirō was prime minister when the cabinet was due to final-
ize the selection of the private sector experts. Mori, who was not sympathetic
to the weakening of the Ministry of Finance as he feared that this might
also lead to the demise of *zoku* politicians, established a different organization, the Fiscal Summit (*zaisei shunō kaigi*), to undercut the functions of
the CEFP. Hashimoto, minister of administrative reform at the time, fought
back against the political forces seeking to undermine the CEFP. Eventually,
Mori agreed to demolish the Fiscal Summit by the time the CEFP began to
operate.

It was under the Koizumi cabinet (2001–2006) that the CEFP became a
true locus of decision making (Makihara 2005; Shiroyama 2003; Uchiyama
2007). Prime Minister Koizumi Jun'ichirō clearly understood the usefulness of the Council in terms of his power struggle against his own party. At
the first meeting of the CEFP under his government, Koizumi defined it as
"the most important council to flesh out structural reform without sanctuar-
ies."[7] Based on discussions at the CEFP, the cabinet issued an "Economic
and Fiscal Reform (Basic Policies)" paper, widely known as "big-boned policy
papers" (*honebuto no hōshin*), every year in June since 2001 to present the
government's policy orientation and priorities as well as a specific menu for
structural reform. Big-boned policy papers became the government's most
important position papers up until 2009 when the DPJ changed the budget-
making process.

Koizumi pursued neoliberal reform in a much more sweeping way than
any previous cabinet had done. He became the LDP president by pledging
to "smash the LDP" and kept his promise by undercutting the power of fac-
tion leaders and *zoku* politicians with respect to appointments of ministers
and policy-making process. He succeeded in reducing the budget for public
works by 10.7% in 2002 and more than 3% each year for the following four

years, to a total reduction of 23.7% during his five-year governance. Given the fact that public works constituted the LDP's major pork barrel, this significant retrenchment should be attributed to Koizumi's personal popularity. His other neoliberal reforms included the privatization of postal services and restraint on social expenditure. The advent of the Koizumi government also reactivated the momentum of deregulation.

During the Koizumi years, the influence of Takenaka Heizō and the four private-sector experts of the CEFP were noticeable. Takenaka, a former Keio University economics professor-turned-politician under Koizumi's patronage, was appointed minister of state for economic and fiscal policy to lead the council's deliberations. He provided the private-sector experts with political support, urging them to present their proposals or "private-sector papers," thereby setting the council's agendas (Ōta 2006). Although the CEFP was ostensibly formed as a council of consultation, the role of private-sector experts was advocacy of neoliberal reform rather than advisory as experts of academia or business. Interestingly, it was Prime Minister Mori who had appointed the experts. Two were economics professors who had worked closely with the government in various advisory councils: Honma Masaaki from University of Osaka, and Yoshikawa Hiroshi from the University of Tokyo. The other two were business leaders: Okuda Hiroshi, chairman of Toyota Motor Corporation and president of Nippon Keidanren, and Ushio Jirō, CEO of Ushio Inc. and former president of Keizai Dōyūkai. It was reported that Mori had selected these four members in consideration of maintaining balance between academia and business as well as between major organizations.[8] However, these members became promoters of neoliberal reform under the Koizumi cabinet due to strong support from Takenaka. The inclusion of such outsiders into the government process, which had previously been all but monopolized by bureaucrats, allowed neoliberal ideas to gradually take root. A predecessor of the CEFP had been the Economic Strategy Council (1998–1999) established by the Obuchi cabinet. This prior council had also included neoliberal economists like Takenaka as well as business leaders like Okuda and Higuchi Kōtarō (Asahi Brewery).[9] However, whereas the Economic Strategy Council had been an ad hoc commission, the CEFP was a formal institution that the prime minister directly chaired, and meetings were held almost weekly. The inclusion of business leaders into the CEFP thus amplified their influence on the government policy.[10]

Partisan Dynamics and Ideational Renewal

My analysis of the mainstreaming of neoliberalism shows that a new mode of partisan dynamics induced political parties to renew their ideational foundation. It is essential to reveal the process of policy repositioning because the strategic adaptation of parties' policy positions ultimately led to policy change. The new mode of partisan competition that emerged in the early

1990s was characterized by the emergence of new centrist anti-LDP parties as well as by the decline of leftist forces. The new parties were formed in an ideational vacuum under the 1955 party system in which the long-term rule of the LDP had largely obstructed the advancement of neoliberal policy demands. The new parties placed the neoliberal agenda at the center of their political platforms in order to effectively challenge and bring an end to the era of conservative rule. Global companies and their employees as well as urban wealthy consumers were the expected constituencies for these new parties.

Facing this challenge from the new parties, the LDP repositioned itself, promoting neoliberal policies of its own. It is true that the LDP had already embraced certain neoliberal policies in the 1980s such as privatization and welfare retrenchment. However, the LDP was not aiming to create flexible labor markets or implement comprehensive structural reform of Japanese capitalism at the time. It was only under the Hashimoto cabinet that the LDP pushed forth a whole array of neoliberal reforms. Although the LDP constantly faced challenges from the neoliberally minded new parties, it did not face the same degree of threat from leftist parties. The former Socialists were split between those who joined the DPJ and those who stayed with the SDP, making their voices and concerns largely marginalized. In this new political context, cooperatism, which peaked in the 1980s, became outmoded. Once employers had divested themselves of the concept, there was no reason for Hashimoto or his successors to defend it any more. However, although the LDP refashioned its ideological position, one of its core values—statism— prevailed. Indeed, statism and neoliberalism complemented each other well in Hashimoto's reform agenda. Hashimoto sought a strong government that would have the capacity to carry out structural reform. The Obuchi cabinet followed suit, and the Koizumi cabinet skillfully deployed the reinforced functions of the state for which Hashimoto had laid the foundation.

The dynamics of the partisan competition that first appeared in 1993 were centripetal in the sense that most parties, with the exception of the socialists and the communists, sought neoliberal reform in some form or other, thus differing from the polarized partisan competition characterizing the 1955 party system. It is often thought that the new electoral system was brought on by the centripetal dynamics, resulting in a quasi two-party system in Japan. The Downsian spatial model predicts that parties pursue policies preferred by the median voter, thereby generating centripetal dynamics (Downs 1957). However, the centripetal partisan dynamics of the 1990s predated electoral reform and were one of the factors that prompted the electoral reform. The causal direction here should not be mistaken. A simple application of the spatial model is problematic, as it treats the policy positions of voters as an exogenous given. Political elites influence the distribution of voter preferences as much as voters do politicians' policy priorities. As Koichi Nakano argues, political parties do not merely reflect pre-existing social cleavages and the preference of the median voter but "actively mold and define the 'popular will' through their advocacy and implementation of policies" (2010, 6). Moreover, it should be noted that centripetal competition is not synonymous with a two-party system. British and US politics illustrate that partisan competition under a two-party system can be both centripetal and centrifugal depending on the political context at any given time. It is, therefore, essential to identify the key agents that introduce new visions and ideas to party politics, as the range of the ideological spectrum established by these agents profoundly affects the dynamics of partisan competition.

Deregulation Panels: Vehicles of Neoliberal Reform

As discussed above, the collapse of the 1955 system and the formation of the Hosokawa cabinet were critical in paving the way for deregulation, including labor market reform. The single most important factor behind the implementation of deregulation was the creation of the deregulation panels in 1995. This was critical to policy change because the formal rules and procedures governing policy-making affect which ideas are transmitted to the policy-making process and thus which ideas are adopted as policy. In short, "institutional filtering" does affect which policies are chosen (Hall 1989). Likewise, the creation of the CEFP in 2001 was also important in expediting a wide array of neoliberal reform.

The deregulation panels existed from 1995 to 2010 as five different committees. The first incarnation was the Deregulation Subcommittee (1995–1997), initially instituted as a sub-organization under the Administrative Reform Committee with a three-year mandate, which survived several reorganizations thereafter to remain in existence until the advent of the DPJ government: first, as the Deregulation Committee (1998–2001; renamed the Regulatory Reform Committee in 1999), then as the Council for Comprehensive Regulatory Reform (CCRR) (2001–2004), followed by the Council for the Promotion of Regulatory Reform (2004–2007), and most recently as the Council for Regulatory Reform (2007–2010).[11] These deregulation panels challenged and, to an extent succeeded altering, the way in which labor laws were formulated. In so doing, the balance of power between workers and employers shifted in favor of the latter not only in the realm of industrial relations but also in policymaking (Miura 2007).

Composition and Procedure

Traditionally, labor laws have been deliberated first at advisory councils under the Ministry of Labour (MOL) or the Ministry of Health, Labour, and Welfare (MHLW), comprising tripartite representatives from public interest organizations (academics and ex-bureaucrats), employers, and workers. Under this system, it was the MOL that led deliberations and proposed frameworks within which employers and workers could express their positions, thereby rendering this policy-making process "bureaucracy-led" (Schwartz 1998). The MOL sought consensus between conflicting parties, which allowed labor representatives to secure a certain degree of influence. Given the fact that unionization rates have been low in Japan (falling from approximately 30% to 20% between 1970 and 2000), this decision-making system compensated for the weakness of labor movements. The deregulation panels fundamentally altered this conventional approach to decision making (Miura 2001, 2002).

First, all the major policies on the deregulation agenda were first proposed by the panels and then approved by the cabinet before the advisory councils reached a consensus, thus constraining the ability of the MOL to negotiate with employers and unions. Second, the composition of the deregulation panel shifted the balance of power in favor of business. The names of the deregulation panels have changed, as have their legal standing and administrative staff, the chairmanship was constantly held by Miyauchi Yoshihiko (chairman of Orix Corp.) from 1996 to 2007.[12] Miyauchi has been one of the most zealous proponents of deregulation and privatization of the public services in Japan. The other approximately ten to fifteen positions on the panels have been dominated by reform-oriented scholars and entrepreneurs. Labor representatives held one post until 2001, but have had no representation in subsequent panels. Consequently, the distribution of representation of social interests on the deregulation panels completely differs from that in the MOL's advisory councils, in which labor has secured one-third of the membership, or at least stands on an equal footing with employers. The transfer of agenda-setting power to the deregulation panels thus tilted the balance of power in favor of business.[13]

The inauguration of the CCRR in 2001 almost coincided with that of the CEFP, which also did not include labor representatives. The absence of labor representatives in these organizations was in stark contrast to the situation during the administrative reforms of the 1980s. The equivalent body to the CEFP at the time was Rinchō (the Second Provisional Council for Administrative Reform), the driving organization behind the administrative reforms, including privatization of the national railways and the public telephone company. Among its nine members, Rinchō included two labor representatives, one from each of the two rival labor confederations, Sōhyō and Dōmei. All the subsequent administrative reform commissions modeled on Rinchō also included at least one labor representative until the advent of the Koizumi cabinet. Labor exclusion, therefore, is a conspicuous feature of structural reform under Koizumi and his successors.[14]

Moreover, as far as labor market reform is concerned, it is important to note that staffing and placement businesses also gained access to the policy-making process. At the MOL's advisory councils, employers' representatives are allowed to attend, but representatives of a particular business are not. Because staffing and placement agencies constitute a type of business rather than an association of employers, they were not qualified to participate in the advisory councils that decided the range of business within which they would be allowed to operate. Thus, access to the policy-making process was crucial for them in order to expand their market opportunities.[15] It is quite symbolic, in this regard, that the CCRR (2001–2004) did not include a single labor representative, but it did include two members—president of a temporary staff agency and an executive of a replacement service corporation—for whom the liberalization of the labor market would bring expanded business opportunities.

How have the deregulation panels succeeded in establishing an active role in the policy-making process? The panels generally made their propositions public in the summer; organized public discussions and held numerous hearings with related organizations and ministries in the fall; then decided on new items to be deregulated, negotiated with respective ministries concerning detailed plans for implementing deregulation, and made public their annual recommendations at the end of each year. By the end of the fiscal year in March, the cabinet revised the Three-Year Plan for Deregulation, basically endorsing the panels' annual recommendations.[16] The panels not only repeated this process every year, but also monitored the extent to which their proposed deregulatory measures had been realized from the previous year. When it found the implementation unsatisfactory, it recommended the same item for deregulation the next year. This procedure exposed any attempts at sabotage by the ministries, thereby creating further impetus for deregulation.

This procedure turned out to be quite effective. As the panels freely proposed deregulatory items and ministries were compelled to explain the raison d'être of each regulation in the public sphere, the deregulatory process became much more transparent. Proponents of deregulation were invited to make propositions to the deregulation panels, which allowed a wide range of issues to be examined. The procedure was designed to establish a national movement for deregulation from the top down. In terms of legal standing, the Deregulation Subcommittee was the only panel that had the authority to advise the executive (*kankoku ken*), none of the other panels being granted such authority (Gyōsei Kaikaku Iinkai OB Kai 1998).

Setting Agendas, Shifting Targets

Table 6.1 summarizes the major propositions issued by the deregulation panels regarding labor market reform, and shows a shift in objectives as well as varying degrees of success. Among the five deregulations panels, the first had the most substantial influence. In 1995, the Deregulation Subcommittee proposed the liberalization of both the staffing business and the placement

TABLE 6.1
The role of deregulation panels in labor law making

	Major propositions	Policy outcomes
Deregulation Subcommittee (1995–1997)	Liberalization of the staffing business	1999 Temporary Work Agency Law
	Liberalization of placement business	1999 Job Security Law
	Expansion of discretionary working hour rules	1998 Labor Standards Law
Regulatory Reform Committee (1998–2001)	Legislation of dismissal rules	2003 Labor Standards Law*
Council for Comprehensive Regulatory Reform (2001–2004)	Monetary resolution system	Not drafted
	Introduction of white-collar exemption	Not drafted
	Abolition of restriction on the term limit for dispatched workers	Not drafted (expansion of the term limit was realized by the 2003 Temporary Work Agency Law)
	Abolition of industry-level minimum wages	2007 Minimum Wage Law*
Council for the Promotion of Regulatory Reform (2004–2007)	Contracting out public placement services	2006 Public Services Reform Law
	Market testing for free-of-charge placement services	Aborted (2009 Public Services Reform Law)
Council for Regulatory Reform (2007–2010)	Paradigm shift of labor law	

*The eventual content of the legislation almost completely contradicted the deregulation panels' original proposals.

business by introducing the negative list method to each. The propositions were implemented by amendments to the Temporary Work Agency Law and the Job Security Law in 1999. The Deregulation Subcommittee also made propositions in 1996 on four items regarding working hour rules, all of which were legislated: expansion of discretionary working hour rules, introduction of irregular annual working hour rules, deregulation of the term of employment, and abolition of restrictions on women working over-time, during holidays, and at night.

Compared to the Deregulation Subcommittee, the achievements of the Regulatory Reform Committee (RRC) were modest. Its propositions were more numerous but mainly covered minor issues of labor law in accordance with the demands of the business organizations represented on the committee. A bolder proposition was made after the panel appointed Kojima Noriaki, labor law professor at University of Osaka, as an adviser to the employment/labor working group.[17] In 1999, the RRC's second report mentioned the need to study dismissal rules, including the possibility of legislation thereof. In its final report issued in 2000, the committee went on to contend that the enactment of dismissal rules was necessary because employment policy should shift from maintaining employment at the company level to securing employment at the societal level in order to assist in smooth labor transfer. This view was shared by Keidanren, as the Toyoda Vision had also indicated a paradigm shift in employment policy. However, experts rather than employers led the agenda setting, as none of the employer organizations demanded the enactment of dismissal rules, at least not publicly. Who was appointed to the panels was thus crucial in determining which ideas were seriously deliberated. The issue of legislating dismissal rules remained on the agenda under the RRC's successor, the CCRR. Professors Yashiro Naohiro and Kojima Noriaki, who advocated a fundamental revision of labor law, remained on the panel as member and adviser, respectively, which allowed a yet wider range of issues onto the agenda. The CCRR proposed the introduction of a white-collar exemption system in its first report and, in its second report, monetary resolution of dismissals and the abolition or expansion of term limit on the use of temporary agency workers. Following these bold recommendations, dismissal rules were indeed legislated, although the details of the legislation differed somewhat from what the CCRR had originally envisioned as they maintained, rather than relaxed, the existing level of employment protection (see also chapter 5). The extension of term limit for temporary agency workers was also realized due to strong support from Prime Minister Koizumi. However, other major policy recommendations were either aborted or not even drafted as bills.

The Council for the Promotion of Regulatory Reform (CPRR), which succeeded the CCRR in 2004, continued to advocate the introduction of a monetary resolution system, but its main focus moved from labor market reform to external contracting of public services. The full name of the CPRR in

Japanese literally meant the Council for Regulatory Reform and Promotion of Opening of Public Services to the Private Sector (*Kisei Kaikaku Minkan Kaihō Suishin Kaigi*). The aim of regulatory reform shifted from liberalizing economic regulation in order to boost entrepreneurship to liberalizing social regulation in order to increase business opportunities for private corporations. The CPRR claimed that the boundaries of the public sector be drawn in the sense that the government should only offer services that the private sector cannot provide. It went on to propose the introduction of market testing in order to clarify the boundaries of the public sector.[18] As the focus of the CPRR shifted away from that of the CCRR, no new items of labor market reform were added to the agenda and the CPRR's second report issued in 2005 disregarded labor market reform altogether. The main target of the report was external contracting of public replacement services through the introduction of market testing (see also chapter 5).

Prime Minister Koizumi's resignation in 2006 was a turning point in the influence of the deregulation panels. In addition to Koizumi's departure, Miyauchi—who had been criticized for expanding his own company's business opportunities by making use of the chairmanship of the deregulation panels—announced his resignation as the CPRR's chairman. A new chairman, Kusakari Takao (chairman of Nippon Yūsen, or NYK Line) was considered to be a much less aggressive business leader in terms of pushing the neoliberal agenda. At the same time, the Abe cabinet appointed Professor Yashiro as a member of the CEFP. Because the CEFP had the authority to determine a wide array of issues, his appointment was likely to strengthen the position of the pro-reformers. Due to persistent pressure from Yashiro, the 2007 big-boned policy claimed that the government would apply market testing to free-of-charge employment services at two Hello Work offices in the Tokyo central area. As the MHLW was vehemently opposed to the idea of privatizing free-of-charge replacement services, Yashiro's appointment finally tilted the balance of power in favor of the pro-reformers. He also launched the "Labor Big Bang," setting up an expert study group on labor market reform under the CEFP. However, the momentum of the Labor Big Bang did not last long, as Abe stepped down after less than a year as prime minister. His successor, Fukuda Yasuo, was not favorably disposed toward neoliberal reform. The expert group discussed a long-term vision of the Japanese labor market and issued four reports before being dissolved in September 2008.[19] Prime Minister Asō Tarō, who succeeded Fukuda a year later, reversed the LDP's policy orientation more openly. He did not reappoint Yashiro as a CEFP member, which tilted the balance of power back. Without Miyauchi and Yashiro, there remained no one in the major government advisory councils who would push for the privatization of Hello Work activities.

In the meantime, the CPRR was reorganized as the Council for Regulatory Reform (CRR) in January 2007. Professor Kojima was replaced by Fukui Hideo, a neoliberal economist at the National Graduate Institute of Policy

Studies, as chairman of the Task Force on Labor Issues. Under Professor Fukui's leadership and in accordance with his personal convictions, the Task Force issued a position paper in May calling for a fundamental revision of labor law. The nomination of Fukui radicalized the CRR to an even greater degree than that seen in the previous deregulation panels.[20] The CRR's second report drafted in December further advanced the neoliberal position, arguing that it was an outmoded myth that strengthening workers' rights contributes to protection of workers. It went on to argue that overstrengthening the rights of female workers would have the effect of reducing employment for women, and that an increase in the level of minimum wages would also risk increasing unemployment and bankruptcy of small businesses. The most important and essential task of labor law, it asserted, is to correct the asymmetry of information concerning labor contacts, and all regulations that interfere with free contracts based on free will should be abolished because such law does not protect workers. More specifically, the CRR proposed to relax the rules governing dismissal in order to expedite firing of workers, to abolish the term limit and restriction of job categories for temporary agency workers, and to revise the obligation imposed on employers to offer a direct work contract to temporary agency workers who worked over the term limit. The second report invited a wide range of criticism from the MHLW, labor unions, and even moderate reformers, not because the reform menu was radical, but because the tone of the report was hostile toward organized workers and tripartite decision making. The MHLW officially publicized its criticism three days later, which was followed by the council's response two months subsequently. Despite the CRR's proactive efforts, political support for the neoliberal reformers had essentially disappeared by the time it compiled its third report at the end of 2008.[21] The government had already changed tack toward re-regulation, deciding to increase the level of minimum wages and ban on-call staffing businesses. In this altered environment, the third report defended the council's position rather than attacking the government's slow decision making, unlike previous reports formulated by the deregulation panels.

It can be said that all of the five deregulation panels succeeded in promoting labor market reform, which would otherwise have been much slower and more modest under the conventional policy-making system coordinated by bureaucrats. However, the degree of success greatly varied. Among the five panels, the first Deregulation Subcommittee was the most effective organ, seeing all its propositions implemented. The fact that it had the authority to advise certainly gave it the legal capital to promote controversial agendas, but political capital was the most valuable resource: Prime Minister Hashimoto's support was also critical. The CCRR also benefited from the political support of Prime Minister Koizumi, leading to the further liberalization of Temporary Work Agency Law. After Koizumi stepped down, the panels' propositions became more ideologically driven, largely due to their reorganized membership, which made it difficult for the government to form a political coalition for legislation. A rapid decline in political capital ultimately saw their propositions sidelined. In sum, though the membership of the Deregulation Panels was decisive in terms of filtering ideas, the prime minister's political support was essential in order for an issue to be implemented.

Legislative Politics: Veto Power at the Diet

I have showed that the LDP began to pursue neoliberal reform after the Hashimoto cabinet and that most political parties had converged on neoliberal policy by the late 1990s. However, neoliberal reform, including labor market reform, was not implemented smoothly. Compared to the scope of the propositions put forward by the reformers, the policies that were actually legislated were more modest, as the Diet amended government bills to mitigate the impact of neoliberal reform. As the Diet is the final veto point in Japan's legislative process, those who oppose government bills must attempt to block or at least amend them at that stage. Under a parliamentary system like Japan's, the government, supported by the parliamentary majority, is usually able to pass its bills without conceding to the opposition.[22] Nevertheless, there are instances when the ruling party agrees to amend its bills. It is thus essential to specify the political conditions under which controversial bills are passed with or without amendment. In the following, I examine case studies on nine controversial labor laws, all proposed or prompted by the deregulation panels. Among these laws, only the 2003 Temporary Work Agency Law and the discretionary working hour rules (the 2003 Labor Standards Law) survived the legislative process unamended. The other pieces of legislation were all subjected to substantial modifications proposed by the DPJ. The ruling coalition's compromises on the Diet floor significantly limited the degree of Japanese labor market reform, and it is important to consider why the LDP made these concessions to the opposition.

Discretionary Working Hour Rules (1998 Labor Standards Law): Concession at the Diet

The 1998 amendment to the Labor Standards Law aimed to introduce discretionary working hour rules under which certain hours set by employer-employee negotiation are counted as working hours regardless of the actual number of hours taken by workers to accomplish a task.[23] Discretionary working hour rules were first adopted in 1987 for professional positions.[24] The 1998 amendment of the Labor Standards Law aimed to expand the coverage to a considerable degree, enabling employers to apply the discretionary working hour rules to white-collar workers involved with planning and drawing up plans in headquarters and the like. On the surface, employers were successful in greatly extending the coverage of the rules. However, through parliamentary deliberations, the DPJ succeeded in inserting detailed conditions for the introduction of discretionary working hour rules that made the new rules practically unusable.[25]

The policy idea of expanding the coverage of discretionary working hour rules per se had already been discussed within the MOL and its policy community in the mid-1990s. The advisory council under the MOL began to deliberate on the issue in 1995, but the ministry made no attempt to hasten negotiations due to fierce opposition from labor representatives. It was only after the Deregulation Subcommittee recommended deregulation of discretionary working hour rules as one of the four items of labor market reform in December 1996 that the MOL began to seek agreement between business and labor. In March 1997, the cabinet set a time limit of the end of July for reaching a conclusion on the basic orientation of working hour regulations. The MOL presented its own proposal to the advisory council in July, which was approved by the council in December.[26] However, Rengō strongly opposed the expansion of coverage of discretionary working hour rules and vigorously lobbied the DPJ, even drafting a counterbill to influence the DPJ's bill. The DPJ did not actually submit its own bill, but instead used it as a bargaining chip vis-à-vis the LDP.[27] The LDP basically accepted the DPJ's propositions, but the SDP, a coalition partner of the LDP, did not, which put an end to parliamentary deliberations. The LDP announced that it would make a fresh start in the next parliamentary session, without any reconsideration of the amended bill to which it had already agreed. A new political environment emerged after the LDP lost its outright majority in the House of Councillors election held in July 1998, securing only 103 seats out of 252. The SDP and Sakigake had left the ruling coalition by that time, which forced the LDP into minority government (until October 1999). The LDP's weak position invited further amendments to the government bill. The Diet decided that the effective date would be delayed by one year and required companies to receive an individual worker's consent to being covered by discretionary working hour rules. The latter provision made it extremely difficult to apply the discretionary working hour rules.

Temporary Work Agency Law (1999): Concessions at the Advisory Council and the Diet

The amendment of the Temporary Work Agency Law (TWAL) in 1999 is a symbol of neoliberal labor market reform, as anti-reformers claim that the law must be amended in order to restore it to its pre-1999 content.[28] The 1999 amendment effected a transformation from the positive list method, according to which only specified job categories were allowed to be legally filled by temporary agency workers, to the negative list method, according to which only jobs that agencies are not allowed to supply with dispatched workers were specified. This change could potentially have opened the door to the creation of a low-cost and flexible labor force.

It was the Deregulation Subcommittee that pushed for the introduction of the negative list method. As labor unions opposed such a radical idea, the MOL was initially reluctant to draft such a legislation. However, Prime Minister Hashimoto ordered Labour Minister Okano Yutaka to implement deregulation of temporary work agencies, which led to the commencement of deliberations at the advisory council. Furthermore, in November 1997, the Hashimoto government issued its Emergency Economic Measures in response to the bankruptcy of the Hokkaido Takushoku Bank, which mentioned that the government would propose a bill to liberalize staffing businesses at the next parliamentary session starting in January. The Hashimoto government expected the deregulatory measures to create jobs. Because the deadline had been set by the cabinet, Soya Noriomi, the director general of the Employment Stability Bureau, was compelled to draft a bill without first obtaining support from the unions.[29] Rengō most fervently opposed the introduction of dispatched labor to the manufacturing sector, where unions were most organized. It even refused to attend the advisory council, which impeded the legislation process and eventually forced the MOL to make a concession, whereby the ministry decided to allow manufacturing jobs to be exempted for a certain period.[30]

Although the most controversial issue was settled before the bill was submitted to the Diet, further amendments were added during parliamentary deliberation. The DPJ, the SDP, and Kōmeitō called for amendments to strengthen protective measures for dispatched workers. The LDP conceded and accepted most of the demands put forth by the three opposition parties.[31] In retrospect, it is interesting that the opposition parties other than the Japan Communist Party did not oppose the government bill and ultimately voted for it. The precarious working conditions of dispatched workers did not come to the public's attention until the mid-2000s. Because dispatched workers usually receive higher wages than *pāto*, the expansion of employment in this field was not generally considered undesirable at the time.

Temporary Work Agency Law (2003): Intransigence

The business community continued to call for further liberalization of the TWAL and the deregulation panels also persistently pressured the government to remove manufacturing jobs from the negative list to open this sector to temporary work agencies.[32] As in the case of the 1999 amendment, political support from the prime minister drove the enactment of the legislation. Facing recession and the large-scale bankruptcy of the Mycal group in the fall of 2001, Prime Minister Koizumi ordered the MHLW to examine the extension of the dispatching period to up to three years and the expansion of fixed-term employment.[33] After deliberations at the advisory council, the MHLW drafted a bill during the winter of 2002 and submitted it to the Diet the following year. The bill aimed to open the manufacturing sector to the staffing business and to extend the term limit from one year to three years, but also to require user companies to offer a direct contract to agency workers who worked for longer than the term limit. Unions opposed the former changes but welcomed the latter, whereas employers took the reverse position. The MHLW thus combined deregulation and re-regulation in order to forge a compromise.

Unlike the case of the 1999 TWAL, the LDP did not amend the bill at the Diet. The DPJ opposed the government bill, but did not submit its own amended bill. At the time, the LDP was allied with Kōmeitō, which allowed the ruling coalition to secure a majority in both houses, as a result of which the LDP was able to pass the bill without making any concessions.

Dismissal Rules (2003 Labor Standards Law): Concession in the Diet

Chapter 5 has examined the legislative process of the dismissal rules. Here, I only wish to emphasize several critical points. The legislation of dismissal rules first made it onto the agenda when the RRC issued its second report in 1999, reflecting Professor Kojima's policy preferences. The MOL was reluctant to proceed to legislation as neither business nor labor had demanded this kind of reform. However, the advent of the Koizumi government pushed bureaucrats to initiate the legislative process for the dismissal rules. The main point of contention was the exact wording of the law, as this would determine the actual degree of employment protection. When the MHLW drafted the bill, the wording of the law appeared rather business-friendly, stipulating the right of employers to dismiss workers, which invited strong opposition from Rengō. In the Diet, the DPJ succeeded in modifying the wording by erasing the very phrase stating that employers have the right to dismiss workers. As a result, the dismissal law as codified in the Labor Standards Law did not alter the existing level of employment protection. It is noteworthy that the DPJ succeeded in amending the government bill despite the fact that the ruling coalition had a secure majority in both houses at the time. This is all the more puzzling in comparison with the DPJ's failure to amend the 2003 TWAL.

Discretionary Working Hour Rules (2003 Labor Standards Law): Intransigence

The 2003 Labor Standards Law also included an amendment of the discretionary working hour rules. The 2003 Labor Standards Law generally loosened the conditions of application of the discretionary working hour rules. Instead of the unanimous agreement of all relevant workers, the consent of four-fifths was now required. Moreover, all workplaces, rather than only headquarters, became able to introduce the rules. This amendment contributed to the spread of the discretionary working hour rules. In the Tokyo metropolis, the number of planning personnel to whom the discretionary working hour rules were applied increased from 1,798 in 2001 to 22,549 in 2006.[34] Unlike the unions' vigorous resistance against the 1998 Labor Standards Law, which resulted in substantial amendments, this time they were not able to effectively mobilize their opposition because they had to concentrate their resources on the issue of the dismissal rules. During parliamentary deliberations, the DPJ questioned the appropriateness of deregulating the discretionary working hour rules, but did not submit any amendments, and the Diet passed the government bill without any serious controversy.

White-Collar Exemption (2007): Concession Prior to Diet Deliberation

Since the mid-1990s employers have advocated the introduction of the white-collar exemption system that would allow some white-collar workers to be exempted from working hour regulations, thereby barring the exempted workers from receiving overtime payment. In 2001, the CCRR recommended that the government should examine a white-collar exemption system and thereafter continued to pressure the MHLW to initiate legislation. In March 2002, the cabinet endorsed the Three-Year Plan for Regulatory Reform (the first revision), which for the first time declared that the government would promptly examine the introduction of a white-collar exemption system. Examination within the MHLW finally began in April 2005 when the ministry set up a study group on the working hour regulations. In February 2006, deliberations began at the MHLW's advisory council, which reached their conclusion in December. Because managers (*kanrishoku*) were already exempted from the working hour regulations, the crucial question was who else was to be exempted. Nippon Keidanren proposed that workers who earned over ¥4 million in annual salary should be exempted. If the four-million-yen threshold had been applied, this would have meant that almost all white-collar workers would be ineligible for overtime payment. The threshold based on annual salary was a very contentious issue and the MHLW refrained from specifying a precise figure in order to forge consensus, although the mass media reported that the MHLW was aiming at a threshold of ¥8 or 9 million. The MHLW's rather moderate stance did not prevent public opinion from becoming critical and skeptical. The mass media covered the deliberation process regarding the white-collar exemption system to an unprecedented degree, despite the fact that they usually pay scant attention to labor law formulation, and named the bill "the no overtime payment law," emphasizing the fact that employers supported the bill as a means of cutting labor costs. Finally, Prime Minister Abe and the LDP gave up on proposing the bill to the Diet in January 2007 in the fear that this framing of the issue by the mass media would have a negative impact on the LDP's performance in the Upper House election scheduled six months later. Rengō had strongly opposed the white-collar exemption system from the beginning, thus it was very likely that the DPJ would have sought to amend the government bill had it been proposed to the Diet. This time, in large part due to the influence of the mass media, the LDP backed down well in advance of parliamentary debate.

Labor Contract Law, Minimum Wage Law, and Overtime Work Premiums (2007–2008): Re-Regulation and Concessions

The Abe cabinet's failure to legislate the white-collar exemption system was a turning point in labor market reform. The combination of deregulation and re-regulation is a method of forging consensus frequently employed by the MOL/MHLW. Initially, the MHLW intended to couple the white-collar exemption system with increases in overtime work premiums and minimum wages as well as improvement of working conditions for part-time workers. The failure of the white-collar exemption bill consequently strengthened the re-regulation aspect.

In March 2007, the Abe cabinet decided to submit three labor bills—the Labor Contract Law, the Minimum Wage Law, and the Labor Standards Law—to the Diet. These government bills were already labor friendly, but the Diet further strengthened the level of protection for workers stipulated therein. The role of the deregulation panels was indirect and the MHLW regained the initiative in the law-making process.

The supplementary resolution of the Labor Standards Law passed at the Diet in 2003 required the government to enact a comprehensive law on labor contracts. The MHLW created a study group to create a blueprint of the law, which issued a report in September 2005.[35] The report contained several controversial issues including that of the monetary resolution system for dismissals. Even though the Ministry had decided to drop the issue by the end of 2002, employers continued to call for its introduction. The study group proposed a detailed plan for the system, but the MHLW never presented a concrete scheme at the advisory council. Deliberations at the advisory council began in October in 2005, but employers and workers held widely divergent opinions on the content of labor contract law, which impeded deliberations and negotiations. The MHLW expanded the issues on the table in March 2006 by asking the same advisory council to discuss new working hour regulations. The CPRR was hostile toward the MHLW's initiative, openly reiterating its position advocating the monetary resolution system. By the end of 2006, the MHLW had dropped most of the controversial points, including the monetary resolution system, in order to forge consensus and drafted its bill in February 2007. The bill restated case law regarding unfavorable changes to work rules, which had triggered opposition from a wide range of actors. However, as both Rengō and the DPJ supported the bill, no concessions were made (see also chapter 4).

The amendment to the Minimum Wage Law was triggered by the recommendation of the CCRR issued in 2003. The target was the abolition of industrial-level minimum wages, which business associations had demanded for a long time. The Koizumi cabinet endorsed the recommendation in 2004, which initiated deliberations at the MHLW. However, when the MHLW began deliberations by setting up a study group, it included re-regulation in the agenda by pointing out the necessity of strengthening the function of regional-level minimum wages. The problem here was that there were instances in which the level of social assistance was higher than that of regional-level minimum wages. The Minimum Wage Law had not stipulated the relationship between minimum wages and social assistance. At the advisory council begun its work in April 2005, employers strongly opposed the reinforcement of regional-level minimum wages, whereas workers resisted the abolition of industrial-level minimum wages. The chairman of the advisory council submitted four separate propositions in an attempt to forge consensus. Finally, in December 2006, the council reached the conclusion that regional-level minimum wages would not be set lower than the social assistance level and that most industrial-level minimum wages would remain intact but fines would not be imposed for infringement (see Nakakubo, 2008).

Largely due to the MHLW's initiative, the three labor bills turned out to be re-regulatory, despite the fact that the CPRR had directly or indirectly set the agenda. By the time the MHLW was ready to submit the bills for the regular Diet session of 2007, Abe was prime minister and had announced his intention to modify Koizumi's structural reform, making "re-challenge" his cabinet's slogan. He even created the Roundtable for Growth Strategy, to which were invited business and labor leaders, in order to forge consensus toward mid-term increases in regional-level minimum wages. Accordingly, minimum wages, which differ from prefecture to prefecture, increased by ¥16 on average, ranging from ¥627 to ¥766 in 2008.[36] This "improvement" was well short of the increase to ¥1,000 that the unions and opposition parties had called for, but the MHLW stated its intention to at least eliminate all cases in which minimum wages are lower than social assistance levels within two to five years. This policy orientation greatly diverged from the demands of the deregulation panels.

Initially, the Abe cabinet intended to pass the three labor bills before the election of the House of Councillors scheduled for July 2007 in order to gain validation for his "re-challenge" policy.[37] However, the parliamentary committee was unable to begin substantive deliberations on the three bills before the election as the outbreak of the pension scandal disrupted the overall schedule.[38] Abe's response to the pension scandal was weak, which resulted in the LDP's electoral defeat and, in turn, allowed the DPJ to secure an outright majority in the Upper House.

The fact that the ruling coalition lost its majority in the House of Councillors considerably increased the DPJ's bargaining power. The DPJ had already created a special team within the party with respect to new working hour regulations in August 2006 and submitted its own bills on the Minimum Wage Law and the Labor Contract Law. After the election, the DPJ could have passed its own bills at the House of Councillors. However, it was likely that the House of Representatives would have voted them down, which would have greatly impeded the passage of labor-friendly government bills. The DPJ prioritized prompt legislation of government bills over the passage of their own bills and, therefore, asked the LDP to sit at the negotiation table.[39]

With respect to the Labor Contract Law, the DPJ extracted a wide range of concessions from the LDP "to a degree unimaginable before the election."[40] Most of the amendments related to the specific wording of the law in parts of the text that Rengō found problematic.[41] Substantial changes included the insertion of "balanced treatment" of different types of workers and "harmony between work and private life" into the principles of labor contract.[42] In the case of the Minimum Wage Law, the DPJ succeeded in adding the phrase, "workers shall have the minimum standard of wholesome and cultural living," as a principle of regional-level minimum wages. This phrase, taken from Article 25 of the constitution (the right to live), aimed to further clarify the legislature's intention that the minimum wage, along with social assistance, guarantee a minimum standard of living. Finally, with respect to the overtime work premium, the government initially proposed that it be increased from 25% to 50% when workers perform over 80 hours per month of overtime work. The DPJ succeeded in reducing the 80-hour threshold to 60 hours during the negotiations that led to the passage of the Labor Standards Law amendment in 2008.[43]

Dynamics of Two-Party Competition

The above cases show that many key government initiatives were either terminated or amended on the Diet floor. A close look at the timing and circumstances of these cases of labor market reform legislation reveals that two factors were decisive in determining whether the LDP would decide to concede to the DPJ: the extent of the LDP's control of the Diet and the range of affected voters. Of the four patterns shown in Table 6.2, the LDP took an uncompromising stance only when its grip on the Diet was strong and the affected voters represented a minority group. Only two cases fulfilled these two conditions: the 2003 TWAL and the 2003 discretionary working hour rules.

TABLE 6.2
The ruling party's attitude toward the opposition

	LDP's grip on the Diet	
Affected voters	Strong	Weak
Majority	Concession (Dismissal rules, White-collar exemption)	Concession (2007 Labor Contract Law, 2008 Overwork premiums)
Minority	Intransigence (2003 TWAL, 2003 DWHR)	Concession (1998 DWHR, 1999 TWAL, 2007 Minimum Wage Law)

Note: TWAL: Temporary Work Agency Law; DWHR: Discretionary Working Hour Rules.

The first dimension in the table is the degree of control of the ruling party at the Diet. The LDP generally made concessions when they did not hold a parliamentary majority. From July 1998 when the LDP lost the House of Councillors election until October 1999 when the Obuchi Cabinet allied with Kōmeitō, the LDP did not hold a majority at the House of Councillors. The LDP's weak grip at one of the Houses compelled it to concede in the case of the 1999 TWAL. In contrast, the LDP's coalition with Kōmeitō allowed it to take a hard-line stance vis-à-vis the opposition parties, as seen in the cases of the 2003 TWAL and the discretionary working hour rules. Despite the fact that unions were able to block the respective pieces of legislation in 1998 and 1999, they were unsuccessful in 2003. Having secured a majority in both houses, the ruling LDP-Kōmeitō coalition did not have any incentive to make concessions to the opposition. In a similar vein, the DPJ's quasi-control of the Upper House between July 2007 and August 2009 had a significant impact on labor law making. With its newly acquired bargaining power, the DPJ succeeded in amending three labor bills in their favor to an unprecedented degree.

The second dimension is the range of affected voters. The LDP appears to have refrained from supporting policies that were hostile to salaried workers. Even though it had secured a parliamentary majority, it made concessions in the case of the dismissal rules and the white-collar exemption system. Although the LDP could have passed the bills without any amendments, it chose to compromise mainly because salaried workers had gained importance as a voting bloc. Urban districts where most salaried workers reside are swing districts. Tax cuts and neoliberal administrative reform are appealing to urban salaried workers, but reducing employment security for regular workers and cutting overtime payments are not. In a context of tight two-party competition, it was not politically expedient to provoke the ire of salaried workers.

The contrasting outcomes of the dismissal rules and the 2003 TWAL could not have been more striking. The two bills were discussed at the Diet at around the same time, but the LDP conceded only in the case of the dismissal rules. The dismissal rules affected all salaried workers, but the amendment of the TWAL only directly affected those who are dispatched by staffing businesses and, indirectly, regular workers in the manufacturing sector. The different range of actors with a stake in the outcome surely influenced the LDP's stance in the respective cases.

Another interesting comparison is between the discretionary working hour rules (1998) and the dismissal rules (2003), and the white-collar exemption system. The former cases were amended at the Diet, allowing the DPJ to claim the credit, whereas in the latter case the LDP had made a concession in favor of salaried workers before the parliamentary deliberations began. If the LDP does indeed care about salaried workers as potential constituencies, it would arguably have been more profitable to amend the former bills while they were still being drafted. That way, the LDP would have been able to claim the credit. The fact that the LDP was slow to respond to union critiques and challenges in the former cases suggests that the attention of the mass media triggered the party's unusual degree of concession in the latter case. Although salaried workers had gained importance as a constituency bloc for the LDP, the party continued to put a priority on business interests unless sensational media coverage threatened to damage their electoral prospects.

As a concluding remark, the political dynamics of labor market reform must be placed in the larger context of Japanese politics. The political reforms enacted in the 1990s, such as the introduction of the single-member district system and the strengthening of the power of prime minister and the cabinet office, specifically aimed to make the Japanese political system closer to the Westminster model, featuring cabinet dominance and concentration of executive power in one party.[44] However, this is not to suggest that the Japanese political system now subscribes entirely to the Westminster model. Aurelia George Mulgan states that "Japan does not have cabinet government, it has party-bureaucratic government" (2002, 146).[45] Her concept of "party-bureaucratic government" accurately captured the feature of the Japanese dual power structure whereby the cabinet leadership was undermined by both the bureaucracy and the LDP *zoku* politicians. However, even though certain institutional features had been reorganized to emulate the Westminster model, Mulgan maintains that party-bureaucratic government still characterized the Japanese political system under Prime Minister Koizumi. My case study on labor law making shows that Japan's strong bicameralism clearly distinguishes Japan from the Westminster model. While political reform in the 1990s certainly introduced top-down decision making by the prime minister in the realm of labor law, thereby eclipsing the power of labor bureaucrats in building consensus at the advisory council, strong bicameralism made it impossible for the governing party to implement reform unless it secured a majority in both houses.

It is thus vital to separate the agenda-setting stage from the negotiation stage. As far as agenda-setting is concerned, the political leadership of prime ministers vis-à-vis the bureaucracy has increased as the locus of agenda-setting has shifted from the bureaucracy to the prime minister and high-level commissions such as the deregulation panels. In contrast, at the negotiation stage, political parties have played a critical role in making deals. The concept of party-bureaucratic government sheds light on the power of the LDP *zoku* politicians who exert influence outside the Diet. However, the new mode of labor policymaking that emerged between 1995 and 2009 increased the role of opposition parties as the locus of decision making moved to the Diet. The active role of the Diet and of opposition parties in legislation deviates from the Westminster model. Given that political reformers have consistently targeted the fusion of power between the executive and the legislature and executive dominance, it is rather surprising that the Diet turned out to be an arena of deal making where opponents of reform were able to modify government bills. Strong bicameralism, coupled with the proportional representation system, made coalition governments or minority governments a "normal" state of politics, which compelled the ruling party to make compromises.[46]

Anti-reformers were thus able to veto absolute implementation of proposed reform plans. Veto power, however, is not the same as transformative power, by which alternative policy ideas are chosen. Although the DPJ has effectively used its veto power, this does not necessarily imply that it will also be able to exert transformative power in office. Veto power is largely determined by institutional and organizational factors, whereas ideational factors play a critical role in determining transformative power. We shall examine the impact of the DPJ's ascension to power in the next chapter.

The Double Movement in Japanese Politics

The Democratic Party of Japan (DPJ) won the general election of 2009, which led to the first power alternation in postwar Japan based on the result of a popular election. This chapter looks at how the DPJ rose to power, how the power alternation changed the dynamism of party competition, and what new ideas the DPJ brought with respect to the Japanese social protection system.

The Declining Appeal of Neoliberal Policy

The DPJ's victory should be understood as a manifestation of what Karl Polanyi (1944) has called "double movement." Polanyi argued that free markets "could not exist for any length of time without annihilating the human and natural substance of society" (1944, 3). This line of argument holds that the market mechanism destroys the social fabric by disconnecting people's economic activities from their social activities, whereby communal values, reciprocity, and redistribution are all subordinated to the impersonal forces of self-regulating markets. In order for society to take measures to protect itself, Polanyi saw that "double-movement" would inevitably occur. I contend that this very mechanism was manifested in Japan in the latter half of the 2000s, which eventually enabled the DPJ to take power. The double movement began after the general election of 2005, following which the Liberal Democratic Party (LDP) gradually reduced its commitment to neoliberal reform and instead showed an interest in strengthening the social protection system. However, such effort on the part of the LDP was undermined by the emergence of the DPJ as a serious contender successfully appealing to those who had suffered as a result of Koizumi's reforms.

In September 2005, the LDP won a landslide victory, securing a total of 296 seats (61.7%).[1] The election was a de facto referendum on Prime Minister Koizumi's postal privatization, his flagship policy of neoliberal reform, and the electoral result delivered a strong mandate for it. After the general election Koizumi reshuffled his cabinet and nominated Yosano Kaoru as minister of state for economic and fiscal policy to replace Takenaka Heizō. Unlike his predecessor, Yosano was a traditional LDP politician who was skeptical of the market economy and openly supported raising the consumption tax.[2] In fact, Takenaka complained that the pace of structural reform slowed under Yosano's chairmanship and was critical of the transformation of the Council on Economic and Fiscal Policy (CEFP) "from an engine of reform to an arena of negotiation" (2006, 318). Despite Takenaka's lament, the truth is that Koizumi no longer needed to rely on the CEFP as he did in the past in order to carry out his pet projects, for he succeeded in putting the LDP under his control by expelling rebels and acquiring a massive number of loyal newcomers (Kamikawa 2010). With his new power base, Koizumi undertook fiscal retrenchment, including the merger of governmental financial institutions, reduction of subsidy to local government, and medical reform.

The LDP's about-face on structural reform, however, became evident soon after Prime Minister Abe succeeded Koizumi in September 2006. Abe Shinzō, the grandson of Kishi Nobusuke (prime minister, 1957–1960), prioritized a conservative agenda, such as the departure from "the postwar regime" and the construction of a "beautiful country," thereby sidelining economic reform.[3] "Re-challenge" replaced structural reform as a symbolic expression of the government's policy orientation. Under the slogan of "re-challenge," Abe cabinet created and expanded programs to support those who had suffered as a result of Koizumi's structural reform. In fact, in a break from the practice followed by the Koizumi cabinet, the 2007 big-boned policy eliminated the term "structural reform" from its title.[4] The CEFP continued to serve as an "arena" rather than as the engine of neoliberal reform. As the private-sector members of the CEFP, Abe nominated two economists (Itō Takatoshi of the University of Tokyo; and Yashiro Naohiro of the International Christian University) and two business leaders (Mitarai Fujio, president and CEO of Canon Inc. as well as chairman of Nippon Keidanren; and Niwa Uichirō, chairman of the Board of Itōchū Corporation and a board member of Keizai Dōyūkai). These appointees continued to advocate a neoliberal agenda, but lacked the political support enjoyed by their predecessors.

In the meantime, the opposition camp underwent a major transformation. The DPJ grew gradually but steadily to the point where it posed a credible threat to the LDP. The beginning of the transformation traces back to the 1996 general election. After the election, the SDP became a marginal force, having secured only 15 seats. In their place, the NFP and DPJ became the two major competitors to the LDP and, eventually, the DPJ consolidated the opposition camp. The first step in this process was its merger with parts of the former NFP in 1998. Ozawa Ichirō disbanded the NFP in December 1997, producing the Liberal Party led by Ozawa and other small parties, which mostly ended up merging with the DPJ in April 1998. The second step was its merger with the Liberal Party in 2003. In that year, at the election of the House of Representatives, the DPJ secured 177 seats and received more votes than the LDP under the proportional representative system. Furthermore, it won the House of Councillors election in 2004 taking 50 seats vis-à-vis the LDP's 49. After its defeat in the general election in 2005, the DPJ won the House of Councillors election in 2007 by securing 60 seats in contrast to the LDP's 37. As a result, the DPJ held 109 seats, outnumbering the ruling coalition (the LDP holding 83 and Kōmeitō 20).

The parliamentary gains made by the DPJ in 2004 and 2007 can be attributed for a considerable part to the failure of the LDP to reestablish public confidence in the pension system.[5] However, the DPJ also made a strategic decision to emphasize the downsides of structural reform after it was badly defeated in the 2005 election, and this decision bore fruit in 2007 as well as in 2009. That this was a strategic move is evident in view of the fact that the DPJ included among its members neoliberal reformers who had come from the LDP and the Japan New Party. As I have already discussed elsewhere, the DPJ has tended to take a position that is closer to the Center-Left on questions of civil liberty and social security than might be expected from its membership (Miura, Lee, and Weiner, 2005). Two factors account for this. First, DPJ politicians tend to be policy experts in their specialized areas. Those who are interested in social policy tend to have come from either the JSP or the DSP, or from citizens' movements, and these politicians are more likely to be assigned to parliamentary committees that deliberate on labor and welfare matters. Their influence on the DPJ's social policy gives it a Center-Left flavor. Second, the DPJ has often made a strategic decision to differentiate itself from the ruling parties. Although the DPJ had adopted a more neoliberal stance than the LDP before Prime Minister Koizumi took power, his embrace of neoliberalism opened up the political space for the DPJ to represent those who were opposed to structural reform.[6]

As a matter of fact, even Maehara Seiji, one of the most right-wing Democrats in terms of both economic policy and defense policy, argued that structural reform had increased inequality in Japanese society in a speech given at the Diet as DPJ leader in early 2006. The DPJ further intensified its criticism of Koizumi's reform once Ozawa succeeded Maehara in April 2006. Ozawa rebuilt the DPJ's relationship with Rengō, which Maehara had weakened, and launched a joint national campaign to appeal to the general voters, proclaiming that the DPJ intended to put a stop to growing inequality. The DPJ also submitted several bills during the parliamentary session of 2007 in order to demonstrate its opposition to "market fundamentalism," openly accusing the LDP of having made Japan the most unequal society among the rich democracies.

The DPJ's self-definition as a party opposed to neoliberal reform and as allies of organized labor further increased the pressure on the LDP, which had already begun to backpedal. The DPJ offensive also encouraged traditional conservatives concerned with local economies and job creation to speak out within the party. The "gap problem" (*kakusa mondai*) or inequality had been widely accepted as a social problem by the time the Abe cabinet came to power.[7] The LDP thus needed to demonstrate its engagement with the problem of increasing inequality in order to prepare for the Upper House election scheduled for July 2007. Abe created the Roundtable for Growth Strategy and invited labor representatives and business leaders to forge a consensus on an increase in the minimum wage. He also made plans to pass labor friendly bills, although he failed to accomplish this before the election. The LDP's defeat in the Upper House election in July 2007 deprived the LDP government of what little political capital it had left with respect to neoliberal reform. Abe resigned in September. His successor, Fukuda Yasuo, proposed "Five Safety Plans" and launched the National Council on Social Security in order to authorize a policy turn to strengthen the social protection system. He managed the cabinet for only one year before stepping down without having achieved any concrete results. The subsequent term of office of Prime Minister Asō Tarō coincided with the Lehman Brothers' bankruptcy and the global financial crisis that broke out in September 2009. Asō reversed a long-standing trend in fiscal policy by formulating a record-breaking budget for the fiscal year 2009.[8] He then set up an advisory panel to address the establishment of a "safe society" and also tinkered with the CEFP's political sympathies by appointing Iwata Kazumasa (economist, former bureaucrat at the Economic Planning Agency, University of Tokyo professor), Yoshikawa Hiroshi (economist, University of Tokyo professor), Chō Fujio (chairman of Toyota Corporation, vice president of Nippon Keidanren), and Mimura Akio (chairman of Nippon Steel Corporation, vice president of Nippon Keidanren) as its private sector members. His choices reflected his government's intention to eschew continuation of Koizumi's policies. However, such repudiation of Koizumi's structural reform did little to boost the popularity of the Asō cabinet.

Asō called a general election in August 30, 2009. During the electoral campaign all the parties pledged to expand the social protection system. The LDP emphasized the realization of a safe society, while the DPJ put forward the slogans of "people's livelihood first" and "from concrete to people," advocating a shift in government spending priorities from public works to people's livelihood. Asō openly proclaimed that Japan should put an end to "excessive market fundamentalism." The major parties' emphasis on social protection is in stark contrast to the 1996 election where all the major parties converged on promises to implement administrative reform.

The electoral result was astonishing, as it led to power alternation based on the result of a general election for the first time under the postwar constitution. The DPJ clinched 308 seats ousting the LDP, which retained only 119 seats. The DPJ's landslide victory is largely attributed to its success in attracting and uniting voters who had been discontent with Koizumi's reforms. Even though the LDP had covertly reneged on its previous commitment to neoliberal reform under the Abe-Fukuda-Asō cabinets, structural reform was synonymous with the LDP. The DPJ's electoral victory thus delivered democratic legitimacy to a policy shift that the LDP had already initiated. Policy adjustment under the post-Koizumi LDP government and the election of the DPJ government indicate that Polanyi's "double movement" came into effect once the damaging consequences of neoliberal reform had become evident. It should be emphasized that Polanyi never assumed that a movement for social protection would necessarily be progressive in character (Evans 2008; Steger 2002). As double movement can assume a variety of forms, we need to explore what kind of social protection the DPJ is likely to implement.

Ideas and Welfare Reform: Statism, Cooperatism, and Productivism

I have argued that three strands of conservatism shaped Japan's welfare through work system: statism, cooperatism, and productivism. Although statism has consistently influenced the conservative political vision, cooperatism, and productivism eventually gave way to neoliberalism. The first wave of the ideational shift took place in the 1980s when political support for productivism began to wane, and risk was transferred from the state to vulnerable individuals. The second wave of the ideational shift occurred in the 1990s when political support for cooperatism also declined during the death throes of the politics of productivity. The marriage of statism and neoliberalism has since represented the dominant ideologies of Japanese conservatives in the 1990s and 2000s.

How has the election of the DPJ government changed the ideational foundation of Japan's social protection system? To what extent has the DPJ inherited the conservative vision and what new ideas, visions, or values does it intend to introduce? I argue that the DPJ is likely to revive cooperatism and productivism in the contemporary context while rejecting the statist vision.

It is possible that cooperatism may be revived under the DPJ government. In an essay written by Prime Minister Hatoyama Yukio after the power alternation, he referred to Hatoyama Ichirō's—his grandfather—*yūai* vision (which I translate as "cooperatism") as a founding principle of the LDP and expressed his intention to redefine it in the contemporary context as a principle of harmonious coexistence of autonomous selves (*jiritsu to kyōsei*) (Hatoyama 2009).[9] The term *yūai* is a translation of "fraternity," which came from *The Totalitarian State against Man* written by Richard N. Coudenhove-Kalergi in 1935. An Austrian count who had once lived in Japan with his Japanese mother, Coudenhove-Kalergi advanced the idea of pan-Europeanism, and his writings reinforced Hatoyama Ichirō's convictions on the need to defend liberal democracy against communism and state socialism.[10] Hatoyama Yukio went on to explain that the principle of *yūai* was substantiated in the 1960s by the LDP's shift to support of management-labor conciliation and was further reaffirmed as the party's official position by the Labor Charter drafted by Ishida Hirohide. Rather than identifying communism or state socialism as the enemies of contemporary liberal democracy, Hatoyama instead opposes the amalgam of the LDP-bureaucracy-business interests and global market fundamentalism. Thus, his *yūai* ideology fosters individualism and acknowledges the primacy of personal independence as an antithesis to traditional conservatism. However, it also cherishes harmony and reciprocity between humans, between countries, and between humans and the environment, as an antithesis to market fundamentalism. Hatoyama's essay indicates that the conservative ideas are not simply historical terms without contemporary meaning. Rather, it shows that the DPJ has inherited at least some part of the traditional conservative ideology.

Hatoyama's reference to the LDP's Labor Charter indicates his intention to revalorize management-labor conciliation, which had been all but ignored by the neoliberal reformers. There is no doubt that the DPJ as a whole attaches great importance to cooperative industrial relations. Rengō, the DPJ's largest support organization, is keen to instigate a return to the politics of productivity. The pertinent question is whether or not the DPJ will be able to inject new life into cooperatism. The critical point here is that the previous pattern of cooperative industrial relations does not provide a solution to the contemporary labor problem. For non-regular workers, who constitute over one-third of the labor force, cooperative relations between enterprise unions and employers provide neither tangible benefits nor normative appeal. For women who have been encouraged to enter the labor market without any state assistance with their domestic care work, the current form of cooperative industrial relations is the problem, not a solution. Cooperative industrial relations are predicated on the gendered dual system. Redefinition of cooperatism in the current economic and social contexts should entail redistribution not only between capital and labor but also between regular and non-regular workers and between men and women. In my view, Hatoyama's reference to the LDP's Labor Charter is inadequate in terms of addressing the contemporary predicament. However, the fact that it does mark a significant departure from the LDP's anti-labor stance should not be underrated.

It appears that the DPJ is also likely to attempt to revive one of the other pillars of conservative social protection: productivism. Productivism justifies welfare programs from the perspective of economic growth. In a broad sense of the term, all welfare states are essentially "productivist" because no government can single-mindedly pursue welfare objectives to the extent that the productive sector of the economy is excessively undermined (Goodin 2001, 14). What I refer to as productivism in this book is a specific and positive interaction between the welfare state and economic production. Productivism asserts that the welfare state enables people to live at their full capacity, thereby contributing to economic growth.[11]

The DPJ's New Growth Strategy deserves attention not least because of its intention to revive productivism in the contemporary context. In December 2009, the DPJ government issued the framework for a New Growth Strategy and compiled a detailed plan with specific numerical targets in June 2010. The strategy indicated the possibility of a return to productivism, signaling a policy change from supply-side to demand-side policy. The document identified the roots of Japan's malaise in the two allegedly misguided policies of reliance on public works and reliance on the market mechanism during structural reform. The strategy proposes a "third way," stressing the importance of stimulating consumer spending through various policies aimed at employment stability, improvement of quality of work, and elimination of fear with regard to people's livelihoods. It then proclaimed that improvement in the quality of work would increase corporate competitiveness and that fair distribution of growth would lead to the expansion of domestic consumption as well as to the next round of economic growth, based on the assumption that people's confidence in the future is essential to increasing domestic demand. With respect to employment policy, the document asserted the necessity of establishing "decent work" by promoting equal/balanced treatment, including the realization of equal pay for comparable work, instituting earned income tax credit, increasing the minimum wage, and realizing a work-life balance. Ambitious numerical targets were established, with the employment rate for 2020 set at 80% for adults aged 20–64, 77% for those ages 20–34, 73% for women ages 25–44, and 63% for adults ages 60–64. With respect to work and family balance, the goals were to reduce by half the number of workers who work longer than 60 hours a week and to enable all parents who wish to return to work to do so by 2017, also targeting 13% as the proportion of men to take childcare leave.

The significance of the New Growth Strategy lies in the fact that it presented an alternative view to the prevailing dominant discourse in Japan— the race to the bottom thesis—which had regarded cheap labor as necessary and appropriate for a Japanese economy under pressure from globalization. The strategy claimed that the availability of cheap labor had dampened economic growth as it made it difficult for Japan to shift its workforce to more profitable sectors and unfair treatment in workplaces had demoralized workers. The positive linkage between fairness and efficiency presented in the New Growth Strategy resonates with the European Union's Lisbon Strategy and Britain's Third Way strategy under the Labour Party.[12] All of these strategies aim to create more and better jobs to make the economy more competitive and sustainable. Although the DPJ's growth strategy is less concerned with learning and with a knowledge-based economy as compared to its European counterparts, the respective strategies all assert a positive link between decent work and economic growth and aim to use welfare policies to promote competitive advantage.

When Ishibashi Tanzan advocated full employment policy in the 1950s, he recognized that the elimination of "underemployment" would lead to the increase of national productive power. When the population is aging and shrinking, the underuse of human potential should be regarded as economically problematic. However, the LDP, having pursued neoliberal policies over the course of a decade, had no intention of reviving productivism, which allowed the DPJ to adopt the concept and redefine it in the context of post-industrialism. In contrast, socialists and communists denounce poor working conditions from the perspective of social justice without any implicit link to economic growth and efficiency. It is, therefore, worthwhile noting that a political force establishing a positive linkage between decent work and economic growth has emerged in the Japanese party system.

Although the DPJ is likely to revive cooperatism and productivism, it is unlikely to inherit the last component of traditional conservatism: statism. As the slogan of "from bureaucratic rule to democratic rule" constitutes a guiding principle of the DPJ, its emphasis on local autonomy and civil society shows a break from statist thinking. The Hatoyama cabinet introduced the concept of the "new public sphere" (*atarashii kōkyō*) to foster development of the voluntary sector positioned between the state and the market, including such organizations as non-profit organizations (NPOs) and social enterprises. The subsequent Kan Naoto cabinet passed a bill that would provide greater tax incentives for donations to NPOs. The voluntary sector is now expected to play a more active role in the provision of social services. The expansion of this sector is essential for the DPJ due to its advocacy of small and efficient government while also committing to a "livelihood first" policy. These two policies are contradictory because the latter entails big spending and a large number of civil servants. The DPJ hopes to reconcile the apparent contradiction by expanding the voluntary sector to enable the realization of a small state that cares about people.

The DPJ's commitment to the "new public sphere" as well as its other important project, the establishment of local government autonomy and sovereignty, which differs from the conservative adherence to statism, portrays it as a liberal party. According to the thinking of statism, the state defines the national interest, which civil society is then expected to serve.[13] In contrast, the DPJ seems to subscribe to a liberal view according to which plural actors should compete and collaborate both in defining the public interest and in undertaking the necessary measures to achieve their thus-defined goals. As the DPJ's liberalism clashes with the generally statist thinking of state bureaucrats, the extent to which the party will be able to wrest power from the bureaucracy is unclear.

Assessment of Policy Change under the DPJ

Next, I examine the extent to which the DPJ has actually been able to implement its preferred policies. In the absence of an environment conducive to the right kind of partisan dynamism, ideational shift by itself cannot bring material results. The following section examines labor market reform as well as welfare reform in order to assess the levels of success of the DPJ in pursuing its agenda during the first two years of its governance under Hatoyama and Kan.

Labor Market Reform: The Case of the Temporary Work Agency Law

I first examine the case of the Temporary Work Agency Law (TWAL) and the failure to amend it because societal awareness of the precarity of dispatched workers was one of the factors that led to the power alternation. The Hatoyama cabinet was formed as a coalition government of the DPJ, SDP, and PNP (the People's New Party)[14] as the DPJ had not secured an outright majority in the House of Councillors. Re-regulation of the staffing business was one area of policy agreement among the three parties.

The 2003 amendment to the TWAL, which enabled the manufacturing sector to use dispatched workers, led to a rapid increase in the overall number of dispatched workers. In 2004, compared to the previous year, the number of female dispatched workers increased by 50% (570,000) and that of male dispatched workers doubled (280,000). Numbers peaked in 2008, recording an increase of 2.3 times (850,000) and 4.2 times (550,000), respectively, compared to the numbers in 2003.[15] In 2005, the Ministry of Health, Labour, and Welfare (MHLW) began deliberations at the advisory council to assess the impact of the 2003 amendment on the labor market and to identify the problems to be addressed by the next round of amendment. In the meantime, the Council for the Promotion of Regulatory Reform proposed in December 2006 to lift the restriction on interviewing agency workers prior to offering a contract and to relax the obligation to provide direct employment after the term limit. Although the deregulation panels had persistently demanded further deregulation, criticism of intolerably large inequalities in wages and status between regular workers and non-regular workers appeared on the public agenda in 2006–2007. The DPJ increased the political and social saliency of the gap problem by repeatedly drawing attention to the negative consequences of structural reform. Further, the MHLW began to study the necessity of regulating the on-call staffing business. However, the level of disagreement between employers and labor was such that the advisory council was not able to establish consensus. The ministry commissioned an expert group in early 2008 to construct a framework around which both employers and labor would be able to deliberate. The expert group issued a midterm report in July, which kicked off deliberations at the advisory council. Eventually, the council agreed on the prohibition of the on-call staffing business as well as of dispatched work contracted for less than 30 days. The government submitted the bill to the Diet in November 2008.

In the meantime, the labor unions that mainly unionize non-regular workers such as the Zenkoku Union, the Rentai Union, and the Haken Union, organized several meetings in Diet members' office buildings to pressure the political parties to amend the TWAL. All the opposition parties and Kōmeitō promised that they would amend the law in order to improve the circumstances of dispatched workers. The SDP, PNP, and JCP each formulated their own bills and the DPJ also prepared a bill in April 2008.[16] Even the LDP announced that it would ask the government to ban on-call staffing. All the parties and the MHLW shared the view that short-term contracts including on-call staffing destabilized the working conditions of dispatched workers. However, they disagreed on the specifics of regulation: the SDP, PNP, and JCP demanded a total ban on the staffing business in all sectors except the current 26 specialized job categories. At the other extreme, the DPJ and the MHLW did not plan to exclude dispatched workers from the manufacturing sector. The difference in opinions between the DPJ and the other three opposition parties made it difficult for them to jointly submit a bill to the Diet.

Why did the SDP, PNP, and JCP single out the manufacturing sector? The idea to ban the staffing business from this sector came from a shared perception that the 2003 amendment to the TWAL under the Koizumi cabinet was the root cause of the precarious working conditions of dispatched workers. Because the manufacturing sector had been exempted from liberalization in 1999 but was not exempted in 2003, it became a symbol of Koizumi's neoliberal reform. Gender bias also played a role here (Miura 2011c). Dispatched workers had predominantly been considered to be women, but those in the manufacturing sector were mostly men. When only women had experienced precarity, little attention was drawn to their plight. However, once men were forced into similar circumstances, political and public concern was quickly roused. Compared to the unyieldingly anti-neoliberal position of the SDP, PNP, and JCP, the MHLW and the DPJ were much more modest in their approach as they did not believe that a return to the positive list method would be an effective solution. The fact that the manufacturing sector already relied on the staffing business precluded the DPJ from proposing a drastic change. Among Rengō's affiliated unions, those in the automobile and electronic industries were reluctant to re-exempt the manufacturing sector. Moreover, the

Jinzai Service General Union—a general union that organizes workers in the staffing business—actively lobbied the DPJ as well as other parties to oppose re-regulation. It was thus difficult for Rengō to propose strong regulation due to these internal divisions.

The formation of the *Haken* village at the end of 2008 abruptly raised public awareness of the seriousness of the problems faced by the working poor. A massive number of dispatched workers were fired after the start of the global financial crisis. Many male dispatched workers working in the manufacturing sector had lived in a company residence. Once fired, they simultaneously lost both their job and their housing. More than 500 people arrived to enter the emergency shelter set up in Hibiya Park in front of the MHLW building and the extensive media coverage of the issue made some sort of political response inevitable.

As early as January 1, 2009, Ozawa Ichirō announced that the DPJ would revise the labor market policy implemented by the Koizumi cabinet and Kan Naoto suggested that it may be necessary to ban staffing agencies from the manufacturing sector. Then, within a week, the DPJ and SDP agreed to jointly submit an amendment bill. Although the DPJ had taken a step forward with respect to banning the staffing business from the manufacturing sector, a number of issues remained to be agreed on by the two parties. In May, the DPJ decided to make another concession to the SDP and PNP, agreeing to prohibit one of two types of dispatched work: that of registering workers for individual contracts that only pay when a job is available (*tōroku-gata haken*). They then submitted their bill in June.

The DPJ's sweeping victory in the general election in August 2009 and its emphasis on strong political leadership led many to expect that it would commit to passing the bill it had submitted together with the SDP and PNP, its coalition partners under the Hatoyama cabinet. Nagatsuma Akira, minister of health, labor, and welfare, decided to consult the same advisory council that had formulated the government bill under the LDP government. (It is a legal requirement that the government consult the opinion of the relevant advisory councils with respect to the formulation of labor-related laws.) Because the minister did not alter the membership of the advisory council, it took rather a hostile position toward the three-party bill and defended the previous government bill to which it had already agreed. Labor bureaucrats then skillfully crafted a new bill, which was essentially a compromise between the two bills.

The lack of DPJ leadership was conspicuous all the way through the legislative process. The SDP and PNP strongly opposed the new government bill because it watered down their proposals and even included a deregulatory item such as the abolition of the ban on interviewing dispatched workers prior to offering contracts. Many female dispatched workers complained that they were illegally interviewed by user companies which, they claimed, only selected young and pretty women. Due to persistent resistance from Minister Fukushima Mizuho (SDP) and Kamei Shizuka (PNP), Deputy Prime Minister

Kan decided to delete the clause permitting pre-contract interviews. With this amendment, the cabinet reached agreement and decided to submit the bill in March 2010. Notably, both Labour Minister Nagatsuma and Junior Minister Hosokawa Ritsuo, who had previously drafted the DPJ's counter bills, kept silent during the negotiations.

The bill was introduced to the Diet, but not deliberated on the floor. The SDP left the coalition in June owing to disagreement over the issue of US military bases in Okinawa and the DPJ lost the election of the House of Councillors in July 2010, resulting in legislative gridlock. The LDP's support was now necessary in order to pass the bill, which meant that it would be impossible for the DPJ to keep its promise to strengthen regulation of the staffing business. In November 2011, the DPJ decided to make a substantial concession to the LDP and Kōmeitō, dropping off the ban on the use of dispatched workers in manufacturing sector as well as registered-type dispatched workers from its reform proposal.[17]

What does the case of the failed TWAL amendment tell us about the DPJ? Although the DPJ has put a high priority on achieving strong political leadership over bureaucratic coordination and sectionalism, its failure with respect to labor market reform is striking. The Hatoyama cabinet abolished the CEFP and the Council for Regulatory Reform, the two main vehicles of neoliberal market reform under the LDP government. It then decided to let the MHLW's advisory council formulate labor law.[18] Under the DPJ government, the new policymaking process returned to the old model. Cooperatism, rather than political leadership, was a guiding principle with respect to labor market reform. Because the DPJ had approved the three-party bill as part of its electoral strategy of alliance with the SDP and PNP, it was not sponsored by any of the DPJ's own members. Without political sponsorship, it comes as no surprise that conventional interest mediation prevailed over political leadership. The DPJ's adherence to cooperatism may justify mediatory politics, but cooperatism is ill-suited to the current political context in which non-regular workers remain unorganized and employers remain staunchly committed to neoliberal reform. Overhaul of the TWAL framework appears to be doomed under the DPJ government.

Welfare Reform: Strengthening the Social Safety Net under Legislative Gridlock

How much did the DPJ succeeded in strengthening Japan's social safety net? In contrast to labor market reform, where the DPJ were unable to effect much in the way of change, the party did succeed in strengthening the social safety net to a certain extent. However, with respect to social transfers such as pensions and family allowances, fierce partisan competition obstructed bipartisan agreement in this field.

First, the DPJ government fortified the "second safety net" for those who are protected neither by social assistance nor by unemployment insurance. Prior to the power alternation, the Asō cabinet had created a program that provided a monthly allowance of ¥100,000 for up to one year to those who were enrolled in officially acknowledged training programs, as well as a housing allowance to those who lost their housing owing to dismissal from their jobs.[19] The DPJ enacted a law to perpetuate the program to assist job seekers and extended the duration of the housing allowance. Because there was no fundamental disagreement between the DPJ and the LDP with respect to correcting "excessive market fundamentalism" and activating those who had lost jobs and housing, the DPJ was able to strengthen the second social safety net.

Second, the DPJ government improved anti-poverty measures. It pressured the MHLW to estimate relative poverty rates, which it had refused to do under the LDP government. It then appointed social activists—Yuasa Makoto and Shimizu Yasuyuki—as cabinet advisors and had them propose specific measures to prevent suicides and improve social services for the unemployed and dispossessed. Kan Naoto, whose political career started as a citizen activist, strengthened the network between the government and citizen's movements first as deputy prime minister and then as prime minister. He then created a special team to discuss the topic of building a "Society That Includes Everyone" (*Hitori Hitori wo Hōsetsu suru Shakai*) and asked Yuasa and Shimizu to intervene in the discussions in order to overcome administrative sectionalism. This team issued the proposition, before Kan stepped down in August 2011, that the government should collect basic data on social risks (which were lacking at the time) and provide personal support services to realize social inclusion. In areas such as these that do not require the Diet's approval, the DPJ clearly advanced its favored policies.

In contrast, in areas that entail allocation of a new budget or legislation, the DPJ's weak grip on the House of Councillors made it difficult to pursue its agenda. The DPJ's defeat in the 2010 Upper House election fueled partisan competition, resulting in legislative gridlock on reforming the social security system. Child allowances and the consumption tax were the two critical issues on which fierce partisan competition precluded bipartisan agreement. A child allowance of ¥26,000 per month regardless of income had been one of the most important electoral pledges in the DPJ's 2009 Manifesto, but it only succeeded in realizing an allowance of ¥13,000 in its first year in power (Miura 2011d). The LDP and Kōmeitō vehemently opposed the DPJ's child allowance for its universality and progressiveness and showed no signs of concession on this matter. When in power, the LDP and Kōmeitō had increased cash allowances for middle income families raising children in order to boost birth rates; however, they opposed the philosophy on which the policy of child allowances was premised, that is, that society should assume responsibility for raising children. The LDP repeatedly claimed that childcare is the responsibility of parents alone, and not of society. It denounced universal child allowances and instead proposed to reinstitute an income threshold in order to establish a clear criterion for eligible recipients.[20] In August 2011, the DPJ finally made a concession, agreeing with the setting of an income threshold and the lowering of benefit levels.

The consumption tax is another issue on which the DPJ has faced difficulties in overcoming legislative gridlock. As a matter of fact, both the LDP and the DPJ have conceded that raising the consumption tax from the current 5% to at least 10% is necessary for fiscal reconstruction in order to sustain the existing social security system. Because the consumption tax is unpopular in Japan, both parties were reluctant to mention the topic during their electoral campaigns and have explored the idea of implementing welfare reform that would justify a tax hike. The Fukuda cabinet set up the National Council on Social Security, which proposed generational redistribution or "functional reinforcement" of the social security system; that is, improvement of benefits for those who have not reached retirement age. Because Japan's social protection system has long been skewed toward the elderly, improving benefits for the younger generations is necessary in order to convince voters of the need to raise taxes. Prime Minister Kan accepted this reasoning, appointing former LDP bigwig Yosano Kaoru as minister of economic and fiscal policy to deal with social security and tax reform. Kan then chaired a government panel to build national consensus, but the opposition parties refused to join. Moreover, internal strife within the DPJ further weakened Kan's leadership. Ozawa Ichirō and his followers criticized Kan's for attempting to modify the 2009 electoral pledges and instead aim at tax increases. When the government panel on social security reform compiled a plan to double the consumption tax in stages by the mid-2010s (interpreted as by March 2016), the Kan cabinet was not able to convince the DPJ to accept the plan, and the cabinet was not able to officially approve it. Those in the party who sought a way to realize a tax hike explored the possibility of allying with the LDP, but both the DPJ and the LDP were divided on the merits of a grand coalition.

Finally, the DPJ has no intention of seriously addressing the issue of gender equality. Although the party encourages women to continue to work after childbearing and has not taken a reactionary position against gender equality, neither has it shown any hint of an intention to overhaul the gendered dual system. The birth of the Hatoyama cabinet coincided with the formulation of the government's Third Action Plan for a Gender Equality Society. Fukushima Mizuho (SDP), minister for gender equality and consumer affairs, put sustained pressure on the Council for Gender Equality to formulate the Third Action Plan. When the Council formulated the Second Action Plan in 2005, the backlash against gender equality and "gender free" education was at its peak as a result of an LDP campaign orchestrated by Abe Shinzō attacking these terms and concepts.[21] Consequently, terms such as "gender," "reproductive rights," and "unpaid work" that are loathed by conservatives were either erased or redefined in a conservative fashion in the Second Action Plan.[22] Although the conservative backlash has not fully dissipated, the power alternation and the appointment of Fukushima facilitated both the reappearance of the above terms in the text and the introduction of "radical" new ideas such as a quota system for political representation, equal pay for comparable work, and a job appraisal system. The alternation of power tipped the balance in favor of pro-gender equality vis-à-vis the conservative backlash. Nonetheless, transformation of the gendered dual system has not figured on the DPJ government's agenda. Fukushima was dismissed in June 2010 and the Kan cabinet thereafter included only one female minister, Renhō, until she was replaced by a male lawmaker to deal with the severe nuclear power plant accident triggered by the Great East Japan Earthquake on March 11. The DPJ leaders have paid little attention to gender equality or the role of women in rebuilding the social protection system.

In essence, the DPJ's adjustments of neoliberal reform have been limited to partial amendments. It has succeeded in strengthening the social safety net to a certain extent, but it has not yet systematically addressed either the dysfunction of the welfare through work system or the gendered dual system on which welfare through work is founded. In other words, although it effectively utilized its veto power in the Diet when in opposition, the DPJ appears to lack the vision to transform the welfare through work system into something fundamentally different. This lack of transformative vision does not mean that the DPJ will not introduce anything new into the social protection system. The DPJ appears likely to attempt to revive productivism by redefining it in the contemporary context and to valorize cooperatism, both of these concepts are being largely ignored by conservatives. As liberalism clashes with the statist tradition, there is room for the concept of social rights to secure greater legitimacy. If the DPJ succeeds in revitalizing these concepts, it will at least be able to restructure welfare through work in a form that is more functional.

Conclusion

In this concluding chapter, I take stock of the key findings of the preceding chapters and elaborate on the theoretical implications of the role of ideas and political parties in the process of forming and reforming the social protection system. This book has argued that Japan's social protection system is best characterized by the concept of welfare through work, where employment maintenance substitutes for income maintenance. The mechanism of the gendered dual system sustains welfare through work regime. This social protection system came into being as an outcome of the interplay between ideas and partisan competition.

Changes and Continuity in Welfare through Work

Scholars disagree over the extent to which neoliberal reform was accomplished in Japan. The various conclusions they reach depend on their respective positions on the merits of establishing a free labor market in Japan. Those who consider neoliberal reform necessary to Japan's recovery contend that the implementation of reform has been too slow and that unnecessary intervention by the state has limited Japan's capacity to adapt to altered circumstances. Conversely, critics of neoliberalism argue that labor market reform proceeded to the extent that it actually dismantled employment protection, resulting in a sudden increase in poverty in Japanese society.

Neither view correctly captures the nature of the actual changes or the mechanism behind the changes. Here, it is vital to distinguish between *labor standards* and *labor conditions* (Flanagan 2006, 7). Labor standards refer to legal requirements created as a result of a political process, and labor conditions refer to the actual working conditions that workers experience and the labor rights they enjoy. It is possible for labor conditions to deteriorate without concomitant downgrading of labor standards. Although Japanese employers have been uncompromising in their calls for labor market reform, their demands were not translated directly into policy. The actual outcome of reform was usually more modest than the initial demands made by employers due to the complexity of the political process.

However, the fact of deterioration is undeniable with respect to labor conditions. Further stratification of workers occurred and more flexibilities were created in conjunction with overall degradation of working conditions. First, the dual structure of the labor market was reinforced, as employment protection for regular workers was preserved while deregulation of the temporary labor market proceeded apace, thereby increasing external flexibility. Second, a significant proportion of regular workers have been replaced by non-regular workers. The share of non-regular workers increased from 20.2% in 1990 to 34.4% in 2010 (men from 8.8% to 18.9%, women from 38.1% to 53.8% [see also Figure 4.2]).[1] Basically, bad jobs drove out good jobs. Third, strong employment protection for regular workers came to entail more internal flexibility, leading to yet longer working hours and related health problems, further exacerbating the incompatibility of work and family responsibilities. Enhanced flexibility in both the internal and external labor markets had a detrimental effect on working conditions regardless of employment status and work style. The result was the deterioration of labor conditions across the board, which cannot be adequately explained by the insider-outsider theories.

In any event, neoliberal labor market reform did not proceed to the extent that reformers had hoped it would. As far as employment protection is concerned, it is certainly true that Japan has not moved toward the liberal market economies. Unlike their US counterparts, Japanese employers do not have the right to dismiss workers at will. However, even a comparatively modest degree of labor market reform has given rise to serious social problems in Japan as a result of the government's failure to upgrade security measures to counteract its adverse consequences. The expansion in numbers of non-regular workers meant that an enormous number of people were excluded from conventional protective measures based on the orthodox style of regular work involving full-time work and open-ended contracts. Consequently, welfare through work has become dysfunctional as a social protection system.

The kind of change that Japan has experienced corresponds to what historical institutionalists call "policy drift." According to Jacob Hacker (2004), policy drift takes place when the effect of a policy gradually changes despite the absence of legal or administrative reform (see also Mahoney and Thelen 2009). Japan's failure to update the social safety net or create protective measures to underwrite the new social risks that emerged as a result of new labor conditions presents a clear case of policy drift. Although welfare through work continues to characterize Japan's social protection system, the process of policy drift has exacerbated the distributional consequences of the model, thereby making welfare through work dysfunctional.

Why, then, did policy drift occur? This book has emphasized the role of ideas in accounting for policy change. I have argued that the visions and values of those in power greatly affect the ways in which social protection systems are formed and reformed. Moreover, I have contended that the policy preferences of actors are not determined by their positions in the economy. Instead, I have proposed that we should empirically reveal how they understand their interests. In other words, their ideas of how the labor market and the social protection system should be organized are politically constructed rather than economically determined. Finally, I have called attention to the role of discourse in policy-making processes.

Political Account of Preference Formation and the Role of Discourse

This book has empirically revealed the policy preferences of actors, notably employers. This methodology differs from functionalist explanations that deduce actors' preferences from their positions in the economy. Some contend that employers prefer liberalization and flexibilization because they pursue maximization of profits, usually at the expense of their workers. Others claim that employers who maintain a competitive strategy based on cooperative industrial relations with skilled labor prefer institutions that provide employment security.[2] Although these two lines of thought disagree on whether the market takes a universal form or a variety of forms, they are both functionalist in the sense that actors' preferences are deduced from their positions in the market economy (Miura 2008b). In contrast, this book has empirically investigated "who wanted what reform" and revealed that employers developed their idea of how the labor market and social protection system should be organized based on their political experiences. Employers are political animals as well as economic animals.

Japanese employers began calling for labor market reform in the 1990s essentially for the purposes of labor cost reduction and effective use of the skilled and unskilled workforces. Such demands might appear universal, given the logic of market mechanism and economic rationality. Globalization, a stagnant economy, and successive recessions lent further weight to the merits of cost cutting by management. Viewed historically, Japanese employers' demands for reform departed from their previous management philosophy, which had prioritized long-term relationships over short-term profits (Dore 2000). Employment protection for regular workers was a cornerstone of the social contract produced by the cross-class coalition that had emerged by the early 1960s. By the 1990s employers began to pursue neoliberal labor market reform, not least because the decline of the leftist labor movement allowed employers to abandon the ideology of cooperatism.

Although employers aggressively pursued reduction of labor costs, they did not publicly advocate the dismantling of employment protection. Rather, they continued to publicly commit to employment protection as an obligatory responsibility of employers. As long as the unions put a high priority on employment protection, employers seek other ways to reduce labor costs, as in fact they did in the realm of labor market flexibility, both internally and externally. This policy preference resulted from the existence of a trade-off between strong employment protection for regular workers and internal and external labor market flexibilities sustained by the gendered dual system. This trade-off has long existed in Japan not only because it is economically sustainable, but also because it is politically constructed and allows for political pay-offs. Employers' policy preferences are neither functionally shaped by their positions in the global economy nor by the way in which the labor market is organized. It is their historical experience of contention with labor movements that shapes their idea of how the labor market and the social protection system are to be organized.

The way in which ideas shape actors' policy preferences is a historical process and it is the researchers' responsibility to reveal the process, as actors might refuse to acknowledge any such causality. What they instead assert are their own justifications for pursuing a certain policy. In so doing, they formulate discourses. A discourse represents "the policy ideas that speak to the soundness and appropriateness of policy programmes and the interactive processes of policy formulation and communication that serve to generate and disseminate those policy ideas" (Radaelli and Schmidt 2005, 11). Actors may mobilize a number of resources to influence policymaking, but discourse is a crucial one as it legitimizes a policy program and has a communicative function in building a coalition. A discourse also helps to reconstruct an actor's understanding of their interests and thus redirect their actions in policy making (see Radaelli and Schmidt 2005; V. Schmidt 2002; Taylor-Gooby 2005). This book has shed light on a number of discourses disseminated by conservatives and employers in order to gather support for neoliberal reform: the "British disease" in the 1970s, the "people's burden rate" in the 1980s, and the "race to the bottom" since the 1990s. The first two discourses attempted to justify welfare retrenchment and the third labor market reform. The foremost beneficiaries of neoliberal reform are quite few in number, being largely limited to owners and managers of global companies and wealthy consumers. In order to broaden the constituency base in favor of neoliberal reform, it was vital to build a coalition with urban salaried workers, a group of vast numbers and flexible identity. If urban salaried workers view themselves as consumers and taxpayers, or even as managers, rather than as workers, it is likely that they will support a neoliberal agenda. The above discourses aimed to garner support from urban salaried workers, and were ultimately successful in this regard as this constituency has indeed supported neoliberal reform relatively consistently since the 1980s.

The discursive triumph of neoliberalism does not in itself necessarily attest to the power of ideas or the causal influence of discourses. The battle of ideas is inextricably linked to the struggle for power. Actors seek to acquire power both in order to shape the discourse of the day as well as by trying to influence it. Throughout the book, I have emphasized the agency of political parties in promoting policy change. What needs to be explored is the interactive process by which the dynamics of partisan competition engenders ideational transformation in, and causes policy repositioning by, political parties, thus producing a new dynamics in partisan competition. The role of discourses should be contextualized in the dynamics of power politics.

Ideas and Partisan Dynamism

The Rise of Neoliberalism

The book takes the position that the visions and values of governing parties determine the dominant characteristics of the social protection system. More specifically, it contends that three strands of conservative ideas—statism, cooperatism, and productivism—fundamentally shaped Japan's system of welfare through work. However, ideas are not fixed entities. Political actors periodically refashion and redefine old ideas in order to navigate the political landscape surrounding them. Therefore, we need to examine how the dynamics of partisan politics influences the process of ideational transformation experienced by political parties. I have pointed out that the political threat from the Left in the 1950s and early 1960s prompted conservatives to preemptively construct the social protection system, albeit on terms favorable to the Right. In the political context of the time, cooperatism and productivism justified the welfare through work system. The political fortunes of the Left declined steadily thereafter before nosediving in the 1980s and essentially reaching their nadir after the end of the Cold War in 1989. In the new political landscape of the 1990s, neoliberalism gained political currency. But what was the mechanism of neoliberal ascendance? How did partisan competition influence ideational transformation among conservatives? And why did the ascendance of neoliberalism lead to policy drift and to the dysfunction of the welfare through work system discussed above?

There were two stages to the ascendance of neoliberalism. First, the Liberal Democratic Party (LDP) refashioned itself in the 1980s to pursue a neoliberal agenda in the realm of administrative reform and welfare retrenchment. This policy turn resulted partly from the ideational reaction of conservatives to welfare expansion in the previous decade and partly from their new electoral strategy in the context of conservative resurgence. A conservative backlash against the welfare state began to gather momentum in the mid-1970s, with the main battlefield at the time being in the realm of public discourse. In the causal and normative framework of conservative thinking at this time, productivism no longer played a part as the welfare state had been discredited without being ascribed any positive role in the economy. It was in the 1980s that conservatives found neoliberal discourse electorally rewarding. Prime Minister Nakasone stated that his policy would allow the LDP to extend its wing toward the Left. Although it might appear paradoxical to presume that left-leaning voters would support neoliberal policy, Nakasone meant that his neoliberal agenda would be appealing to urban salaried workers who paid a comparatively large amount of taxes and thus would prefer a small government with a limited tax burden. Having benefited from the welfare through work system, this group insisted that core workers be protected and that their tax burden be minimized. Such salaried workers were mostly organized by the private sector unions, which were staunch advocates of administrative reform and privatization, while at the same time espousing cooperatism at the workplace.

The second stage was after the end of the Cold War, which triggered a sea change in the ideological landscape of Japanese politics. A substantial new political space emerged that was ripe for the taking by new political forces. Neoliberal reformers dominated this new space because they positioned themselves in opposition to perpetual conservative rule. The LDP's fall from power in 1993 accelerated the new partisan dynamics in which a number of new parties emerged to challenge what the LDP had been. Although the LDP had obtained a measure of support from urban voters in the 1980s, it continued to rely on rural voters and protected industries. As the LDP had maintained power through electoral machines lubricated by its distributional policy, neoliberal reformers attacked the organs of distribution which, they claimed, distorted the efficient allocation of resources necessary for the Japanese economy to recover. The ascendance of neoliberal forces in political circles led to the LDP's repositioning. Prime ministers Hashimoto and Koizumi, bolstered by strong popular support, succeeded in pushing the party toward a neoliberal orientation and embarked on structural reforms such as the financial Big Bang, welfare retrenchment, deregulation, reduction of public works, and postal privatization, as well as labor market reform. Because employers had abandoned the ideology of cooperatism, neoliberal labor market reform was able to make it onto the public agenda. This discussion shows that partisan dynamics determines which ideas are politically rewarding with respect to alliance formation and vote seeking.

The LDP's disengagement with cooperatism-productivism had the effect of fortifying the policy framework of welfare through work. Policymakers customarily come up with policy solutions consistent with existing policy frameworks. Welfare retrenchment in the 1980s was a logical extension of welfare through work—as long as jobs are abundantly available, welfare spending can be and should be constrained. However, even when labor demand shrinks, as was the case in the 1990s and early 2000s, the policy framework of welfare through work continued to prioritize job creation rather than expansion of the social safety net. The framework justifies further flexibilization of the labor market because bad jobs are considered better than no jobs. Prime ministers Hashimoto and Koizumi chose to expand the temporary labor market through the amendment of the Temporary Work Agency Law in the hope that this would mitigate the impact of rising unemployment rates caused by their structural reforms. As temporary workers were predominantly either married women and thus not the primary breadwinner or they lived with their parents and could at least afford a place to sleep, they were not thought to be in danger of falling into precarious circumstances. The expansion of non-regular workers was considered a desirable solution under the policy framework of welfare through work. Policy drift was thus a logical extension of, and the desirable solution under, the welfare through work system.

The Double Movement

As inevitable and desirable under this framework as policy drift was, this policy solution eventually hit the wall of its own limitations. The logic of Polanyi's (1944) "double movement" set in, with society protecting itself against the impersonal forces of the self-regulating market. In fact, by the mid-2000s, anti-neoliberalism had gained political currency as the gap problem and rising poverty started to cause significant social concern. A new political landscape thus emerged, which the Democratic Party of Japan (DPJ) was quick to take advantage of, strategically shifting its position to represent those who were discontent with neoliberal reform. The DPJ's landslide victory in 2009 speaks to the success of this electoral strategy.

We must consider how the vision and values of the DPJ might affect policy drift with respect to the welfare through work system. The book argues that the DPJ is likely to revive cooperatism and productivism, while discarding statism. This means that the party has no intention of transforming Japan's social protection system into something fundamentally different from welfare through work. Rather, it intends to remake welfare through work as a more functional social protection system. Whether or not it succeeds in this regard will depend on the specific dynamics of partisan competition that it experiences while in power. Because the DPJ does not control the Upper House, the impact of party politics looms large. If it seeks an alliance with, or even cooperation from, the LDP, the odds on further policy drift rise. However, if the DPJ somehow manages to revalorize cooperatism and productivism, there is a possibility that welfare through work will be remade. The key questions are whether the DPJ will be able to successfully argue the merits of social protection reform in light of competitive advantage and how urban salaried workers will perceive their own interests.

A new direction of reform that the DPJ may embark on involves a new politics of work and welfare. Workers have been stratified to the extent that it is difficult to maintain or create solidarity among them, whereas employers are unified with a shared preference for blocking re-regulation. In order to build a coalition in such circumstances, the ability to formulate a persuasive discourse is crucial, as support cannot be gathered from pre-existing organizations but must be carefully cultivated among diverse groups of people.

I have pointed out that urban salaried workers were the hidden agents behind the ascendance of neoliberalism. In the 1980s, the marriage of cooperatism and neoliberalism allowed them to support neoliberal policy. In contrast, the divorce of these concepts in the 1990s has made adherence to the same policy position problematic. Although the employment of core workers is still protected, the number of core workers has shrunk and the increased flexibility of the internal labor market has degraded their working conditions. The expansion of non-regular workers has had a negative impact on the labor conditions experienced by regular workers. However, the discourse of insider-outsider theory propagates that urban salaried workers benefit from increased numbers of non-regular workers as they enjoy employment protection at the expense of non-regular workers. If they are convinced by this discourse, it is likely that they will, at least tacitly, support the neoliberal labor market. Therefore, the DPJ needs to win the battle of ideas over the understanding of interests held by urban salaried workers. Such a process would involve an effective dissemination of discourse linking the lassitude of the Japanese economy with the dysfunction of the social protection system and justifying reform from the perspective of competitive edge. The DPJ's New Growth Strategy made a step in this direction as it argued that an improvement in the quality of work would increase corporate competitiveness and that employment stability, in addition to fair distribution of growth, would stimulate consumer spending. Put another way, it suggested a positive-sum relation between regular and non-regular workers as well as between corporate competitiveness and quality of work. The prospects for the remaking of welfare through work thus depend on the DPJ's ability to convince urban salaried workers through the formulation of feasible policy programs based on productivism.

Although it is quite a challenging task for the DPJ to carry this out, I must emphasize that reviving cooperatism and productivism in the hope of remaking welfare through work system is likely to end in disappointment. This is because the underlying cause of the dysfunction of the welfare through work system lies in the excessive strain placed on the gendered dual system. Japan's shrinking population inevitably pushes maternal employment further onto the agenda, but the current legal framework and corporate practices merely take the gendered dual system for granted, thereby posing an unbearable burden on working mothers. Without a strong political will to remedy the distortions of the gendered dual system, policy drift seems all but certain to be perpetuated.

Notes

Introduction

1. For instance, Swenson argues that Swedish employers in the 1950s supported universalistic welfare policies because such policies stabilized centralized bargaining arrangements, which had been under stress due to tight constraints on the labor market. With the introduction of comprehensive health insurance and generous sick pay, employers were able to avoid competition over benefit levels (Swenson 2002). See also Estévez-Abe, Iversen, and Soskice (2001); Manow (2001); Mares (2001); C. Martin (1995, 2000); Swenson (1997); and Thelen (2000).

2. On political settlement, see Zysman (1983). See also Pontusson (2005b) on the tension between approaches that stress political (class) struggle and those that focus on employer coordination. See also Korpi (2006).

3. On discussions of the relationship between occupationalism and clientelism, see Lynch (2006).

4. See Itō (2007) on how conservative elites—bureaucrats, judges, and legal scholars—succeeded in preventing the substantialization of the right to life by sabotaging the legislation of positive law and propagating conservative interpretations of the constitution.

5. On the LDP's various attempts and plans for constitutional revision, see Izeri (2008). The *Yomiuri Shimbun,* a conservative daily paper, has proposed the amendment to Art. 25 with the aim of encouraging self-endeavor and mutual collaboration (May 3, 2004).

6. See also Katzenstein (1996) and Gao (1997) on the role of cultural norms and ideologies in Japan.

7. The political reasoning of social insurance advocated by cooperatist thinking is the same as that advanced by what is known as "state corporatism." I use "cooperatism" in lieu of "corporatism" in order to avoid misunderstanding, as the latter is often used to refer to tripartite decision making in favor of organized labor. Moreover, "cooperatism" better conveys the sense of the Japanese term *kyōchō shugi.*

8. On conservative parties in the West, see Béland (2007); Béland and Waddan (2007); Hacker (2002, 2006); Palier and Martin (2008); Pierson (1994). In the

context of Japanese politics, rare examples shedding light on the role of political parties in policymaking include Noble (1998) on industrial policy and Nakano (2010) on decentralization policy.

Chapter 1

1. Instead of social expenditure per GDP, the proportion of GDP spent on tax-financed social programs can be used to measure the extent to which states aim to redress undesirable market outcomes ex post facto. This indicator excludes spending on contributory social insurance programs because "social insurance cannot be seen as a compensatory social policy, as it basically prolongs (labor) market outcomes instead of modifying them" (Bonoli 2003: 1012). Continental European countries—France, Germany, Belgium, the Netherlands, and Italy—tend to spend less on tax-financed social programs due to their heavy reliance on social contributions. Although this indicator accurately designates the degree of ex post income replacement measures, it does not capture the degree to which labor markets and welfare states are intertwined. In order to understand and highlight the mechanisms of "welfare without work" and "welfare through work," the proportion of social expenditure to GDP is an appropriate indicator.

2. It is possible that a higher proportion of self-employed workers in the workforce may raise employment rates. However, in Japan, the share of employees (i.e., neither self-employed nor unpaid family workers) among the total workforce was 83% in 2000, which is close to the average share in the 20 OECD countries (OECD Labour Force Statistics Database). Even among workers ages 55–64, the share of self-employed and unpaid family workers in the workforce is 22% (Ministry of Internal Affairs and Communications, *Labour Force Survey*, 2004, http://www.stat.go.jp/data/roudou/). It is, therefore, safe to assume that the effect of the self-employed on employment statistics is not particularly large in Japan when compared to other advanced economies.

3. For data on employment rates for workers over 65, see ILO LABORSTA (http://www.ilo.org).

4. Different definitions of unemployment make international comparisons difficult. It is often argued that the Japanese government's definition of unemployment has tended to underestimate real unemployment. Responding to this critique, the Ministry of Labour has countered that Japanese unemployment rates would be lower compared to the US definition of unemployment (Ministry of Labour, 1999, 106–107). For instance, Japan's unemployment rate in 2003 was 5.3% according to the Japanese government definition, and 4.5% according to the American definition (Japan Institute for Labour Policy and Training, 2004, 118–119).

5. Statistical data on the Japanese labor market are compiled from *Employment Outlook* (OECD, various years) and *Labour Force Survey*.

6. Belgium, France, Germany, and Italy provide the typical examples of welfare without work. In Esping-Anderson's original work on welfare states without work, he included the Netherlands and Spain. The Netherlands' unemployment rates have improved significantly since 1998, but Spain's rates remain very high. If we include these two countries, the average rates become 11.0% and 7.8% in the respective time periods (Source: OECD Employment and Labour Market Statistics).

7. Sources available at ILO LABORSTA (http://www.ilo.org). The ranking of the major OECD countries in terms of the proportion of the female population aged 60–64 active in the labor market in 1995 was as follows: Sweden, Norway, Japan, the United States, New Zealand, Canada, Denmark, Finland, Australia, Spain, France, Germany, Austria, the Netherlands, Italy, and Belgium.

8. These data are based on OECD (2004, 112).

9. Data available at http://stats.oecd.org/Index.aspx.

10. The replacement rates were reduced to 50–80% in 2003.

11. Since the 2000 reform, the maximum duration was extended to 330 days for those who lose their jobs due to bankruptcy or dismissal, are between the ages 45 and 59, and have a payment record longer than 20 years.

12. The numbers indicate the average of the gross unemployment benefit replacement rates for two earnings levels, three family situations, and three durations of unemployment (OECD 2004).

13. The low level of unemployment benefits means that insurance premiums are also low in Japan. The unemployment insurance premium was 1.95% (employers paying 1.15% and workers paying 0.8%) in 2005. In contrast, social contributions for unemployment insurance were 6.18% in France, 6.5% in Germany, and 5.42% in Sweden in the late 1990s. Japan's low premium is partially compensated by state subsidy. A quarter of the unemployment insurance account is financed by the government's general budget, whereas in the United States and France such state subsidies do not exist. Germany has a similar system, although the rate was 15% as of 1999. Data here are from documents prepared by the Ministry of Health, Labour, and Welfare (MHLW).

14. The *Nihon Salt Manufacturing* case, Supreme Court, 2nd Petty Bench, April 25, 1975, the *Kōchi Hōsō* case, Supreme Court, 2nd Petty Bench, January 31, 1997. See Sugeno (1997, 47–48, 53–55; 2000, 442–453), Nogawa (2000). See also chapter 3.

15. Mori(2001) points out that the four requirements were not applicable to workers in small- and medium-size firms and in fact the court tended to require only two. On the historical development of court interpretation, see also Yamakawa (2002).

16. Ōtake and Fujikawa (2001) show that the plaintiff victory rate stayed at approximately 50% during the 1970s and 1980s, increasing to 80% after 1995. They also raise the possibility that dismissals at small and medium-size firms have increased since 1995 due to the severity of the economic climate.

17. For instance, Gordon argues that the near-total control held by managers over job transfers and job definitions in exchange for refraining from dismissals was "a tremendous gain for business in an era of continuous technological innovation" (1985, 400). See also chapter 3.

18. The *Toa Paint* case, Supreme Court, July 14, 1986.

19. The French Regulation School uses the concept of "unlimited duties" (Yamada 2000). On the mobilization mechanism of "total commitment," see Gordon (1998) and Kumazawa (1997). Hisamoto Norio (1998) develops a theory of "employee-ization" (*shainka*) in order to explain the "transfer flexibilities" common among Japanese firms. Kumazawa and Hisamoto differ in terms of value judgments on Japanese industrial relations as well as the role of enterprise unions, but both agree that Japanese-style human resource management has induced long working hours as well as the duality in the Japanese labor market.

20. Definitions of part-time workers vary between countries and even differ within a country depending on the criteria employed by different surveys. Different statistical surveys in Japan show various numbers for the share of part-timers in the workforce (Japan Institute of Labour 2000). The Part-Time Labor Law defines part-time workers as workers for whom fewer weekly work hours are prescribed than for regular employees employed by the same establishment.

21. *Labour Force Survey.*

22. Estimated from data provided in "The General Survey of Part-Time Workers" (*Pātotaimu Rōdōsha Sōgō Jittai Chōsa*), Ministry of Health, Labour, and Welfare, 2001

(http://www.mhlw.go.jp/toukei/itiran/roudou/koyou/keitai/01/index.html)   and
2006 (http://www.mhlw.go.jp/toukei/itiran/roudou/koyou/keitai/06/index.html).
In 2001, there were 11 million workers who worked for fewer than 35 hours, and the
number of *pāto* also amounted to 11 million. Approximately 20% of the former were
categorized either as regular workers or as temporary agency workers, whereas 30%
of the latter worked for more than 35 hours. The MHLW estimated the number of
part-time *pāto* to be approximately 8 million. See Ministry of Health, Labour, and
Welfare, "The Final Report of the Study Group on Part-Time Employment" (*Pāto
Rōdo no Kadai to Taiō no Hōkōsei*], July 2002 (http://www.mhlw.go.jp/shingi/2002/07/
s0719-3f.html).

23. White-collar fixed-term workers are conventionally referred to by two different names, "entrusted employee" (*shokutaku shain*) and "contract employee" (*keiyaku
shain*). Those in the former group are employed in some capacity by the same company after their retirement from positions as regular workers, whereas the latter do
not have this kind of relationship with their employers. Blue-collar fixed-term workers
are referred to as "fixed-term laborers" (*kikan kō*).

24. *Labour Force Survey.* The MHLW estimated the number of workers dispatched
by temporary agencies to be 3.2 million in 2006, whereas *Labour Force Survey* put the
figure at 1.3 million the same year. The MHLW annually receives business reports
from staffing companies and estimates the number of dispatched workers based on
the reports.

25. In 1992, 8.7% of full-time *pāto* experienced promotions and 54.3% received
regular raises (Ministry of Labour, 1992).

26. Ministry of Health, Labour, and Welfare, *Wage Structure Basic Survey*
(http://stat.jil.go.jp/jil63/plsql/JTK0300?P_TYOUSA=R1).

27. See Economic Planning Agency, 1996. The Japanese figure is calculated using
data from the *Wage Structure Basic Survey* (http://stat.jil.go.jp/jil63/plsql/JTK0300?P_
TYOUSA=R1). My own estimate, using the *Wage Structure Basic Survey*, indicates that
female regular workers earned less than 60% of the wages of male regular workers
before 1987, and the figure reached 65.4% in 1999, and 69.0% in 2008.

28. When education, length of employment, and firm size are controlled for, female workers are receive approximately 75% of male wages (Japan Institute of Labour
2000, 182–183).

29. See Nitta (2008) and Brinton (1993). It should be noted that male temporaries
were not completely replaced by female *pāto*. Gordon (1985, 407–409) reveals that
these two types of workers functioned differently from each other.

30. See Kinoshita (1999) on a brief history of wage systems in Japan.

31. The data is based on the Ministry of Labour's *Survey on Employment Management
(Koyō Kanri Chōsa)*, see Ministry of Labour, 1976.

32. See Gordon (1998) on the development of the wage system in typical cases
in large Japanese firms. Endō (1999) provides a comprehensive study on Japanese
personnel assessment in companies. He argues that the lack of effective employment
discrimination law in Japan allows Japanese employers to abuse the personnel assessment system and discriminate against women and leftist unionists.

33. Personnel assessment is not unique to Japan. However, according to Endō
(1999), distinctive features of the Japanese version are (i) the wide application
thereof, being also extended to low rank employees, (ii) the relatively heavy weight
given to personal traits, and (iii) vagueness of job description. Workers are often required to set objectives by themselves, which, due to vague job descriptions, can result
in unreasonably high objectives (Endō 1999, 157). Severe competition among employees, induced in large part by the specter of personnel assessment, results in long
working hours.

Chapter 2

1. Esping-Andersen initially used the term corporatist regime. It is now more common to use the term Christian democratic regime, thereby highlighting the political forces instrumental in the creation of the regime (see Levy 1999).

2. Originally, Esping-Andersen (1990) located Japan as of medium conservatism and highly liberal. On hybrid regimes, see Esping-Andersen (1997) and Uzuhashi (1997).

3. For example, Pempel and Shinkawa (1996) stress the role of occupational pensions. The high ratio of occupational pensions to public pensions, they argue, reveals Japan to be a liberal regime. Uzuhashi (1997) compares the policy outcomes of the childcare package and concludes that Japan can be categorized as a typical liberal welfare regime in this particular respect. Hiroi (1999) argues that the Japanese social insurance system is being shifted from a corporatist type to a liberal type by increasing state subsidies.

4. For the childcare package, see Uzuhashi (1997, 160). The level of entitlement can be measured by gross spending on each item by GDP but also by benefit replacement rates, qualifying conditions, and take-up rates.

5. On statutory social security contributions, family allowances and non-statutory contributions, see Takegawa and Satō (2000).

6. For the definition of social welfare here, see the website of the Institute of National Institute of Population and Social Security Research (http://www.ipss.go.jp).

7. After the power alternation in 2009, the Ministry of Health, Labour, and Welfare changed its position that it was unable to estimate the take-up rate and published six types of estimates ranging from 15.3 % to 87.4% (as of 2004 and 2007). The variation in these figures results from the different surveys and estimation methods used. For details, see http://www.mhlw.go.jp/stf/houdou/2r98520000005olmimg/2r98520000005oof.pdf.

8. In terms of benefit replacement rates, which is the ratio of annual benefit level to annual income of the average production worker, the Japanese pension level for wage earners is not internationally low (Allan and Scruggs 2004; Estévez-Abe 2008). This is not the case for those who only receive the People's Pension. Overall, "transfer-heavy" features cannot be applied to Japan.

9. Pempel (1998, 188) points out that Japan's welfare expansion in the 1970s resembles the Bismarckian model more than the Beveridgeian, as it was created by a conservative government rather than a social democratic government.

10. My assertion that employment maintenance can be substituted for income maintenance (Miura 2002) is largely accepted by Japanese scholars (see, e.g., Miyamoto 2008; Ōsawa 2007).

11. Bonoli (2003) focuses on two sorts of labor market-based social policy instruments namely, the legal regulation of the labor market and self-regulation by collective bargaining which are functionally equivalent to income replacement programs.

12. On the relationship between welfare regimes and types of labor market institutions, see Kolberg (1992); Kolberg and Esping-Andersen (1992). On the usefulness of comparative research on subcategories of welfare states, see Kasza (2002).

13. Japan concentrates its social spending on the elderly (see Lynch 2006; Miyamoto 2008).

14. Chapter 4 briefly discusses how similar levels of production market regulation in Continental European countries and Japan resulted in significantly different levels of employment maintenance, which attests to the importance of the role played by labor market policy.

15. The occupation forces in the postwar period did influence the development of the Japanese welfare state by imparting liberal tendencies, but this influence was largely negated after Japan's independence in 1952. More important, certain kinds of liberal tradition already existed in Japan even in the prewar period. The emphasis on self-help can be found in conservative discourses (Garon 1997; Ishida 1989).

16. Garon (1997) stresses the importance of ideology in the development of Japanese welfare state.

17. For a succinct review of partisan theory, see M. Schmidt (2010).

Chapter 3

1. I follow the periodization offered by Curtis (1988).

2. The Japan Democratic Party's platform is reprinted in Jiyū Minshutō (1987, 1132–1134).

3. The platform of the Reform Party, declared in 1952 on Empire Day (February 11; today known as National Foundation Day), a day symbolic of Japan's prewar regime, states that the party aimed to pursue socialistic policies in order to correct the problems of capitalism. The platform is reprinted in Jiyū Minshutō (1987, 1128–1130).

4. *Asahi Shimbun,* April 8, 1953.

5. When the right-wing Socialist Party clarified its seven major policies in 1952, the construction of a welfare state was not included. See Amamiya (1997, 102). In 1955 and thereafter, the JSP stated in its policy platform that it aimed to transform the Japanese state into a welfare state and a cultural state.

6. See also Miyazaki (1988) and Hiwatari (1991).

7. It was because of pressure from Ishibashi (1970, 215–216) that the Japan Democratic Party included full employment in its policy pledges. Ishibashi (1959) did not only advocate countercyclical fiscal policy, but also argued that Japan was in a situation of "disguised full employment" in which full employment was achieved in some sectors, but not in others. In such conditions, he argued, government intervention should not be limited to fiscal and monetary policy but extended to various industrial policies.

8. Under the Hatoyama cabinet, Ishibashi was not appointed finance minister. Hatoyama nominated Ichimada Hisato instead, pursuing a policy of austerity. Ishibashi's commitment to full employment was nonetheless included as part of Hatoyama's Five-Year Economic Independence Plan.

9. *Nihon Keizai Shimbun* (December 15, 1956), reprinted in Ishibashi (1970, 325–326).

10. Although Ishibashi was clearly more interested in fiscal expansion than tax cuts, he decided to implement a relatively large tax cut simply because it was the most popular policy at the time (Ōtake 1991). Later, Kōsai Yutaka (1981, 113), a prominent economist, evaluates this "100 billion tax cut, 100 billion projects" very favorably as a model for fiscal policy during the high-speed economic growth period.

11. Historians reveal that the income doubling plan had two origins: one developed by Kishi and Ōkita Saburō at the Economic Planning Agency and the other by Ikeda and Shimomura Osamu at the Ministry of Finance. The former, based on Keynesian theory, stressed the demand-side economy, whereas the latter proposed supply-side policy influenced by Schumpeter (Kouno 2002, 198–204; see also Asai 2000). Kishi's appointment of Ikeda as minister of international trade and industry led to the materialization of Ikeda's income doubling idea as part of Kishi's economic plan.

12. Translated by the Japan Productivity Center (reorganized as the Japan Productivity Center for Socio-Economic Development in 1994). See http://www.jpcsed.or.jp/eng/mission/principle.html.

13. On Sōhyō's critique, see Tsutsui (1998: 141–146). Sōhyō's arguments are nicely documented in a journal published by the Japan Productivity Center, which collected important official statements made by Sōhyō and related intellectuals regarding the productivity movement (Seisansei Kenkyū, vol. 19, 1960).

14. See also Garon and Mochizuki (1993).

15. Enterprise-level unions appeared sympathetic to the productivity movement from the beginning (Nihon Seisansei Honbu 1985). Sōhyō did not oppose cooperation for the purpose of productivity increase per se, but opposed the movement as organized by the Japan Productivity Center and business leaders. The anti-productivity movement was designated as its first goal of struggle in 1957 and 1958, only to be replaced, in 1959, by opposition to revision of the US-Japan Security Treaty. Thereafter, anti-productivity was framed more broadly in terms of struggle against rationalization (Nihon Rōdō Kumiai Sōhyōgikai, 1974).

16. The term was co-invented by James C. Abegglen and his translator (Kameyama 1994; Nomura 2007). Abegglen published *The Japanese Factory* in 1958 in which he used the term "lifetime commitment," which was then translated into Japanese as "lifetime employment."

17. See also Gordon (1985, 386–396) on the process resulting in the creation of the myth of permanent employment.

18. Both Kuraishi and Ishida were career politicians in a long line of Hatoyama Liberals. They were very close to Ishibashi Tanzan, worked tirelessly to establish Ishibashi's cabinet, and supported Ishibashi's "Small Japan Thesis" (Shō Nippon shugi) which, criticizing Japan's prewar military expansion, proposed that Japan should become a non-military economic superpower.

19. On differences between Kuraishi and Ishida, see, for instance, Sorai (1993, 137). On Kuraishi's views, see Iijima (1987, 347).

20. The LDP's New Labor Policy Outline was published in its monthly journal, *Seisaku Geppō* (August 1957: 64–73).

21. Nakakita Kōji provides a thorough historical analysis of the formation of the 1955 system, arguing that the Five-Year Economic Independence Plan and the productivity movement had the same political goal; namely, to counter mounting socialist influence. See Nakakita (2002, 239).

22. The National Health Insurance System Law passed in 1958, and the National Pension System Law and the Welfare Pensions for the Aged, Mothers, and Children, and Disabled Persons Law passed the following year.

23. The term "universality" describes "the provision of a specific welfare benefit independently of individual income and/or other individual characteristics" (Bergh 2004, 745). Though the Japanese social insurance system achieved comprehensive coverage, coverage remained segmented and thus was not universal.

24. For instance, the Reform Party pressured the government to revive military pensions (*gunjin onkyū*).

25. When Kishi commented in 1956 that the LDP would pursue comprehensive coverage of health insurance and pensions, this statement followed immediately on the heels of a comment on the necessity to strengthen home security to counter international communist activities, which suggests that Kishi's agenda with respect to social security was linked to his anti-communist stance. *Asahi Shimbun*. March 25, 1956.

26. Soeda (1995) is critical of the impact of the Asahi litigation and the mass movement and instead emphasizes the autonomous role of welfare bureaucrats who were willing to substantiate the right to life. See Milly (1999, ch. 7) on litigations based on Article 25.

27. Ministry of Finance, *Zaisei Tōkei* (various years), Tokyo: Ōkurashō Insatsukyoku.

28. For detailed accounts of the new programs facilitating employment adjustment, see Ministry of Labour (1978), Ujihara (1989), Kume (1998, 1995), Takanashi (1995), and Hamaguchi (2004).

29. Employment policy became integrated with industrial policy. In particular, enactment of the Provisional Measure for Laid-Off Workers in Designated Depressed Industries Law (1977) and the Provisional Measure for Laid-Off Workers in Designated Depressed Areas Law (1978) resulted in the use of the Employment Stability Fund as a subsidy for industrial restructuring rather than for the compensation of employees hit by cyclical fluctuations in business conditions.

30. Seasonal workers recurrently received benefits as an integral part of their yearly income, and young female workers received them even if they then left the labor force. Although the JSP and JCP opposed cutbacks, opposition parties did not use the argument that young female workers were not bona fide recipients. In fact, the argument that young female workers abused the system repeatedly appeared in later reform deliberations.

31. The idea of using the unemployment insurance account for the purpose of employment maintenance originated in the 1950s. By 1974, employment maintenance programs de facto accounted for approximately 35% of the expenditure from the unemployment insurance account. This was because the account consistently produced surpluses thanks to low unemployment rates and the fact that there was a need at the time to financially assist structurally depressed industries such as the coalmining, shipbuilding, and fiber industries. The MOL intended to institutionalize this practice by enacting the Employment Insurance Law.

32. For instance, Murakami Yasusuke, a prominent economic sociologist, edited a volume on the future of the Japanese type of welfare society, presenting the concept of welfare society (Murakami and Rōyama 1975).

33. These include Morishima Michio's *Watashi no Mita Eikoku Byō* (Kansai Keizai Kenkyū Sentā, 1975), Nakamura Chūichi's *Igirisu Byō, Itaria Byō, Nihon Byō* (Tōyō Keizai Shinpōsha, 1976), Kayama Ken'ichi's *Eikoku Byō no Kyōkun* (PHP Kenkyūjo, 1978), Murata Kunio's *Igirisu Byō no Seijigaku* (Kōyō Shobō, 1990), Sako Kanzō's *Thatcher: Josei Saishō to Igirisu Byō* (Kyōikusha, 1980). Among these, Kayama's book was probably the most well read. He is thought to have been one of the writers of Group 1984 (Shinkawa 1993: 117). Peter Wiles's *British Disease, Soviet Disease, Japanese Disease: A Sovietologist's View of Japan* (Shinpyōsha, 1979) was also published only in Japanese.

34. These include Paul Einzig's *Decline or Fall? Britain's Crisis in the Sixties* (Macmillan, 1969), Robert Bacon and Walter Eltis's *Britain's Economic Problem: Too Few Producers* (Macmillan, 1976), George Mikes' *How to Be Decadent* (Deutsch, 1977), Andrew Glyn and John Harrison's *The British Economic Disaster* (Pluto Press, 1980), Louis Heren's *Alas, alas for England: What Went Wrong with Britain* (Hamilton, 1981). The fact that none of these books used the "British Disease" in their titles suggests that translators or publishers considered the term appealing to the Japanese audience. These imported "British Disease" analyses were not all neoliberal propaganda. Glyn and Harrison are radical Marxist economists and Mikes is a well-known humorous essay writer. Interestingly, the US Library of Congress lists only three books that contain the words the "British Disease" in their tittles published in the 1970s. None of them were translated into Japanese. This suggests that Japanese publishing industry developed its own " British Disease" business without much reference to debates in the English language.

35. On the affinity between statism and neoliberalism, see also Crouch (2005). See Levy (2006) on the new activities of the state in the context of post-industrial society.

36. For a critical assessment of the people's burden rate, see Satomi (1994). Satomi also argues that the people's burden rate has the effect of exaggerating the size of

the Japanese government. The standard way to measure the size of the government is the total tax revenue as a percentage of GDP rather than national income. Because national income is smaller than GDP, the people's burden rate tends to overemphasize the size of the government as compared to the standard measurement. Similarly, Sumiya Mikio, a prominent social policy scholar, has also criticized the people's burden rate, labeling it a "fake" (*inchiki*) concept manufactured by the Ministry of Finance (*Shūkan Shakai Hoshō Kenkyū* 1731 [1993.3.15], 9). The Social Security System Advisory Council (Shakai Hoshō Seido Shingikai), headed by Professor Sumiya, notably avoided referring to the people's burden rate in its report on the Future of Social Security published in February 1993.

37. Ministry of Health, Labour, and Welfare, *Shakai Fukushi Gyōsei Gyōmu Hōkoku* (Social Assistance Administration Report). See http://www.ipss.go.jp/s-info/j/seiho/seiho.asp.

38. See Shinozuka (1989) for a critical assessment of the Employment Adjustment Allowance and Nitta (2008) on its role for forming a social consensus. The Employment Stability Fund funded various employment-related enterprises such as the construction of refreshment centers, gymnasiums, swimming pools, convention centers, and housing for displaced workers. These enterprises were often administered by organizations that accepted retired bureaucrats from the MOL. The Employment Stability Fund thus not only served to bolster employment maintenance in general but also the employment security of MOL officials in particular.

39. There is disagreement among scholars as to whether welfare reform in the 1980s should be interpreted as retrenchment. Although copayment of health-care insurance was reintroduced for the aged, the MHW also expanded various health service activities. See Campbell (1984), Shinkawa (1993), and Estévez-Abe (2008). The long-term care insurance introduced in 2000 also sparked a similar debate in academia. One of the program's aims was to reduce the burden borne by medical insurance due to the lack of welfare institutions for the bedridden elderly. For a critical view, see, for instance, Itō (2001) and Niki (2007).

Chapter 4

1. The 1994 pension reform extended the pensionable age for the flat-rate basic pension from 60 to 65, taking effect in 2001 for men and 2006 for women. The 2000 reform further extended the pensionable age for the income-related public pension from 60 to 65, which will become effective in 2013 for men and 2018 for women. Completion of both extensions is scheduled to take twelve years.

2. For instance, see the *National Westminster Bank* case (the third provisional disposition), Tokyo District Court, January 21, 2000, *Rōdō Hanrei* 782: 23.

3. Interview with a Rengō official (October 22, 2008). See also Araki (2005).

4. The dismissal law was moved from the Labor Standards Law (Art. 18–2) to the Labor Contract Law (Art. 16) in 2007.

5. Ministry of Health, Labour, and Welfare, "Kongo no Rōdō Keiyaku Hōsei no Arikata ni kansuru Kenkyūkai Hōkokusho" (Report of the Study Group on the Future of the Labor Contract Law System), September 15, 2005 (http://www.mhlw.go.jp/shingi/2005/09/s0915-4.html).

6. Controversial issues included the white-collar exemption system (see chapter 5), a monetary resolution system for unfair dismissals, and labor-management councils.

7. The *Shūhoku Bus* case (1968) and the *Daishi Ginkō* case (1997) provide the framework and standards for determinations of reasonableness. See Sugeno (2002, 120–125).

8. For instance, Zenrōren, the communist labor unions, and the ACW2 (Hataraku Josei no Zenkoku Sentā), an NGO created by women's unions, expressed their

opposition to the Labor Contract Law. The Japan Lawyers Association for Freedom (Jiyū Hōsōdan) and a group of thirty-five labor law scholars also issued statements, warning that the legislation of the Labor Contract Law would actually change legal practices to the disadvantage of workers.

9. More precisely, the government amended the implementation guidance under Article 44 of the Job Security Law, thereby relaxing the criteria of eligibility for labor supply businesses.

10. The government determined as early as 1963 that female labor force should be more effectively utilized (Keizai Shingikai, 1963). In 1966, the advisory council on women and minors within the Ministry of Labour focused on middle-age women as a human reserve for part-time labor.

11. Thirteen job types were originally listed, which was eventually extended to twenty-six job types.

12. Medical services are also exempted. The ministerial order lists types of medical services in which staffing businesses are not allowed to operate.

13. The one-year term limit was not applied to the original twenty-six job types listed in the former positive list because policymakers claimed that replacement of regular workers was unlikely to take place in these fields. Without legal basis, however, the MOL de facto set a three-year term limit on these twenty-six job types. This restriction was lifted in 2003.

14. The Job Security Law was amended in 1999, replacing the positive list with the negative list method in the realm of fee-charging placement services.

15. For instance, French law recognizes a limited list of cases in which client companies are able to accept temporary agency workers and forbids recourse to temporary placement in certain cases such as replacement of an employee on strike, dangerous work or following economic redundancies (Macaire and Michon 2006). Such regulation of the use of temporary agency workers is absent from Japanese law, although some unionists and experts have called for the introduction thereof.

16. Ministry of Health, Labour, and Welfare, "The General Survey of Part-Time Workers" (Pātotaimu Rōdōsha Sōgō Jittai Chōsa), 2001 (http://www.mhlw.go.jp/toukei/list/8-13.html).

17. Ministry of Health, Labour, and Welfare, "Kongo no Rōdōsha Haken Seido no Arikata ni Kansuru Kenkyūkai Hōkokusho" (Report of the Study Group on the Future of the Dispatching Manpower System), July 28, 2008 (http://www.mhlw.go.jp/houdou/2008/07/h0728-1.html).

18. Ministry of Health, Labour and Welfare, "Yūki Keiyaku Rōdōsha no Koyō Kanri no Kaizen ni Kansuru Kenkyūkai Hōkoku" (Report of the Study Group on the Improvement of Employment Management of Fixed-Term Workers), July 2008 (http://www.mhlw.go.jp/shingi/2008/07/s0729-1.html).

19. For regular workers, the case of the Toshiba Yanagimachi Factory (Supreme Court, 1974) set the precedent for subsequent cases, and for part-time workers, the case of Maruko Keiki (Nagano District Court, 1997) established the case law.

20. Ministry of Internal Affairs and Communications, *Labour Force Survey, Labour Force Special Survey* (http://www.stat.go.jp/data/roudou/).

21. Part-time workers as defined in the Part-Time Labor Law are workers whose total weekly working hours are fewer than the total hours worked by regular workers employed in the same workplace.

22. Art.3. Employers shall endeavor to promote effective utilization of Part-Time Workers' abilities in an effective manner, in due consideration of the actual work conditions of Part-Time Workers concerned, and *maintain balance with regular workers* by securing proper working conditions, implementing education and training, improving their welfare and improving employment management (translation by the Japan Institute of Workers' Evolution; italics added).

23. One of the key actors who contributed to the legislation of the Part-Time Labor Law was Ōwaki Masako, a labor law expert as well as a member of the House of Councillors (Japan Socialist Party, later DPJ). Ōwaki (2007) provides her account of the legislative process.

24. The official name of the study group is "Pātotaimu Rōdō ni Kakawaru Koyō Kanri Kenkyūkai."

25. The Japanese name of the study group is "Pātotaimu Rōdō Kenkyūkai." The Study Group on Part-Time Workers released a final report titled "Pāto Rōdō no Kadai to Taiō no Hōkōsei" (Challenges and Direction for Actions concerning Part-Time Work) on July 2002. See http://www.mhlw.go.jp/shingi/2002/07/s0719-3f.html.

26. Minutes of Proceedings, the Committee of Health, Labour and Welfare, House of Representatives, the 166th Diet, Issue No. 10, April 4, 2007.

27. The Japan Institute of Labour Policy and Training, "Tanjikan Rōdōsha Jittai Chōsa," December 2010 (http://www.jil.go.jp/press/documents/20101227.pdf).

28. Limitations on overtime work were set at 360 hours per year for men and 150 hours for women. Women in managerial positions and professional and technical positions became exempt to the limitation on overtime work for women. Maternity leave after childbirth was extended from four to six weeks.

29. As of 1991, 42.3% of large companies employing over 5,000 workers introduced course-based employment management. The share had increased to 55% in 2006. See Ministry of Health, Labour, and Welfare, *Joshi Koyō Kanri Kihon Chōsa*, 2006 (http://www.mhlw.go.jp/toukei/list/71-18.html).

30. In the mid-1990s, the proportion of women on the managerial track among the 300 large firms was 4.3% (Hiroishi 1995).

31. Ministry of Labour, "Kōsu-tō de Kubun shita Koyō Kanri ni tsuiteno Ryūi Jikō," June 2000 (http://tokyo-roudoukyoku.jsite.mhlw.go.jp/library/tokyo-roudoukyoku/seido/kintou/image/01_kintou/course_pamphlet.pdf).

32. Ministry of Health, Labour, and Welfare, "Kōsu betsu Koyō Kanri Seido no Jisshi Jōkyō to Shidō-tō Jōkyō ni tsuite," press release, October 5, 2001 (http://www.jil.go.jp/mm/siryo/20011010a.html); "Kōsu betsu Koyō Kanri Seido no Jisshi Jōkyō to Jogen-tō Jōkyō," press release, November 2, 2006 (http://www.mhlw.go.jp/houdou/2006/11/dl/h1102-3a.pdf).

33. The 1995 amendment of the Childcare Leave Law created provisions for family care leave, and changed the name of the law to the Childcare Family Care Leave Law. Those who take such leave are entitled to 25% of their basic salary during the period of leave. This was increased to 40% of basic pay in 1999 and to 50% in 2007 (as a provisional measure). The basic salary does not include various allowances, which usually account for 15–20% of monthly pay and biannual bonuses, which account for approximately one-third of annual income.

34. Employers vigorously opposed the creation of new protective measures and succeeded in restricting the criteria for eligibility. As a result, those who raise after-school-age children were excluded. The MOL subsequently also issued a directive that stated that workers who live with persons over the age of 16 are not able to claim this right.

35. These include criteria concerning (i) the worker's height, weight, or physical strength; (ii) the worker's availability for reassignment that results in relocation of the worker's residence; and (iii) whether or not the worker has experience of having been reassigned to a workplace other than that where the worker had formerly worked. The third criterion relates to the promotion of workers.

36. The EEOL provides a legal foundation for actions taken by the MHLW vis-à-vis employers. Even though the EEOL and subsequent ordinances have limited the specific criteria that are relevant to questions of indirect discrimination, there is still a possibility that the courts may apply the concept of indirect discrimination more broadly.

37. According to a survey conducted in 2006, 83.4% of companies that operate course-based employment management used the acceptance of relocation as a condition for the managerial track. Given that the corresponding figure in 2001 was 94.4%, gender discrimination based on family responsibilities has decreased, albeit to a limited degree. See the Ministry of Health, Labour, and Welfare, "Kōsu betsu Koyō Kanri Seido no Jisshi/Shidō-tō Jōkyō," October 5, 2001; November 2, 2006 (http://www.jil.go.jp/mm/siryo/20011010a.html).

38. Committee on the Elimination of Discrimination against Women, "Concluding Observations of the Committee on the Elimination of Discrimination against Women, Japan," August 7, 2009 (http://www2.ohchr.org/english/bodies/cedaw/docs/co/CEDAW.C.JPN.CO.6.pdf).

39. Ministry of Health, Labour, and Welfare, "Kōsu betsu Koyō Kanri Seido no Jisshi/Shidō-tō Jōkyō," press release, December 24, 2008. See http://www.mhlw.go.jp/houdou/2008/12/h1224-1.html. The survey is based on the MHLW's investigation of 123 companies that used employment management categories: 84.7% of the companies responded that the share of women on the managerial track was under 10%, whereas the share of women on the secretarial track was 77.9% overall and 90.0% among companies employing over 5,000; 30.1% of the companies only employed women on the secretarial track.

40. Ministry of Health, Labour, and Welfare, *Wage Structure Basic Survey* (http://www.mhlw.go.jp/toukei/itiran/roudou/chingin/kouzou/detail/index.html). I used scheduled wages per hour to estimate the wage gaps.

41. Women are more stratified in this respect than men. See Miura (2011b).

42. Although not stipulated by the law, the MHLW issued a directive in 2002 stating that the law should be applied to fixed-term workers who work in an equivalent manner to regular workers because of frequent renewal of contracts. The 2003 Labor Standards Law extended the limit of fixed-term labor contracts from one year to three years, which triggered the change in the Childcare Family Care Leave Law as it was not possible to justify not granting one year-long childcare leave to workers hired under three-year contracts.

43. Ministry of Health, Labour, and Welfare, press release, December 24, 2009 (http://www.mhlw.go.jp/stf/houdou/2r98520000003civ.html).

44. Cabinet Office, 2010, 3 and 2011, 59.

45. Takanashi Akira, the chairman of the advisory council that discussed the enactment of the Temporary Work Agency Law in 1985, later admitted this point in an interview by Takenobu Mieko, an *Asahi Shimbun* journalist (*Asahi Shimbun*. November 7, 2008). The complete elimination of protective measures for women, with the exception of maternity protection, was not implemented until the amendment of the Labor Standards Law in 1997.

46. See also Rueda (2007) for a political explanation of the insider-outsider gap.

47. A quarter of male workers ages 35–39 worked longer than 60 hours a week. See the Ministry of Health, Labour and Welfare, 2005, 319. The data are based on *Labour Force Survey*.

48. Data from the Ministry of Health, Labour, and Welfare. *Karōshi* includes deaths from both brain and heart disease as well as suicide.

49. *Nihon Keizai Shimbun*, August 4, 2008.

50. Osaka Karōshi Mondai Renrakukai (http://homepage2.nifty.com/karousiren rakukai/7 = Q&Atop.htm.)

51. *The Nikkei Marketing*, May 26, 2008. See also Weathers and North (2009/2010) for the trial cases against leading companies.

52. Ministry of Health, Labour and Welfare, "The General Survey of Part-Time Workers," (Pātotaimu Rōdōsha Sōgō Jittai Chōsa), 2001 (http://www.mhlw.go.jp/toukei/list/8-13.html).

53. Ministry of Internal Affairs and Communications, *Employment Status Survey,* 2007 (http://www.stat.go.jp/english/data/shugyou/index.htm).

54. These numbers are from the Ministry of Health, Labour and Welfare, *Shakai Fukushi Gyōsei Gyōmu Hōkokurei* (Social Assistance Administration Report). See http://www.ipss.go.jp/s-info/j/seiho/seiho.asp and http://www.mhlw.go.jp/toukei/list/381a.html.

55. Ōtake (2005) points out a growing income gap among youth as well as a growing gap in consumption expenditure among the young and middle-aged populations, which reflect a trend toward a growing gap in lifetime incomes.

56. The National Consumption Survey is conducted every five years by the Ministry of Internal Affairs and Communications. The Economic Planning Agency used the National Consumption Survey to compute the Gini coefficient in order to provide data to the OECD (see Nishizaki et al. 1998).

57. Ministry of Health, Labour and Welfare (http://www.mhlw.go.jp/toukei/saikin/hw/k-tyosa/k-tyosa10/).

58. Tachibanaki and Urakawa (2008) show that the poverty rate rose from 15.2% in 1995 to 16.2% in 1998 and 17.0% in 2001.

59. With respect to poverty, Japan is certainly closer to "Liberal American" than to "Socialist European." See Pontusson (2005a).

60. Ministry of Internal Affairs and Communications, *Labour Force Survey.* Temporary agency workers peaked in 2008 (8%) and have declined since then.

61. The OECD uses the indicator of "product market regulation" to measure the degree to which policies promote or hinder competition. The indicator covers formal regulations such as state control of business enterprises, legal and administrative barriers to entrepreneurship, and barriers to international trade and investment. See OECD Stat at http://stats.oecd.org.

62. *Asahi Shimbun,* January 20, 2009.

63. On the number of unemployment benefit recipients, see the Ministry of Health, Labour, and Welfare, 2006. On the numbers of unemployed, see *Labour Force Survey.* If we calculate only those who have quit or been fired from a job—that it, excluding first-time job seekers—the proportion of recipients is 30%.

Chapter 5

1. Regarding the approach of using revealed preferences instead of actual stated preferences, see Vogel (2006, 52).

2. Nikkeiren (1995b).

3. Nikkeiren (1998).

4. Excerpt of Okuda's speech at Nikkeiren's management top seminar on August 5–6, 1999 (*Shūkan Rōdō News,* August 30, 1999) (translated by the author).

5. *Nikkeiren Times,* November 4, 1999.

6. Ishihara Takashi, chairman of Keizai Dōyūkai (1985–1991) and president of Nissan (1977–1985), paved the way for this fundamental transformation (Kikuchi 2005).

7. Keizai Dōyūkai, "Kojin no Jiritsu to Chōwa: Nihongata Koyō Kankō no Chūchōki Tenbō," 1994; "2010 nen ni Mukete Korekara no Rōdō no Arikata," 1992.

8. *Asahi Shimbun,* May 19, 2007.

9. On the internal division of Japanese business between the domestic sector and the international sector, see Pempel (1998).

10. The extent to which the Industrial Revitalization Law (IRL) actually brought about labor force reductions remains a point of controversy. Unions and some sections of the press condemned the law, arguing that the IRL would encourage lay-offs. It may be the case that government support under the IRL scheme reduced the scope

of personnel reductions that Japanese companies would have otherwise carried out. Headline-making restructuring plans such as those of Nissan, NTT, and Mitsubishi Motors were announced before the IRL became effective. With regard to the submission of restructuring plans, companies that applied for government support under the IRL proclaimed that they did not intend to dismiss their regular employees as part of their restructuring plans. See the Ministry of Economy, Trade and Industry's web page at http://www.meti.go.jp/policy/business_infra/4.html. Similarly, Tiberghien (2007, 136) argues that the IRL was a comparatively milder tool than the direct restructuring tools used by Korea and France.

11. Although business associations embrace conflicting interests and must formulate abstract policies that please everyone, individual business leaders freely voice their personal convictions. Pempel (1998, 215) points out that Keidanren, which is publicly supportive of the principles of deregulation, is internally divided on most specifics. See also Vogel (2006, 56–58).

12. These policy proposals are collected from various official position papers and official demands made public by either Nikkeiren or Keidanren in the 1990s. The main documents were Nikkeiren and Keidanren's "Demands for Removal and Deregulation of Government Regulation" (the exact title varies each time), which were regularly submitted to the Deregulation Subcommittee (1995–1997), the Regulatory Reform Committee (1998–2000), and the government as well as Nikkeiren's annual reports and proposals on industrial relations (Nikkeiren, 1992, 1993, 1994, 1995a, 1996, 1997, 1998, 1999, 2000). Not all of their proposals made it onto the agenda of formal policy-making procedure. The list does not take account of chronological shifts in preferences or the intensity of preferences. It simply compiles all the demands made during the 1990s.

13. Nikkeiren (1995a).

14. Nomura (2007) argues that there are various definitions of "base-up," which makes it easier to fabricate a standardized base-up while allowing an individual company to drift significantly from a standard wage level.

15. In the spring offensive of 2006, unions succeeded in securing wage increases in certain industries such as the automobile and electronics industries, ending five consecutive years of wage decreases.

16. Bank of Japan, *Outlook for Economic Activity and Prices* (April 2007), released on May 1, 2007 (http://www.boj.or.jp/en/type/release/teiki/tenbo/index.htm).

17. Ministry of Health, Labour, and Welfare, *Rōdō Sōgi Tōkei Chōsa* (various years) (http://www.mhlw.go.jp/toukei/list/14-22.html).

18. The Supreme Court, General Office and Administration Office, "Rōdō Kankei Minji/Gyōsei Jiken no Gaikyō", *Hōsō Jihō*, 52(8), 62(8).

19. Kisei Kaikaku Iinkai, "Kisei Kaikaku ni tsuite no Dainiji Kenkai," December 14, 1999 and "Ronten Kōkai," July 26, 2000.

20. *Asahi Shimbun*, June 7, 2001.

21. Kisei Kaikaku Iinkai, "Kisei Kaikaku ni tsuite no Kenkai," December 12, 2000.

22. *Asahi Shimbun*, May 11, 2001.

23. "Kisei Kaikaku Suishin Sankanen Keikaku (Kaitei)" endorsed by the cabinet on March 29, 2002.

24. *Nihon Keizai Shimbun*, November 8, 2001.

25. *Keiei Times*, November 14, 2002.

26. *Shūkan Rōdō News*, November 12, 2001; *Nihon Keizai Shimbun*, November 7, 2001.

27. See Miura (2005) on the precise wording in Japanese.

28. In 1969, Nikkeiren issued a report titled "Meritocratic Management" (*nōryokushugi kanri*).

29. The *Toa Paint* case, Supreme Court, July 14, 1986. See also chapter 1.

30. On informal groups, see Gordon (1998). Hisamoto (1998) argues that pie theory was not appealing to ordinary workers, which necessitated the use of informal groups to convince workers.

31. Nitta (2008) argues that both employers and workers have understood lifetime employment in a flexible way: employers endeavor to avoid dismissals as much as possible and workers and unions cooperate with employers in order to avoid being dismissed. Acceptance of relocation is an instance of worker cooperation in this regard.

32. Sasamori Kiyoshi, "Nihon teki Rōshi Kankei no Henkaku," *Business Labor Trends,* November 2006.

33. Ministry of Health, Labour, and Welfare, "Koyō Kanri Chōsa" (2006) (http://www.mhlw.go.jp/toukei/itiran/roudou/koyou/kanri/kanri04/index.html). Massive scale solicitations of voluntary retirement took place shortly after the financial crisis of 1998–1999 and the economic recession of 2001–2003. See *Nikkei Sangyō Shimbun,* August 18, 1999; Tokyo Shoko Research, Keizai Kenkyūshitsu (http://www.tsr-net.co.jp/new/data/1187858_818.html).

34. Ministry of Internal Affairs and Communications, *Labour Force Survey* (http://www.stat.go.jp/data/roudou/).

35. See also Miura (2008a), and Suzuki (2009) which supports my view.

36. Ministry of Economy, Trade and Industry, *Kaigai Jigyō Katsudō Kihon Chōsa* (http://www.meti.go.jp/statistics/tyo/kaigaizi/index.html).

37. Dai-ichi Life Research Institute Inc., *Economic Trends,* March 6, 2007 (http://group.dai-ichi-life.co.jp/dlri/kuma/pdf/k_0703b.pdf).

38. Overseas profits include exports and profits made by overseas subsidiaries.

39. Tokyo Stock Exchange, "2008 Shareownership Survey" (http://www.tse.or.jp/english/market/data/shareownership/english2008.pdf).

40. Bank of Japan, *Outlook for Economic Activity and Prices* (April 2007) (http://www.boj.or.jp/en/type/release/teiki/tenbo/index.htm).

41. For the data on 1993, see Nikkeiren (1995a). Other data can be found in the various annual editions of the same position papers.

42. Japan Institute of Labour Policy and Training, *Dēta Bukku Kokusai Rōdō Hikaku* (various years).

43. Ministry of Finance, *Trade Statistics* (http://www.customs.go.jp/toukei/info/index.htm).

44. The race to the bottom can be triggered not only by capital flight but also by trade and migration (Flanagan 2006).

45. Ministry of Health, Labour, and Welfare, annual press release on the business reports of temporary work agencies as well as their annual press release on the business reports of private placement services.

46. *Nihon Keizai Shimbun,* June 1, 2006.

47. The Association of Job Journals of Japan, the Japan Executive Search and Recruitment Association, and the Japan Staffing Services Association organized a study group to explore the future of labor market services, which in March 2002 published a proposition titled "Proposition for the Vitalization of the Labor Market Service Industry."

48. Among the three areas of Hello Work activities, which had already been exposed to market testing, the government decided to continue with market testing only in the case of career exchange plazas. The results of market testing showed that the public sector provided the services at lower cost and more effectively. Among the three areas, the cost gap between the public and private sectors was relatively small in the career exchange plazas (although the public sector performed better), which is the main reason why the government decided to continue to use market testing in that

area (personal communication with the Ministry of Health, Labour, and Welfare, September 8, 2009).

Chapter 6

1. *Zoku* politicians, or policy tribes, are middle-ranking LDP politicians who ally with a certain ministry or agency in order to appropriate budgets and in return wield a strong influence over policy on a day-to-day basis. These tribes are compartmentalized according to ministerial boundaries and mainly pressure bureaucrats to address their electoral concerns.

2. *Nihon Keizai Shimbun,* August 7, 1996; October 3, 1996.

3. Note that the total number of seats was reduced from 511 to 500.

4. During the electoral campaign, the DPJ pledged to create an Administrative Surveillance and Evaluation Committee under the Diet, which differentiated it from the LDP and the NFP.

5. Other members are the minister of finance, the minister of internal affairs and communications, the minister of economy, trade and industry, and the governor of the Bank of Japan.

6. Mizuno Kiyoshi, secretary general of the Administrative Reform Conference, advocated the inclusion of non-government representatives, such as academic economists and businesspersons, to counterbalance the Ministry of Finance, despite opposition from the ministry. Further, during the deliberations of the Administrative Reform Conference, the CEFP was not conceived as a business-friendly commission, but the inclusion of labor representatives was also discussed.

7. *Nihon Keizai Shimbun,* May 19, 2001.

8. *Nihon Keizai Shimbun,* December 20, 2000.

9. On the Economic Strategy Council, see Tiberghien (2007).

10. Frustrated with bureaucratic coordination, big business sought direct access to political decision making. Keidanren frequently lobbied the LDP to propose politician-sponsored bills in order to bypass the advisory councils. For example, Keidanren and the LDP's Commerce and Industry Committee worked together to draft a bill to revise the Commerce Act, which has been revised every year since 1997 (*Nihon Keizai Shimbun,* January 8, 2002).

11. The repeated reorganization resulted from the fact that the deregulation panels were the successors of the third Provisional Council for the Promotion of Administrative Reform, which also had a three-year mandate.

12. From April 1995 until April 1996, Shiina Takeo (chairman of Japan IBM) chaired the Deregulation Subcommittee. Shiina resigned as his one-year appointment expired.

13. Regarding the concept of agenda, I follow Kingdon's definition referring to "the list of subjects or problems to which governmental officials, and people outside of government closely associated with these officials, are paying some serious attention at any given time" (1984/1995, 3).

14. On the relationship between Rengō and the LDP during this period, see Miura (2011a).

15. Representatives of temporary staff agencies now attend the meetings as observers.

16. In March 1995, the Murayama cabinet endorsed the Deregulation Plan, the first such plan to be officially approved. It was annually revised in the following years. The Three-Year Deregulation Plan has been endorsed since 1998.

17. It was the Economic Strategy Council that had proposed to rename the Deregulation Committee as the Regulatory Reform Committee and expand membership.

18. The idea of market testing had already appeared in the CCRR's final report issued December 2003.

19. For the reports and minutes, see the CEFP's website at http://www5.cao.go.jp/keizai-shimon/special/work/index.html.

20. Hamaguchi (2007) points out that the CPRR had already changed its position by the summer of 2007, displaying a negative attitude toward the monetary resolution system for dismissals that it had previously demanded. Instead, it adopted an even more radical position by claiming that dismissal should be freely implemented without monetary compensation.

21. The Task Force on Labor Issues was dissolved in June 2007. The Task Force on Employment Opportunities, led by the economist Hatta Tatsuo, became the arena within the CRR for discussion of employment policy, and focused on employment opportunities rather than labor market reform.

22. The Japanese Diet has amended government bills more frequently than other parliamentary democracies such as the United Kingdom, France, and Germany (Iwai 1988). Several legislative rules allow opposition parties to block legislation, thereby giving the cabinet and the ruling party an incentive to incorporate demands made by opposition parties: the short term of the ordinary session (150 days), the principle holding that any matters unresolved during one session of the Diet should not be carried over to the next session, and the Diet law stipulating that only one extension is allowed for the ordinary session and two extensions for special and provisional sessions.

23. See Miura (2005) for details.

24. Professional jobs included designers, producers, directors, information technicians, and research and development engineers. Another six professional job-types were added to the list in 1997.

25. On the detailed preconditions for introducing the discretionary working hour rules to planning personnel (*kikaku gyōmu-gata sairyō rōdōsei*), see Sugeno (2000: 296–299). Both Rengō and Nikkeiren admitted that the new rules based on the 1998 amendment would not facilitate the introduction of the discretionary working hour rules (interview with Kumagai Ken'ichi, director of Labor Law Division, Rengō, July 21, 2000; interview with Nikkeiren's Labor Law Department, September 7, 2000).

26. Rengō opposed the expansion of discretionary working hour rules, but some of its affiliated industrial federations—the Japan Automobile Workers' Union and the Japan Electrical Electronic and Information Union—supported it, which made it difficult for Rengō to take concerted action at the advisory council.

27. Interview with a policy secretary of a DPJ politician involved in the legislation (September 19, 2000).

28. See Miura (2005) for details.

29. The Hashimoto cabinet pressured Soya by suspending his promotion to vice minister, which was eventually announced two days after the bill was submitted to the Diet in October 1998 (*Asahi Shimbun,* July 14, 2007).

30. Although the main text of the law did not place the manufacturing sector on the negative list, an exception clause made such an allowance.

31. As Weathers (2004) shows, the 1999 Temporary Work Agency Law does not provide enough protection to temporary agency workers. However, compared to the original government bill, the amendments at the Diet bolstered some of the protective measures therein.

32. See Miura (2005) for details.

33. *Asahi Shimbun,* September 19, 2001.

34. See a press release from the Tokyo Labor Bureau (http://www.roudoukyoku.go.jp/news/2007/20070608-sairyo/20070608-sairyo.html).

35. Ministry of Health, Labour, and Welfare, "Kongo no Rōdō Keiyaku Hōsei no Arikata ni kansuru Kenkyūkai Saishū Hōkoku" (Report of the Study Group on the

Future of the Labor Contract Law System), September 15, 2005 (http://www.mhlw.
go.jp/shingi/2005/09/s0915-4.html).

36. In 12 prefectures, minimum wages were lower than social assistance when one
compares a monthly wage at the minimum wage level based on a 40-hour working
week to the average social assistance allowance. Based on the passage of the 2007
Minimum Wage Law, the government aimed to correct this incongruity within two to
five years (*Asahi Shimbun,* September 13, 2008). The government had also increased
the minimum wage in 2007 by ¥14 on average, which was triple the increase of the
previous year.

37. Abe cabinet amended the Part-Time Labor Law in 2007 with the same political
motivation. See chapter 4 on the content of the Part-Time Labor Law.

38. In February 2007, responding to a demand from the DPJ, the Social Security
Agency revealed that, as of June 2006, 50 million public pension transactions could
not be linked to the identification numbers of those who had paid contributions. The
LDP's mismanagement of the record-keeping debacle led to its defeat in the Upper
House election in July of the same year.

39. Hosokawa Ritsuo, a DPJ member of the Parliamentary Committee on Health,
Labour, and Welfare, who negotiated with the LDP regarding the amendment of the
government bill, has recalled that he was afraid that the LDP would abort all three of
the labor bills without sitting at the negotiation table. He believed that the DPJ should
not adopt an obstinate stance on labor policy and, instead, should prioritize negotiation with the LDP. See his comments in the roundtable talk published in RENGO,
February 2008, 20–23.

40. This was an expression used by Hosokawa Ritsuo (Habermeyer 2008, 66). See
the same source for more on the negotiation process between the DPJ and the LDP.

41. Rengō claimed that the actual wording of the government bill differed from the
basic items of the bill (*hōan yōkō*) on which the advisory council had agreed. Rengō
raised six issues and the DPJ was successful in amending the wording in each case.

42. The DPJ had proposed to insert "equal treatment," but the LDP counterpro-
posed the term "balanced treatment" (Habermeyer 2008, 71). As discussed in chapter 4, the conflict between "balanced treatment" and "equal treatment" has a long
history. Japanese conservatives consistently and tenaciously oppose the concept of
equality.

43. For between 45 and 60 hours overtime work per month, employers and unions
became able to set the premium at over 25%. However, small and medium-size companies were exempted from the new regulations for at least the first three years, which
meant that 80% of workers were not covered. The DPJ unsuccessfully demanded that
the law be applied to all workers.

44. Arendt Lijphart (1999) lists ten characteristics of the Westminster model: (1)
concentration of executive power in one-party and bare majority cabinets, (2) cabinet
dominance, (3) a two-party system, (4) a majoritarian and disproportional system of
elections, (5) interest group pluralism, (6) a unitary and centralized system of government, (7) concentration of legislative power in a unicameral legislature, (8) constitutional flexibility, (9) absence of judicial review, and (10) a central bank controlled by
the executive (9–47). Mulgan (2002, 169–170) points out that Japan exhibits all these
features except those relating to the concentration of executive power and executive
(cabinet) dominance, a two-party system and constitutional flexibility (due to the existence of a written constitution).We need to add that asymmetric bicameralism is also
absent in Japan, as Japan features strong bicameralism.

45. In Japanese academia, the term "bureaucratic cabinet system" (*kanryō naikakusei*) is often used to describe the same structure (see Iio 2007).

46. Lijphart (1999) argues that strong cabinet leadership depends on majority
support in the lower house and the cohesiveness of the majority party. Therefore,

cabinets lose some of their predominance when either or both of these conditions is absent. He also argues that a disciplined two-party system gives rise to executive dominance.

Chapter 7

1. The LDP polled 47.8% of the votes under the single-member districts and 38.2% of the votes under the proportional representation system. With the votes polled by its coalition partner, Kōmeitō, the ruling parties secured 327 seats (68.1%). Under the single-member districts, they secured 227 seats (75.7%), but received only 49.2% of the votes. This discrepancy was facilitated by the first-past-the-post system. The number of seats under proportional representation had been reduced from 300 to 280 in 2000, leaving a total of 480 seats.

2. For Yosano (2008) for his views.

3. Koizumi refused to give party endorsement to those who opposed his postal privatization bill and, further, endorsed "assassins" to run against the rebels. However, Abe reversed Koizumi's decision and accepted any rebels who wished to return to the LDP and Abe's successor, Prime Minister Fukuda, even nominated Noda Seiko, a leading figure in the opposition to postal privatization, as minister of consumer affairs.

4. From 2001 to 2006 under the Koizumi cabinet, the big-boned policy was officially called "Basic Policies for Economic and Fiscal Management and Structural Reform." From 2007 to 2009 under the Abe, Fukuda, and Asō cabinets, it was referred to as the "Basic Policies for Economic and Fiscal Management."

5. In 2004, the government revised the Pension Law such that the premiums for employee pension programs would increase annually for fourteen years until becoming fixed at 18.3% of a worker's annual salaries, and benefits would be kept at 50% of average disposable incomes. Public confidence in this measure was low due to political scandals that erupted in the spring of 2004 involving the failure of certain politicians to pay pension premiums. Many observers believe that guaranteeing a 50% benefit ratio is unrealistic.

6. On the DPJ's neoliberal stance, see Schoppa (2006b).

7. NHK (Japan Broadcasting Corporation) broadcasted a documentary, "The Working Poor: Not Becoming Affluent despite Working Hard," in July 2006 and Yuasa Makoto's books ringing alarm bells about rising poverty were published the same year.

8. The Asō cabinet compiled a supplementary budget of ¥ 13.9 trillion, which far surpassed the measures enacted by Prime Minister Obuchi in 1998 to secure the previous record of ¥7.7 trillion. See *Nihon Keizai Shimbun*, April 16, 2009, evening edition. Prime Minister Hatoyama's government broke the record again in 2010.

9. The same message was translated into English and published in the *New York Times* (August 26, 2009) under the title "A New Path for Japan."

10. It is not clear as to why Hatoyama Ichirō chose the term *yūai* instead of *hakuai*, the usual translation of "fraternity." Hatoyama Yukio explains that his grandfather chose the term *yūai* in order to emphasize that fraternity is a strong and combative concept underlying revolution. The word *yūai* originated from the Friendly Society created by Suzuki Bunji and represents the principle of cooperatism. Whether or not it was deliberate, his choice of the term *yūai* must have conveyed the message that Hatoyama Ichirō supported cooperatism.

11. Esping-Andersen argues that Sweden practices "productivist social justice," as it "invests in optimizing people's capacity to be productive citizens" (1994, 722; see also Esping-Andersen 1999). This idea later developed into the concept of the "social investment state" wherein the welfare state invests in the younger generation's acquisition of human capital (see, e.g., Lister 2004). I contend that productivist elements in the DPJ's vision as well as in that of Ishibashi Tanzan are a variant of this kind of

productivist thinking, although the Japanese version does not explicitly use the term "investment" and is less focused on education.

12. In 2000, the European Council set up the Lisbon Strategy, which aimed to make the European Union the most competitive and dynamic knowledge-based economy in the world by 2010, formulating various policy initiatives to create jobs and sustain economic growth. On Third Way thinking, see Lewis and Surender (2004).

13. The LDP government had relied on societal partners to economize on welfare spending, such as regionally organized social welfare councils, social welfare corporations, welfare commissioners, and NPOs (Estévez-Abe 2003). Though the state defined what these organizations should and can do under LDP rule, the DPJ appears more willing to loosen the state's control over the initiatives of civil society.

14. The People's New Party was created by former LDP politicians who opposed Koizumi's postal reform such as Kamei Shizuka and Watanuki Tamisuke. These politicians criticize neoliberal reform from a conservative perspective. For instance, Kamei, as minister of transport in the 1990s, opposed the deregulation of the airplane industry, arguing that such policy would degrade the working conditions of flight attendants.

15. Ministry of Internal Affairs and Communications, *Labour Force Survey* (http://www.stat.go.jp/data/roudou/).

16. The DPJ created a non-regular employment measures project team, which began deliberations on temporary agency workers in September 2007. In April 2008, both the DPJ's department meeting (*bumon kaigi*) on welfare and labor issues and the shadow cabinet (*nekusuto kyabinetto*) endorsed the bill.

17. The Diet passed the revised bill agreed by the DPJ, LDP, and Kōmeitō in March 2012.

18. In contrast, the DPJ changed the membership of the advisory council on medical insurance issues (*chūō shakai hoken iryō kyōgikai*) in order to facilitate implementation of its policy in this area.

19. Previously, Japan provided neither housing allowances nor adequate quantities of public housing for low-income workers. It was often the case that dispatched workers lived in company domiciles. On Japanese housing policy, see Hirayama and Ronald (2006).

20. The family allowance system under the LDP government provided ¥10,000 per month for children under 3 and ¥5,000 for children over 3 until graduation from elementary school at the age of 12. The DPJ's child allowance not only increased the amount of the allowance but also extended the duration thereof until graduation from junior high school at the age of 15 and discontinued the income threshold. As a result, the budget for child allowances more than doubled. However, the DPJ abolished the tax exemption for heads of households raising children up to 15 years of age. Because tax exemption is highly regressive, the DPJ's reform package was rather progressive, which is another reason behind the LDP's disapproval.

21. In the 1990s, some Japanese schoolteachers began to use the term "gender free" in the context of gender sensitive educational programs and practices. The enactment of the Basic Law for a Gender Equal Society in 1999 triggered a backlash against gender equality, which led to the LDP's campaign against "gender free sex education" in the early 2000s. As a consequence, in 2006, the Cabinet Office notified local governments that they were not to use the term "gender free" in order to avoid confusion. Many local governments canceled lectures and social education programs that included the term and removed books with the titles including the terms "gender" or "gender free" from public libraries (*Asahi Shimbun,* May 12, 2006). See also Wakakuwa and Fujiwara-Fanselow (2011).

22. The term "gender" has been defined in official Japanese documents as a socially and culturally constructed sex. However, the Second Action Plan removed the

word "culturally." The plan stated that Japanese people do not support "gender free" activities that aim to eliminate masculinity and femininity and renounce Japanese culture and festivals based on traditional gendered roles. It also made the point that Japan does not officially endorse freedom of abortion, despite the fact that the Japanese government has accepted the concept of reproductive rights as internationally defined.

Conclusion

1. Ministry of Internal Affairs and Communications, *Labour Force Survey*. See http://www.stat.go.jp/data/roudou/.

2. Neoclassical economists and Marxists deduce actors' interests from their position in the economy. Explanations focusing on the *Varieties of Capitalism* (Hall and Soskice 2001) emphasize differences in competitive strategies between nations, which shape actors' preferences.

References

Abegglen, James C. 1958. *The Japanese Factory.* Glencoe: Free Press.

Adema, Willem. 2001. "Net Social Expenditure, 2nd edition." OECD Labour Market and Social Policy Occasional Papers No. 52. Paris.

Ahmadjian, Christina L., and Gregory E. Robbins. 2005. "A Clash of Capitalisms: Foreign Shareholders and Corporate Restructuring in 1990s Japan." *American Sociological Review* 70(3): 451–471.

Allan, James P., and Lyle Scruggs. 2004. "Political Partisanship and Welfare State Reform in Advanced Industrial Societies." *American Journal of Political Science* 48(3): 496–512.

Amamiya, Shōichi. 2007. "Kishi Nobusuke to Nihon no Fukushi Taisei." *Gendai Shisō* 35(1): 154–158.

———. 1997. *Senji Sengo Taiseiron.* Tokyo: Iwanami Shoten.

Arai, Kazuhiro. 1996. *Koyō Seido no Keizaigaku.* Tokyo: Chūō Keizaisha.

Araki, Takashi. 2005. "Corporate Governance Reforms, Labor Law Developments, and the Future of Japan's Practice-Dependent Stakeholder Model." *Japan Labor Review* 2(1): 26–57.

Arima, Motoharu. 1966. *Koyō Taisaku Hō no Kaisetsu.* Tokyo: Nikkan Rōdō Tsūshinsha.

Asai, Yoshio. 2000. "Seisaku Shisō toshiteno Keinzu-shugi no Juyō: Nihon no Baai." In *Kingendai Nihon no Shinshiten,* edited by Nakamura Masanori, 202–226. Tokyo: Yoshikawa Kōbunkan.

Baumgartner, Frank, Christoffer Green-Pedersen, and Bryan D. Jones. 2009. *Comparative Studies of Policy Agendas.* London: Routledge.

Becker, Gary. 1993. *Human Capital: A Theoretical and Empirical Analysis with Special Reference to Education.* Chicago: University of Chicago Press.

Bergh, Andreas. 2004. "The Universal Welfare State: Theory and the Case of Sweden." *Political Studies* 52(4): 745–766.

Béland, Daniel. 2007. "Neo-Liberalism and Social Policy: The Politics of Ownership." *Policy Studies* 28(2): 91–107.

Béland, Daniel, and R. H. Cox. 2010. *Ideas and Politics in Social Science Research.* New York: Oxford University Press.

Béland, Daniel, and Alex Waddan. 2007. "Conservative Ideas and Social Policy in the United States." *Social Policy & Administration* 41(7): 768–786.

Bertola, Giuseppe, Tito Boeri, and Giuseppe Nicoletti. 2001. *Welfare and Employment in a United Europe: A Study for the Fondazione Rodolfo Debenedetti*. Cambridge: MIT Press.

Björklund, Anders. 2000. "Going Different Ways: Labour Market Policy in Denmark and Sweden." In *Why Deregulate Labour Markets?* edited by Gøsta Esping-Andersen and Marino Regini, 148–180. Oxford: Oxford University Press.

Blau, Francine D., and Lawrence M. Kahn. 1995. "The Gender Earnings Gap: Some International Evidence." In *Differences and Changes in Wage Structures*, edited by Richard B. Freeman and Lawrence F. Katz, 105–143. Chicago: University of Chicago Press.

Blyth, Mark. 2002. *Great Transformations: Economic Ideas and Institutional Change in the Twentieth Century*. Cambridge: Cambridge University Press.

Bonoli, Giuliano. 2003. "Social Policy Through Labor Markets: Understanding National Differences in the Provision of Economic Security to Wage Earners." *Comparative Political Studies* 36(9): 1007–1030.

——. 1997. "Classifying Welfare States: A Two-Dimension Approach." *Journal of Social Policy* 26(3): 351–372.

Brinton, Mary C. 1993. *Women and the Economic Miracle: Gender and Work in Postwar Japan*. Berkeley: University of California Press.

Cabinet Office. 2010–11. *Danjo Kyōdō Sankaku Hakusho*. Tokyo: Chūwa Insatsu.

Calder, Kent. 1988. *Crisis and Compensation*. Princeton: Princeton University Press.

Campbell, John Creighton. 1992. *How Policies Change: The Japanese Government and the Aging Society*. Princeton: Princeton University Press.

——. 1984. "Problems, Solutions, Non-Solutions, and Free Medical Care for the Elderly in Japan." *Pacific Affairs* 57(1): 53–64.

Campbell, John L. 2002. "Ideas, Politics, and Public Policy." *Annual Review of Sociology* 28: 21–38.

Carew, Anthony. 1987. *Labour under the Marshall Plan: The Politics of Productivity and the Marketing of Management Science*. Manchester: Manchester University Press.

Carlile, Lonny E. 2005. *Divisions of Labor: Globality, Ideology, and War in the Shaping of the Japanese Labor Movement*. Honolulu: University of Hawaii Press.

Castles, Francis G. 2004. *The Future of the Welfare State*. Oxford: Oxford University Press.

Castles, Francis G., and Deborah Mitchell. 1993. "Worlds of Welfare and Families of Nations." In *Families of Nations: Patterns of Public Policy in Western Democracies*, edited by Francis G. Castles, 93–128. Brookfield: Dartmouth.

Chūma, Hiroyuki. 1998. "'Kaikoken Ranyō Hōri' no Keizai Bunseki: Koyō Keiyaku Riron no Shiten kara." In *Kaisyahō no Keizaigaku*, edited by Miwa Yoshiro, Kanda Hideki, and Yanagawa Noriyuki, 425–451. Tokyo: Tokyo Daigaku Shuppankai.

Christensen, Raymond. 1996. "The New Japanese Election System." *Pacific Affairs* (Spring): 49–70.

Crompton, Rosemary, ed. 1999. *Restructuring Gender Relations and Employment: The Decline of the Male Breadwinner*. Oxford: Oxford University Press.

Crouch, Colin. 2005. *Capitalist Diversity and Change: Recombinant Governance and Institutional Entrepreneurs*. Oxford: Oxford University Press.

Crump, John. 2003. *Nikkeiren and Japanese Capitalism*. London: Routledge Curzon.

Curtis, Gerald L. 1988. *The Japanese Way of Politics*. New York: Columbia University Press.

Dore, Ronald. 2000. *Stock Market Capitalism: Welfare Capitalism: Japan and Germany versus the Anglo-Saxons*. Oxford: Oxford University Press.

——. 1973. *British Factory, Japanese Factory: The Origins of National Diversity in Industrial Relations*. Berkeley: University of California Press.

Downs, Anthony. 1957. *An Economic Theory of Democracy*. New York: Harper & Row.

Drezner, Daniel W. 2007. *All Politics Is Global: Explaining International Regulatory Regimes.* Princeton: Princeton University Press.

Economic Planning Agency. 1996. *Kokumin Seikatsu Hakusho.* Tokyo: Kokuritsu Insatsukyoku.

———. 1961. *Kokumin Shotoku Baizō Keikaku.* Tokyo: Ōkurashō Insatsukyoku.

Endō, Kōshi. 1999. *Nihon no Jinji Satei.* Kyoto: Minerva Shoten.

Eshita, Takashi. 1957. *Kanzen Koyō: Mondai to Seisaku.* Tokyo: Rōdō Hōrei Kyōkai.

Esping-Andersen, Gøsta. 1999. *Social Foundations of Postindustrial Economies.* New York: Oxford University Press.

———. 1997. "Hybrid or Unique? The Japanese Welfare State between Europe and America." *Journal of European Social Policy* 7(3): 179–189.

———. 1996. "Welfare States without Work: The Impasse of Labour Shedding and Familialism in Continental European Social Policy." In *Welfare States in Transition: National Adaptation in Global Economies,* edited by Gøsta Esping-Andersen, 66–87. London: Sage

———. 1994. "Welfare States and the Economy." In *The Handbook of Economic Sociology,* edited by Neil. J. Smelser and Richard Swedberg, 711–732. Princeton: Princeton University Press.

———. 1990. *The Three Worlds of Welfare Capitalism.* Princeton: Princeton University Press.

———. 1985. *Politics against Markets: The Social Democratic Road to Power.* Princeton: Princeton University Press.

Esping-Andersen, Gøsta, and Marino Regini, eds. 2000. *Why Deregulate Labour Markets?* New York: Oxford University Press.

Estévez-Abe, Margarita. 2008. *Welfare and Capitalism in Postwar Japan: Party, Bureaucracy, and Business.* Cambridge: Cambridge University Press.

———. 2003. "State-Society Partnerships in the Japanese Welfare State." In *The State of Civil Society in Japan,* edited by Frank J. Schwartz and Susan J. Pharr, 154–172. Cambridge: Cambridge University Press.

Estévez-Abe, Margarita, Torben Iversen and David Soskice. 2001. "Social Protection and the Formation of Skills: A Reinterpretation of the Welfare State." In *Varieties of Capitalism: The Institutional Foundations of Comparative Advantage,* edited by Peter A. Hall and David Soskice, 145–183. Oxford: Oxford University Press.

Evans, Peter. 2008. "Is an Alternative Globalization Possible?" *Politics & Society* 36(2): 271–305.

Flanagan, Robert J. 2006. *Globalization and Labor Conditions: Working Conditions and Worker Rights in a Global Economy.* Oxford: Oxford University Press.

Foote, Daniel. 1996. "Judicial Creation of Norms in Japanese Labor Law: Activism in the Service of Stability?" *UCLA Law Review* 43(3): 635–709.

Förster, M., and M. Mira d'Ercole. 2005. "Income Distribution and Poverty in OECD Countries in the Second Half of the 1990s." *OECD Social Employment and Migration Working Papers,* No. 22. Paris: OECD.

Frieden, Jeffry. 2006. *Global Capitalism: Its Fall and Rise in the Twentieth Century.* New York: W.W. Norton.

Fujimoto, Takeshi. 1967. *Saitei Chinginsei.* Tokyo: Iwanami Shoten.

Fukui, Hideo. 2006. "Kaiko Kisei ga Jochō suru Kakusa Shakai." In *Datsu Kakusa Shakai to Koyō Hōsei,* edited by Ōtake Fumio and Fukui Hideo, 37–58. Tokyo: Nihon Hyōronsha.

Gao, Bai. 1997. *Economic Ideology and Japanese Industrial Policy: Developmentalism from 1931 to 1965.* Cambridge: Cambridge University Press.

Garon, Sheldon. 1997. *Molding Japanese Minds: The State in Everyday Life.* Princeton: Princeton University Press.

———. 1987. *The State and Labor in Modern Japan.* Berkeley: University of California Press.

Garon, Sheldon, and Mike Mochizuki. 1993. "Negotiating Social Contracts." In *Postwar Japan as History*, edited by Andrew Gordon, 145–166. Berkeley: University of California Press.

Garret, Geoffrey. 1998. *Partisan Politics in the Global Economy*. Cambridge: Cambridge University Press.

Goodin, Robert E. 2001. "Work and Welfare: Toward a Post-Productivist Welfare Regime." *British Journal of Political Science* 31(1): 13–39.

Goodman, John, and Louis Pauly. 1993. "The Obsolescence of Capital Controls?" *World Politics* 46(October): 50–82.

Gordon, Andrew. 1998. *The Wages of Affluence: Labor and Management in Postwar Japan*. Cambridge: Harvard University Press.

——. 1985. *The Evolution of Labor Relations in Japan: Heavy Industry, 1853–1955*. Cambridge: Harvard University Press.

Gurūpu 1984. 1975. "Nihon no Jisatsu." *Bungei Shunjū* 53(2): 92–124.

Gyōsei Kaikaku Iinkai OB Kai. 1998. *Gyōsei Kaikaku Iinkai: Sōri eno Zenteigen*. Tokyo: Gyōsei Kanri Kenkyū Sentā.

Habermeyer, Noriko. 2008. "Rōdō Keiyaku-hō no Shūsei to Seiritsu no Katei wo Furikaeru." *Kikan Rōdōhō* 221(Summer): 66–77.

Hacker, Jacob S. 2006. *The Great Risk Shift: The New Economic Insecurity and the Decline of the American Dream*. Oxford: Oxford University Press.

——. 2004. "Privatizing Risk without Privatizing the Welfare State: The Hidden Politics of Social Policy Retrenchment in the United States." *American Political Science Review* 98(2): 243–260.

——. 2002. *The Divided Welfare State: The Battle over Public and Private Social Benefits in the United States*. Cambridge: Cambridge University Press.

Hall, Peter. 1989. *The Political Power of Economic Ideas*. Princeton: Princeton University Press.

Hall, Peter, and David Soskice, ed. 2001. *Varieties of Capitalism: The Institutional Foundations of Comparative Advantage*. Oxford: Oxford University Press.

Hamaguchi, Keiichirō. 2007. "Kaiko Kisei no Hōseisaku." *Kikan Rōdōhō* 217 (Summer): 173–199.

——. 2004. *Rōdōhōseisaku*. Kyoto: Minerva Shobō.

Harvey, David. 2005. *A Brief History of Neoliberalism*. Oxford: Oxford University Press.

Hatoyama, Yukio. 2009. "Watashi no Seiji Tetsugaku." *Voice* 381(September): 132–141.

Hemerijck, Anton, Philip Manow, and Kees Van Kersbergen. 2000. "Welfare without Work? Divergent Experiences of Reform in Germany and the Netherlands." In *Survival of the European Welfare State*, edited by Stein Kuhnle, 106–127. London: Routledge.

Hirayama, Yōsuke, and Richard Ronald, eds. 2006. *Housing and Social Transition in Japan*. London: Routledge.

Hiroi, Yoshinori. 1999. *Nihon no Shakai Hoshō*. Tokyo: Iwanami Shoten.

Hiroishi, Tadashi. 1995. "Kigyō ni okeru Josei Koyō Kanri no Jittai." *Jurist* 1079: 23–30.

Hisamoto, Norio. 1998. *Kigyōnai Rōshi Kankei to Jinzai Keisei*. Tokyo: Yūhikaku.

Hiwatari, Nobuhiro. 1991. *Sengo Nihon no Shijō to Seiji*. Tokyo: Tokyo Daigaku Shuppankai.

Hoshino, Shinya. 1995. "Fukushi Kokka Chūryū Kaisōka ni Torinokosareta Shakai Fukushi: Zenkoku Shōhi Jittai Chōsa no Dēta Bunseki (1)." *Jinbun Gakuhō* 261: 23–85.

Hosokawa, Morihiro. 1992. "'Jiyū Shakai Rengō' Kettō Sengen," *Bungei Shunjū* (June): 94–106.

Huber, Evelyne, and John D. Stephens. 2001. *Development and Crisis of the Welfare State: Parties and Policies in Global Markets*. Chicago: University of Chicago Press.

——. 1998. "Internationalization and the Social Democratic Model: Crisis and Future Prospects." *Comparative Political Studies* 31(3): 353–397.

Iijima, Hiroshi. 1987. *Kuraishi Tadao: Sono Hito to Jidai.* Tokyo: Kuraishi Tadao Sensei Kenshōkai.

Iio, Jun. 2007. *Nihon no Tōchi Kōzō: Kanryō Naikakusei kara Giin Naikakusei e.* Tokyo: Chūō Kōronsha.

International Labour Organization (ILO). 2009. *The Financial and Economic Crisis: A Decent Work Response.* Geneva.

Inagami, Takeshi, and David Hugh Whittaker. 2005. *The New Community Firm: Employment, Governance and Management Reform in Japan.* Cambridge: Cambridge University Press.

Ishibashi, Tanzan. 1970. *Ishibashi Tanzan Zenshū.* Vol. 14. Tokyo: Tōyō Keizai Shinpōsha.

——. 1959. *Nihonkeizai no Shinro: Furu Enpuroimento wo Mezashite.* Tokyo: Tōyō Keizai Shinpōsha.

Ishida, Takeshi. 1989. *Nihon no Seiji to Kotoba: Jiyū to Fukushi.* Tokyo: Tokyo Daigaku Shuppankai.

Ishida, Hirohide. 1986. *Watashi no Seikai Shōwashi.* Tokyo: Toyō Keizai Shinpōsha.

——.1963. "Hoshu Seitō no Bijon." *Chūō Kōron* 78(1): 88–97.

Itō, Shūhei. 2007. *Kenri, Shijō, Shakaihoshō: Seizonken no Kiki kara Saikōchiku e.* Tokyo: Aoki Shoten.

——. 2001. *Kaigo Hoken wo Toinaosu.* Tokyo: Chikuma Shobō.

Iversen, Torben. 2005.*Capitalism, Democracy and Welfare: The Changing Nature of Production, Elections, and Social Protection in Modern Capitalism.* New York: Cambridge University Press.

Iwai, Tomoaki. 1988. *Rippō Katei.* Tokyo: Tokyo Daigaku Shuppankai.

Izeri, Hirofumi. 2008. *Kenpō Kaisei Shianshū.* Tokyo: Shūeisha.

Japan Institute of Labour. 2000. *Yūsufuru Rōdō Tōkei 2000.* Tokyo: Japan Institute of Labour.

Japan Institute of Labour Policy and Training. Various years. *Dēta Bukku Kokusai Rōdō Hikaku.* Tokyo: Japan Institute of Labour Policy and Training.

Jiyū Minshutō. 1987. *Jiyū Minshutō Shi: Shiryō Hen.* Tokyo: Jiyū Minshutō.

——. 1979. *Nihongata Fukushi Shakai.* Tokyo: Jiyū Minshutō Kōhō Iinkai Shuppankyoku.

Kameyama, Naoyuki. 1994. "Shūshin Koyō." *Nihon Rōdō Kenkyū Zasshi* 408: 38–39.

Kamikawa, Ryūnoshin. 2010. *Koizumi Kaikaku no Seijigaku: Koizumi Jun'ichirō wa Hontō ni "Tsuyoi Shushō" datta noka?* Tokyo: Tōyō Keizai Shinpōsha.

Kamo, Toshio. 1994. "Gendai Nihongata Seiji Shisutemu no Seiritsu: Ikeda-Satō Seiken to Hoshu Shihai no Kōzō." In *Sengo Kaikaku to Gendai Shakai no Keisei,* edited by Banno Junji et al., 331–369. Tokyo: Iwanami Shoten.

Kasza, Gregory J. 2006. *One World of Welfare: Japan in Comparative Perspective.* Ithaca: Cornell University Press.

——. 2002. "The Illusion of Welfare 'Regimes.'" *Journal of Social Policy* 31(2): 271–287.

Katzenstein, Peter J. 1996. *Cultural Norms and National Security: Police and Military in Postwar Japan.* Ithaca: Cornell University Press.

Keizai Shingikai. 1963. *Keizai Hatten ni okeru Jinteki Nōryoku Kaihatsu no Kadai to Taisaku.* Tokyo: Ōkurashō Insatsukyoku.

Kikuchi, Nobuteru. 2005. *Zaikai towa Nanika.* Tokyo: Heibonsha.

Kingdon, John W. 1984/1995. *Agendas, Alternatives, and Public Policies.* Boston: Little Brown.

Kinoshita, Takeo. 1999. *Nihonjin no Chingin.* Tokyo: Heibonsha.

Kishi, Nobusuke. 1953. "Shin-hoshutōron." *Kaizō* (May): 90–95.

Koike, Kazuo. 1999. *Shigoto no Keizaigaku.* Tokyo: Toyo Keizai Shinpōsha.

Kolberg, Jon Eivind, ed. 1992. *Between Work and Social Citizenship*. Armonk, NY: M.E. Sharpe.

Kolberg, Jon Eivind, and Gøsta Esping-Andersen. 1992. "Welfare States and Employment Regimes." In *Between Work and Social Citizenship*, edited by Jon Eivind Kolberg, 3–35. Armonk, NY: M.E. Sharpe.

Komamura, Kōhei. 2002. "Sēfuthi Netto no Saikōchiku." *Shūkan Shakai Hoshō* 2208: 24–27.

Konno, Harutaka, and Honda Yuki. 2008. "Hataraku Wakamono tachi no Genjitsu." *Sekai* 783 (October): 179–190.

Korpi, Walter. 2006. "Power Resources and Employer-Centered Approaches in Explanations of Welfare States and Varieties of Capitalism: Protagonists, Consenters, and Antagonists." *World Politics* 58 (January): 167–206.

——. 2001. "Contentious Institutions: An Augmented Rational-Action Analysis of the Origins and Path Dependency of Welfare State Institutions in Western Countries." *Rationality and Society* 13(2): 235–283.

——. 1983. *The Democratic Class Struggle*. London: Routledge and Kegan Paul.

——. 1974. "Conflict, Power and Relative Deprivation." *American Political Science Review* 68 (4): 1569–1578.

Kōsai, Yutaka. 1981. *Kōdo Seichō no Jidai: Gendai Nihon Keizaishi Nōto*. Tokyo: Nihon Hyōronsha.

Kōseishō Nenkin-kyoku, ed. 1962. *Kokumin Nenkin no Ayumi*. Tokyo: Kōseishō Nenkinkyoku.

Kōseishō 50nen Shi Henshū Iinkai, ed. 1988. *Kōseishō 50nen Shi: Kijutsu Hen*. Tokyo: Chūō Hōki Shuppankai.

Kouno, Yasuko. 2002. *Sengo to Kōdo Seichō no Shūen*. Tokyo: Kōdansha.

Krugman, Paul. 1994. "Competitiveness: A Dangerous Obsession." *Foreign Affairs* 73(2): 28–44.

Kumazawa, Makoto. 1997. *Nōryokushugi to Kigyō Shakai*. Tokyo: Iwanami Shoten.

Kume, Ikuo. 1998. *Disparaged Success: Labor Politics in Postwar Japan*. Ithaca: Cornell University Press.

——. 1995. "Institutionalizing the Active Labor Market Policy in Japan: A Comparative View." In *The Japanese Civil Service and Economic Development: Catalysts of Change*, edited by Hyung-ki Kim, Michio Muramatsu, T. J. Pempel and Kozo Yamamura, 311–336. Oxford: Clarendon Press.

Kurzer, Paulette. 1993. *Business and Banking: Political Change and Economic Integration in Western Europe*. Ithaca: Cornell University Press.

Lee, Sangheon, Deirdre McCann, and Jon C. Messenger. 2007. *Working Time around the World: Trends in Working Hours, Laws and Policies in a Global Comparative Perspective*. London: Routlledge.

Levy, Jonah D., ed. 2006. *The State after Statism: New State Activities in the Age of Liberalization*. Cambridge: Harvard University Press.

——. 1999. "Vice into Virtue? Progressive Politics and Welfare Reform in Continental Europe." *Politics and Society* 27(2): 239–273.

Lewis, Jane. 1993. "Introduction: Women, Work, Family and Social Policies in Europe." In *Women and Social Policies in Europe: Work. Family and State*, edited by Jane Lewis, 1–24. Aldershot: Edward Elgar.

Lewis, Jane, and Rebecca Surender, eds. 2004. *Welfare State Change: Towards a Third Way?* Oxford: Oxford University Press.

Lewis, Paul M. 1980. "Social and Political Causes of the Passage of the 1959 National Pension System Law." *Kikan Shakai Hoshō Kenkyū* 15(4): 52–60.

Lijphart, Arend. 1999. *Patterns of Democracy: Government Forms and Performance in Thirty-Six Countries*. New Haven: Yale University Press.

Lindbeck, Assar, and Dennis J. Snower. 2002. "The Insider-Outsider Theory: A Survey." Institute for the Study of Labor Discussion Paper No. 534. Bonn, Germany.

——. 1988. *The Insider-Outsider Theory of Employment and Unemployment.* Cambridge: MIT Press.

Lister, Ruth. 2004. "The Third Way's Social Investment State." In *Welfare State Change: Towards a Third Way?* edited by Jane Lewis and Rebecca Surender, 157–181. Oxford: Oxford University Press.

Lodovici, Manuela Samek. 2000. "The Dynamics of Labour Market Reform in European Countries." In *Why Deregulate Labour Market?* edited by Gøsta Esping-Andersen and Marino Regini, 30–65. New York: Oxford University Press.

Lynch, Julia. 2006. *Age in the Welfare State: the Origins of Social Spending on Pensioners, Workers and Children.* Cambridge: Cambridge University Press.

Macaire, S., and F. Michon. 2006. "Temporary Agency Work: National Reports, France." European Foundation for the Improvement of Living and Working Conditions. Available at http://www.eurofound.europa.eu/publications/htmlfiles/ef0226.htm.

Mahoney, James, and Kathleen Thelen, eds. 2009. *Explaining Institutional Change: Ambiguity, Agency, and Power.* Cambridge: Cambridge University Press.

Maier, Charles S. 1987. *In Search of Stability: Explorations in Historical Political Economy.* Cambridge: Cambridge University Press.

Makihara, Izuru. 2005. "'Sengo Seiji no Sōkessan' ga Mamonaku Owaru: Rekishi kara mita Keizai Zaisei Shimon Kaigi to sono Shōraizō." *Ronza* (August): 53–62.

Manow, Philip. 2001. "Comparative Institutional Advantages of Welfare State Regimes and New Coalitions in Welfare State Reforms." In *The New Politics of the Welfare State,* edited by Paul Pierson, 146–164. Oxford: Oxford University Press.

Mares, Isabela. 2001. "Enterprise Reorganization and Social Insurance Reform: The Development of Early Retirement in France and Germany." *Governance* 14(3): 295–319.

Marshall, Thomas H. 1950. *Citizenship and Social Class and Other Essays.* Cambridge: Cambridge University Press.

Martin, Cathie. J. 2000. *Stuck in Neutral: Business and the Politics of Human Capital Investment Policy.* Princeton: Princeton University Press.

——. 1995. "Nature or Nurture: Sources of Firm Preferences for National Health Reform." *American Political Science Review* 89(4): 898–913.

Martin, John P. 1996. "Measures of Replacement Rates for the Purpose of International Comparisons: a Note." *OECD Economic Studies* 26: 99–115.

McKenzie, Richard, and Dwight Lee. 1991.*Quicksilver Capital: How the Rapid Movement of Wealth Has Changed the World.* New York: Free Press.

Mehta, Jal. 2011. "The Varied Roles of Ideas in Politics: From 'Whether' to 'How.'" In I*deas and Politics in Social Science Research,* edited by Daniel Béland and Robert Henry Cox, 23–46. Oxford: Oxford University Press.

Milly, Deborah J. 1999. *Poverty, Equality, and Growth: The Politics of Economic Need in Postwar Japan.* Cambridge: Harvard University Asia Center.

Ministry of Finance (various years). *Zaisei Tōkei.* Tokyo: Ōkurashō Insatsukyoku.

Ministry of Health, Labour, and Welfare. 2006. *Koyō Hoken Jigyō Nemp&omacr.* Tokyo: Kōsei Rōdōshō Shokugyō Antei Kyoku.

——.2005. *Rōdō Keizai Hakusho.*Tokyo: Kokuritsu Insatsukyoku.

Ministry of Labour. 1999. *Rōdō Hakusho.* Tokyo: Nihon Rōdō Kenkyū Kiko.

——. 1992. *Pātotaimā no Jittai.* Tokyo: Ōkurashō Insatsu-kyoku.

——. 1978. *Shiryō Rōdō Undō-shi.* Tokyo: Rōmu Gyōsei Kenkyūjo.

——. 1976. *Koyō Kanri Chōsa Hōkoku.* Tokyo: Rōdō Daijin Kanbō Seisaku Chōsabu Koyō Tōkeika.

——. 1966. *Rōdō Hakusho.* Tokyo: Ōkurashō Insatsukyoku.

Mishra, Ramesh. 1999. *Globalization and the Welfare State*. Cheltenham: Edward Elgar.

Miura, Mari. 2011a. "The Impact of Two-Party Competition on Neo-Liberal Reform and Labor Unions." In *Evolution of Japan's Party System: Politics and Policy in an Era of Institutional Change*, edited by Leonard J. Schoppa, 177–204. Toronto: Toronto University Press.

——. 2011b. "Rōdō Seiji no Jendā Baiasu: Shinjiyūshugi wo Koeru Kanōsei." In *Kabe wo Koeru: Seiji to Gyōsei no Jendā Shuryūka*, edited by Tsujimura Miyoko, 145–167. Tokyo: Iwanami Shoten.

——. 2011c. "Rōdō Seisaku no Hōkōtenkan ni okeru Seiji Shudō to Shingikai." *Jendā to Hō* 8: 66–77.

——. 2011d. "Minshutō wa 'Tōchi naki Meisō' wo dassuruka? Shin-seichō Senryaku to Kodomo Teate." In *Minshutō Seiken no Seisaku to Kettei Shisutemu: Hatoyama Seiken wo Chūshin ni*, Rengō Sōken Bukkuretto No.6, 41–48. Tokyo: Rengō Sōken.

——. 2008a. "Labor Politics in Japan during 'the Lost Fifteen Years': From the Politics of Productivity to the Politics of Consumption." *Labor History* 49(2): 161–176.

——. 2008b. "Shinjiyūshugi no Seiji Bunseki: Shūren Ronsō no naka no Nihon" (Political Analysis of Neoliberal Reform: Japan in the Convergence Debates). In *Gurōbaru na Kihan/Rōkaru na Seiji: Minshushugi no Yukue*, edited by Kishikawa Takeshi and Nakano Koichi, 31–68. Tokyo: Sophia University Press.

——. 2007. "Koizumi Kaikaku to Rōdō Seiji no Henyō: 'Tasūha Shihaigata' no Seisaku Katei no Shutsugen." *Nenpō Gyōsei Kenkyū* 42: 100–122.

——. 2005. "Rengō no Seisaku Sanka." In *Suitai ka Saisei ka? Rōdō Kumiai Kasseika eno Michi*, edited by Nakamura Keisuke, 169–192. Tokyo: Keisō Shobō.

——. 2002. "Rōdō Kisei." In *Ryūdōki no Nihon Seiji: 'Ushinawareta 10nen no Seijigakuteki Kenshō*, edited by Nobuhiro Hiwatari and Mari Miura, 259–277.Tokyo: Tokyo Daigaku Shuppankai.

——. 2001. "Daihyōsei, Setsumei Sekinin, Seisaku Yūkōsei: Hakenhō Kaisei no Seisaku Kettei Katei wo Seisaku Hyōka Suru Ichi Shiron." *Nihon Rōdō Kenkyū Zasshi* 497: 33–43.

Miura, Mari, Kap Yun Lee, and Robert Weiner. 2005. "Who Are the DPJ? Policy Positioning and Recruitment Strategy." *Asian Perspective*, 9(1): 49–78.

Miyamoto, Tarō. 2008. *Fukushi Seiji: Nihon no Seikatsu Hoshō to Demokurashī*. Tokyo: Yūhikaku.

Miyazaki, Ryūji. 1988. "Nihon ni okeru 'Sengo Demokurashī' no Koteika: 1955 Taisei no Seiritsu." In *Sengo Demokurashī no Seiritsu*, edited by Indō Kazuo et al., 151–222. Tokyo: Iwanami Shoten.

Mori, Seigo. 2001. "Seiri Kaiko Hōri no Igi to Genkai." *Rōdō Hōritsu Junpō* 1497: 6–20.

Morioka, Kōji. 2005. *Hatarakisugi no Jidai*. Tokyo: Iwanami Shoten.

Moses, Jonathon. 1994. "Abdication from National Policy Autonomy: What's Left to Leave?" *Politics and Society* 22(2): 125–148.

Mulgan, Aurelia George. 2002. *Japan's Failed Revolution: Koizumi and the Politics of Economic Reform*. Canberra: Asia Pacific Press at the Australian National University.

Murakami, Yasusuke, and Rōyama Shōichi, eds. 1975. *Shōgai Sekkei (Raifu Saikuru) Keikaku: Nihongata Fukushi Shakai no Bijon*. Tokyo: Nihon Keizai Shimbunsha.

Muramatsu, Michio, and Ellis S. Krauss. 1987. "The Conservative Policy Line and the Development of Patterned Pluralism." In *The Political Economy of Japan*. Vol. 1, edited by Kozo Yamamura and Yasukichi Yasuba, 516–554. Stanford: Stanford University Press.

Nakakita, Kōji. 2006. "Reisenki Amerika no Tainichi Rōdō Seisaku: Hankyōsanshugi to Shakai Minshushugi no Sōkoku." In *Kensei no Seijigaku*, edited by Junji Banno, Muneyuki Shindo, and Masaya Kobayashi, 125–151. Tokyo: Tokyo Daigaku Shuppankai.

——. 2002. *1955nen Taisei no Seiritsu*. Tokyo: Tokyo Daigaku Shuppankai.

Nakakubo, Hiroya. 2008. "Saitei Chingin Hōsei no Atarashii Shuppatsu." *Kikan Rōdōhō* 222 (Autumn): 55–65.

Nakamura, Keisuke. 2006. *Seika Shugi no Shinjitsu.* Toyo Keizai Shinpōsha.

Nakano, Koichi. 2010. *Party Politics and Decentralization in Japan and France: When the Opposition Governs.* London: Routledge.

———. 1998. "The Politics of Administrative Reform in Japan, 1993–1998: Toward a More Accountable Government?" *Asian Survey* 38(3): 291–309.

Nakano, Mami. 2006: *Rōdō Danpingu: Koyō no Tayōka no Hateni.* Tokyo: Iwanami Shoten.

Nihon Rōdō Kumiai Sōhyōgikai. ed. 1974. *Sōhyō 20nenshi.* Tokyo: Rōdō Junpōsha.

Nihon Seisansei Honbu. 1985. *Seisansei Undō 30 nenshi.* Tokyo: Nihon Seisansei Honbu.

Niki, Ryū. 2007. *Kaigo Hoken Seido no Sōgōteki Kenkyū.* Tokyo: Keisō Shobō.

Nikkeiren (Nihon Keieisha Dantai Renmei). 2000. *Hito no Kao wo shita Shijō Keizai wo Mezashite: Heisei 12-nendo Rōdō Mondai Kenkyū Iinkai Hōkoku.* Tokyo: Nihon Keieisha Dantai Renmei Kōhōbu.

———. 1999. *Dainamikkude Toku no aru Kuni wo Mezashite: Heisei 11-nendo Rōdō Mondai Kenkyū Iinkai Hōkoku.* Tokyo: Nihon Keieisha Dantai Renmei Kōhōbu.

———. 1998. *Kiki karano Dasshutsu: Daisan no Michi wo Motomete: Heisei 10-nendo Rōdō Mondai Kenkyū Iinkai Hōkoku.* Tokyo: Nihon Keieisha Dantai Renmei Kōhōbu.

———. 1997. *Koyō Antei to Kokumin-Seikatsu no Shitsu-teki Kaizen wo Mezasu Kōzō Kaikaku— Dai 3 no Michi no Mosaku: Heisei 9-nendo Rōdō Mondai Kenkyū Iinkai Hōkoku.* Tokyo: Nihon Keieisha Dantai Renmei Kōhōbu.

———. 1996. *Kōzō-Kaikaku niyoru Dainamikku na Nihon Keizai no Jitsugen ni Mukete: Heisei 8-nendo Rōdō Mondai Kenkyū Iinkai Hōkoku.* Tokyo: Nihon Keieisha Dantai Renmei Kōhōbu.

———. 1995a. "Nihon Keizai no Sai-Kasseika to Keieisha, Rōshi no Kadai." *Heisei 7-nendo Rōdō Mondai Kenkyū Iinkai Hōkoku.* Tokyo: Nihon Keieisha Dantai Renmei Kōhōbu.

———. 1995b. "Shinjidai no 'Nihonteki Keiei': Chōsen Subeki Hōkō to Sono Gutaisaku." *Shin Nihonteki Keiei Shisutemu-tō Kenkyū Purojekuto.* Tokyo: Nihon Keieisha Dantai Renmei.

———. 1994. *Shinkokuka suru Chōki Fukyō to Koyō Iji ni Mukete no Rōshi no Taiō: Heisei 6-nendo Rōdō Mondai Kenkyū Iinkai Hōkoku.* Tokyo: Nihon Keieisha Dantai Renmei Kōhōbu.

———. 1993. *Atarashii Kokusaika Jidai ni okeru Nihon to Rōshi no Sentaku: Heisei 5-nendo Rōdō Mondai Kenkyū Iinkai Hōkoku.* Tokyo: Nihon Keieisha Dantai Renmei Kōhōbu.

———. 1992. *Shin-Jidai no Keizai Shakai to Rōshi Kankei wo Motomete: Heisei 4-nendo Rōdō Mondai Kenkyū Iinkai Hōkoku.* Tokyo: Nihon Keieisha Dantai Renmei Kōhōbu.

Nippon Keidanren (Nihon Keizai Dantai Rengōkai). 2003. *Keiei Rōdō Seisaku Iinkai Hōkoku.* Tokyo: Nippon Keidanren Shuppan.

Nishizaki, Bunpei, Yamada Yasushi, and Andō Eisuke. 1998. *Nihon no Shotoku Kakusa: Kokusai Hikaku no Shitenkara.* Tokyo: Ōkurashō Insatsukyoku.

Nitta, Michio. 2008. "Koyō no Ryōteki Kanri." In *Nihon teki Koyō Sisutemu,* edited by Nitta Michio and Hisamoto Norio, 27–72. Kyoto: Nakanishiya Shuppan.

———. 2003. *Henka no Naka no Koyō Sisutemu.* Tokyo: Tokyo Daigaku Shuppankai.

———. 1998. "Rōshi Kankeiron to Shakai Seisaku ni Kansuru Oboegaki: Nakayama Ichirō Kyōju to Seisansei Kōjō Undō." In *Shakai Seisaku Gakkai 100nen,* edited by Shakaiseisaku Sōsho Henshū Iinkai, 109–130. Tokyo: Keibunsha.

Noble, Gregory. 1998. *Collective Action in East Asia: How Ruling Parties Shape Industrial Policy.* Ithaca: Cornell University Press.

Nogawa, Shinobu. 2000. "Kaiko no Jiyū to Sono Seigen." In *Rōdō Keiyaku,* edited by Nihon Rōdōhō Gakkai, 154–177. Tokyo: Yūhikaku.

Nomura, Masami. 2007. *Nihonteki Koyō Kankō.* Kyoto: Minerva Shobō.

Ogawa, Hiroshi. 2000. "Hinkon Setai no Genjō: Nichiei Hikaku." *Keizai Kenkyū* 51(3): 220–231.

Organization for Economic Co-operation and Development (OECD). 2006. *OECD Economy Surveys: Japan.* Paris.

——. 2004. *Employment Outlook.* Paris.

Orloff, Ann Shola. 1993. "Gender and the Social Rights of Citizenship: The Comparative Analysis of Gender Relations and Welfare States." *American Sociological Review* 58(3): 303–328.

Osaka Karōshi Mondai Renrakukai. 2003. *Q&A Karōshi Karōjisatsu 110 ban.* Tokyo: Minjihō Kenkyūkai.

Ōsawa, Mari. 2007.*Gendai Nihon no Seikatsu Hoshō Sisutemu: Zahyō to Yukue.* Tokyo: Iwanami Shoten.

——. 1993. *Kigyō Chūshin Shakai wo Koete: Gendai Nihon wo Jendā de Yomu.* Tokyo: Jiji Tsūshinsha.

Ōta, Hiroko. 2006. *Keizai Zaisei Shimon Kaigi no Tatakai.* Tōyō Keizai Shinpōsha.

Ōtake, Fumio. 2005. *Nihon no Fubyōdō: Kakusa Shakai no Gensō to Mirai.* Tokyo: Nihon Keizai Shimbunsha.

——. 2000. "90 nendai no Shotoku Kakusa." *Nihon Rōdō Kenkyū Zasshi* 480: 2–11.

Ōtake, Fumio, and Keiko Fujikawa. 2001. "Nihon no Seiri Kaiko." In *Koyō Seisaku no Keizai Bunseki,* edited by Inoki Takemori and Ōtake Fumio, 3–28. Tokyo: Tokyo Daigaku Shuppankai.

Ōtake, Fumio, and Hiroko Okudaira. 2006. "Kaiko Kisei wa Koyō Kikai wo Herashi Kakusa wo Kakudai saseru." In *Datsu Kakusa Shakai to Koyō Hōsei,* edited by Ōtake Fumio and Fukui Hideo, 165–186. Tokyo: Nihon Hyōronsha.

Ōtake, Hideo. 1994. *Jiyūshugiteki Kaikaku no Jidai: 1980 nendai zenki no Nihon Seiji.* Tokyo: Chūō Kōronsha.

——. 1991. "Hatoyama Kishi Jidai ni okeru 'Chiisai Seifu' ron: 1950nendai Kōki ni okeru Genzei Seisaku." *Nempo Seijigaku:* 165–185.

Ōwaki, Masako. 2007. "Rippō no Genba ni Tatte." *Rōdō Hōritsu Junpō* 1644: 32–36.

Palier, Bruno, and Claude Martin. 2008. *Reforming the Bismarckian Welfare Systems.* London: Wiley-Blackwell.

Pempel, T. J. 1998. *Regime Shift: Comparative Dynamics of the Japanese Political Economy.* Ithaca: Cornell University Press.

Pierson, Paul. 2001. "Post-Industrial Pressures on the Mature Welfare States." In *The New Politics of the Welfare State,* edited by Paul Pierson, 80–104. Oxford: Oxford University Press.

——. 1994. *Dismantling the Welfare States? Reagan, Thatcher, and the Politics of Retrenchment.* Cambridge: Cambridge University Press.

Piven, Frances Fox. 1995. "Is It Global Economics or Neo-Laissez-Faire?" *New Left Review* I/213: 107–114.

Polanyi, Karl. 1944. *The Great Transformation.* Boston: Beacon Press.

Pontusson, Jonas. 2005a. *Inequality and Prosperity: Social Europe vs. Liberal America.* Ithaca: Cornell University Press.

——. 2005b. "Varieties and Commonalities of Capitalism." In *Varieties of Capitalism, Varieties of Approaches,* edited by David Coates, 163–188. New York: Palgrave Macmillan.

Radaelli, Claudio M., and Vivien A. Schmidt. 2005. *Policy Change and Discourse in Europe.* London: Routledge.

Regini, Marino. 2000. "The Dilemmas of Labour Market Regulation." In *Why Deregulate Labour Markets?* edited by Gøsta Esping-Andersen and Marino Regini, 11–29. Oxford: Oxford University Press.

Rhodes, Martin. 2001. "The Political Economy of Social Pacts: 'Competitive Corporatism' and European Welfare Reform." In *The New Politics of the Welfare State*, edited by Paul Pierson, 165–194. Oxford: Oxford University Press.

——. 1997. "Southern European Welfare States: Identity, Problems, and Prospects for Reform." In *Southern European Welfare States: Between Crisis and Reform*, edited by Martin Rhodes, 1–22. London: Frank Cass.

Rinji Gyōsei Chōsakai. 1983. *Rinchō Saishū Teigen*. Tokyo: Gyōsei Kanri Kenkyū Sentā.

Rodrik, Dani. 1997. *Has Globalization Gone Too Far?* Washington DC: Institute for International Economics.

Rueda, David. 2007. *Social Democracy Inside Out: Government Partisanship, Insiders, and Outsiders in Industrialized Democracies*. Oxford: Oxford University Press.

Rupert, Mark. 1995. *Producing Hegemony: The Politics of Mass Production and American Global Power*. Cambridge: Cambridge University Press.

Sainsbury, Diane, ed. 1999. *Gender and Welfare State Regimes*. Oxford: Oxford University Press.

——. 1996. *Gender, Equality and Welfare States*. Cambridge: Cambridge University Press.

Saint-Paul, Gilles. 2000. *The Political Economy of Labour Market Institutions*. Oxford: Oxford University Press.

——. 1996. *Dual Labor Markets*. Cambridge: MIT Press.

Sako, Mari. 1997. "Shunto: The Role of Employer and Union Coordination at the Industry and Inter-sectoral Levels." In *Japanese Labour and Management in Transition*, edited by Mari Sako and Hiroki Sato, 315–331. London: Routledge.

Sasaki, Kenshō. 2007. *Henbō suru Zaikai: Nihon Keidanren no Bunseki*. Shinnihon Shuppansha.

Satomi, Kenji. 1994. "Shakai Hoshō to 'Kokumin Futan': 'Kokumin Futan no Zōdai Yokuseiron no Yūdōsei to Sōsasei." *Shakai Mondai Kenkyū* 44(1): 1–35.

Scharpf, Fritz W., and Vivien A. Schmidt. 2000. *Welfare and Work in the Open Economy*. New York: Oxford University Press.

Scheiner, Ethan. 2006. *Democracy without Competition in Japan: Opposition Party Failure in a One-Party Dominant State*. New York: Cambridge University Press.

Schoppa, Leonard J. 2006a. *Race for the Exits: The Unraveling of Japan's System of Social Protection*. Ithaca: Cornell University Press.

——. 2006b. "Neoliberal Economic Policy Preferences of the 'New Left': Home-grown or an Anglo-American Import?" In *The Left in the Shaping of Japanese Democracy*, edited by Rikki Kersten and David Williams, 117–139. London: Routledge.

Schmidt, Manfred G. 2010. "Parties," in Francis G. Castles et al (eds.), *The Oxford Handbook of the Welfare State*, Oxford: Oxford University Press.

Schmidt, Vivien A. 2002. "Does Discourse Matter in the Politics of Welfare State Adjustment?" *Comparative Political Studies* 35(2): 168–193.

Schwartz, Frank J. 1998. *Advice and Consent: The Politics of Consultation in Japan*. Cambridge: Cambridge University Press.

Shinagawa, Masaji, and Ushio Jirō. 2000. *Nihon Kigyō no Kōporēto Gabanansu wo Tou*, Tokyo: Shōji Hōmu Kenkyūkai.

Shinkawa, Toshimitsu. 2005. *Nihongata Fukushi Regīmu no Hatten to Henyō*. Kyoto: Minerva Shobō.

——. 1993. *Nihongata Fukushi Kokka no Seiji Keizaigaku*. Tokyo: Sanichi Shobō.

——. 1984. "1975 Shuntō to Keizai Kiki Kanri." In *Nihon Seiji no Sōten*, edited by Ōtake Hideo, 189–232. Tokyo: Sanichi Shobō.

Shinkawa, Toshimitsu, and T. J. Pempel. 1996. "Occupational Welfare and the Japanese Experience." In *The Privatization of Social Policy? Occupational Welfare and the Welfare State in America, Scandinavia and Japan*, edited by Michael Shalev, 280–326. New York: St. Martin's Press.

Shinozuka, Eiko. 1989. *Nihon no Koyō Chōsei: Oil Shock Ikōno Rōdō Shijō*. Tokyo: Tōyōkeizai Shinpōsha.

Shiota, Sakiko. 2000. *Nihon no Shakai Seisaku to Jendā: Danjo Byōdō no Keizai Kiban*. Tokyo: Nihon Hyōronsha.

Shiroyama, Hideaki. 2003. "Seisaku Katei ni okeru Keizai Zaisei Shimon Kaigi no Yakuwari to Tokushitsu: Unyō Bunseki to Kokusai Hikaku no Kantenkara." *Kokusai Kōkyō Kenkyū* 3: 34–45.

Soeda, Yoshiya. 1995. *Seikatsu Hogo Seido no Shakaishi*. Tokyo: Tokyo Daigaku Shuppankai.

Sohara, Toshimitsu. 1985. "Tei Shotoku Setai to Seikatsu Hogo." In *Fukushi Seisaku no Kihon Mondai*, edited by Shakai Hoshō Kenkyūjo, 183–200. Tokyo: Tokyo Daigaku Shuppankai.

Sorai, Mamoru. 1993. "Jimintō Ittō Shihai Taisei Keisei Katei toshiteno Ishibashi/Kishi Seiken, 1957–1960." *Kokka Gakkai Zasshi* 106(1/2): 107–160.

Steger, Manfred B. 2002. *Globalism: The New Market Ideology*. Lanham, MD: Rowman and Littlefield.

Stephens, John D. 1974. *The Transition from Capitalism to Socialism*. London: Macmillan.

Sugeno, Kazuo. 2002. *Shin Koyō Shakai no Hō*. Tokyo: Yūhikaku.

———. 2000. *Rōdōhō*. 5th ed. Tokyo: Kōbundō.

———. 1997. *Koyō Shakai no Hō*. Tokyo: Yūkikaku.

Sugii, Shizuko. 1990. "Pātotaimu no Haigūsha Kōjo to Josei no Jiritsu." *Chingin to Shakai Hoshō*, 1036: 10–16.

Suzuki, Akira. 2009. "Nihon no Rōdō Undō." In *Rōdō to Fukushi Kokka no Kanōsei: Rōdō Undō Saisei no Kokusai Hikaku*, edited by Shinkawa Toshimitsu and Shinoda Tōru, 31–50. Kyoto: Minerva Shoten.

Swank, Duane. 2001. "Political Institutions and Welfare State Restructuring: The Impact of Institutions on Social Policy Change in Developed Democracies." In *The New Politics of the Welfare State*, edited by Paul Pierson, 197–237. Oxford: Oxford University Press.

Swenson, Peter. 2002. *Capitalists against Markets: The Making of Labor Markets and Welfare States in the United States and Sweden*. New York: Oxford University Press.

———. 1997. "Arranged Alliance: Business Interests in the New Deal." *Politics and Society* 25(1): 66–117.

Sykes, Robert, Bruno Palier, and Pauline M. Prior. 2001. *Globalization and European Welfare States: Challenges and Change*. New York: Palgrave.

Tachibanaki, Toshiaki. 2009. *Confronting Income Inequality in Japan: A Comparative Analysis of Causes, Consequences, and Reform*. Cambridge: MIT Press.

———. 1998. *Nihon no Keizai Kakusa*. Tokyo: Iwanami Bunko.

Tachibanaki, Toshiaki, and Kunio Urakawa. 2008. "Trends in Poverty among Low-Income Workers in Japan since the Nineties." *Japan Labor Review* 5(4): 21–46.

Takahashi, Mutsuko. 1997. *The Emergence of Welfare Society in Japan*. Aldershot: Avebury.

Takanashi, Akira. 1995. *Aratana Koyō Seisaku no Tenkai*. Tokyo: Rōmu Gyōsei Kenkyūsha.

Takeda, Makoto. 1993. *Ōji Seishi Sōgi, 1957–1960*. Tokyo: Taga Shuppan.

Takegawa, Shōgo, and Satō Hiroki, eds. 2000. *Kigyō Hoshō to Shakai Hoshō*. Tokyo: Tokyo Daigaku Shuppankai.

Takenaka, Heizō. 2006. *Kōzō Kaikaku no Shinjitsu*. Tokyo: Nihon Keizai Shimbunsha.

Tatebayashi, Masahiko. 2004. *Giin Kōdō no Seiji Keizaigaku: Jimintō Shihai no Seido Bunseki*. Tokyo: Yūhikaku.

Taylor-Gooby, Peter, ed. 2005. *Ideas and Welfare State Reform in Western Europe*. Houndmills: Palgrave.

Thelen, Kathleen. 2000. "Why German Employers Cannot Bring Themselves to Dismantle the German Model." In *Unions, Employers and Central Banks*, edited by Torben Iversen, Jonas Pontusson, and David Soskice, 138–169. New York: Cambridge University Press.

Thelen, Kathleen, and Ikuo Kume. 1999. "The Effects of Globalization on Labor Revisited: Lessons from Germany and Japan." *Politics and Society* 27(4): 477–505.

Thelen, Kathleen, and Christa Van Wijnbergen. 2003. "The Paradox of Globalization: Labor Relations in Germany and Beyond." *Comparative Political Studies* 36(8): 859–880.

Tiberghien, Yves. 2007. *Entrepreneurial States: Reforming Corporate Governance in France, Japan, and Korea.* Ithaca: Cornell University Press.

Tominaga, Ken'ichi. 2001. *Shakai Hendō no nakano Fukushi Kokka: Kazoku no Shippai to Kokka no Atarashii Kinō.* Tokyo: Chūō Kōronsha.

Tsuji, Hideo. 1978. "Atarashii Seiji no Bijon wo Motomete: Rōdō Kenshō Sōan to Kōryō Sōan." In *Ishida Rōsei: Sono Sokuseki to Tenbō,* edited by Rōsei Kenkyūkai, 289–331. Tokyo: Rōmu Gyōsei Kenkyūjo.

Tsutsui, William M. 1998. *Manufacturing Ideology: Scientific Management in Twentieth-Century Japan.* Princeton: Princeton University Press.

Uchiyama, Yū. 2007. *Koizumi Seiken.* Tokyo: Chūō Kōronsha.

Ujihara, Shōjirō. 1989. *Nihon Keizai to Koyō Seisaku.* Tokyo: Tokyo Daigaku Shuppankai.

Uzuhashi, Takafumi. 1997. *Gendai Fukushikokka no Kokusai Hikaku: Nihon Moderu no Ichizuke to Tenbō.* Tokyo: Nihon Hyōronsha.

Van Kersbergen, Kees. 1995. *Social Capitalism: A Study of Christian Democracy and the Welfare State.* London: Routledge.

Vogel, Stephen K. 2006. *Japan Remodeled: How Government and Industry Are Reforming Japanese Capitalism.* Ithaca: Cornell University Press.

Wakakuwa, Midori, and Kumiko Fujiwara-Fanselow. 2011. "Backlash against Gender Equality after 2000." Translated by Minata Hara. In *Transforming Japan: How Feminism and Diversity Are Making a Difference,* edited by Kumiko Fujimura-Fanselow, 337–359. New York: Feminist Press.

Watanabe, Osamu. 1994. "Hoshu Gōdō to Jiyū Minshutō no Kessei." In *Sengo Kaikaku to Gendai Shakai no Keisei,* edited by Banno Junji et al., 1–36. Tokyo: Iwanami Shoten.

Weathers, Charles. 2004. "Temporary Workers, Women, and Labour Policy-Making in Japan." *Japan Forum* 16(3): 423–447.

Weathers, Charles, and Akira Ebizuka, eds. 2004. *Nihon Seisansei Undō no Genten to Tenkai.* Tokyo: Shakai Keizai Seisansei Honbu Seisansei Rōdō Jōhō Sentā.

Weathers, Charles, and Scott North. 2009/2010. "Overtime Activists Take on Corporate Titans: Toyota, McDonald's and Japan's Work Hour Controversy." *Pacific Affairs* 82(4): 615–636.

Whiteford, Peter, and Willem Adema. 2007. "What Works Best in Reducing Child Poverty: A Benefit or Work Strategy?" OECD Social, Employment and Migration Working Papers, No. 51. Paris: OECD Publishing.

Wilensky, Harold. 1975. *The Welfare State and Equality: Structural and Ideological Roots of Public Expenditures.* Berkeley: University of California Press.

Wilson, J. Q. 1980. *The Politics of Regulation.* New York: Basic Books.

Yamada Toshio, 2000. "Japanese Capitalism and the Companyist Compromise." In *Japanese Capitalism in Crisis: A Regulationist Interpretation,* edited by Robert Boyer and Toshio Yamada, 19–31. London: Routledge.

Yamakawa, Ryūichi. 2002. "Nihon no Kaiko Hōsei: Rekishi, Hikakuhō, Gendai teki Kadai." In *Kaiko Hōsei wo Kangaeru: Hōgaku to Keizaigaku no Shiten,* edited by Ōtake Fumio, Ōuchi Shinya, Yamakawa Ryūichi, 3–32. Tokyo: Keisō Shobō.

Yokoyama, Kazuhiko, and Hidenori Tada, eds. 1991. *Nihon Shakai Hoshō no Rekishi.* Tokyo: Gakubunsha.

Yosano, Kaoru. 2008. *Dōdōtaru Seiji.* Tokyo: Shinchōsha.

Yoshinaga, Jun, Gotō Michio, and Karakama Naoyoshi. 2010. "Bōdai na 'Hogo kara no Haijo' wo Shimesu." *Chingin to Shakai Hoshō* 1523 (October): 4–16.

Zysman, John. 1983. *Governments, Markets, and Growth: Financial Systems and the Politics of Industrial Change.* Ithaca: Cornell University Press.

Index

Abe, Shinzō, 77, 112–13, 128, 135–37, 142, 144–45, 154
Abegglen, James C., 171n16
administrative reform, 61, 64, 115–20, 124, 138, 144, 160–61
Administrative Reform Committee, 116–17, 123
Administrative Reform Conference, 119–20
advisory council
  in labor law making, 43, 77, 104, 123–25, 131–36, 139, 149–52, 174n10, 176n45
  political parties and, 180n10, 184n18
  Social Security System, 173n36
Ahmadjian, Christina L., 108
Amamiya, Shōichi, 40, 49, 170n5
Asō, Tarō, 113, 128, 144–45, 153
Australia, 14–16, 18–19, 25, 27, 32, 34–35, 67, 83–84, 89, 166n7
Austria, 14, 16–18, 20, 31, 89, 166n7

balanced treatment, 68, 75–78, 137, 147
Baumgartner, Frank, 37
Becker, Gary, 104
Béland, Daniel, 5, 6, 36, 165n8
Belgium, 14, 16–18, 20, 31, 33, 66–67, 88–89, 166n1, 166nn6–7
Bergh, Andreas, 171n23
Blau, Francine D., 27
Blyth, Mark, 6
Bonoli, Giuliano, 33–34, 166n1, 169n11

Brinton, Mary C., 168n29
Britain. See United Kingdom
British Disease, 59, 159

Calder, Kent, 53, 119
Campbell, John C., 36, 53, 55, 173n39
Campbell, John L., 6
Canada, 14, 16, 18, 20, 32, 67, 87, 89, 91, 166n7
Carlile, Lonny E., 46
Castles, Francis G., 19, 34, 35, 109
CEDAW (Committee on the Elimination of Discrimination against Women), 80
child allowance
  DPJ's, 82, 153–54
  LDP's childcare allowance, 52, 55, 184n20
Childcare Leave Law/Childcare Family Care Leave Law, 68, 79, 82
Chō, Fujio, 144
clientelism, 4–5
Committee on the Elimination of Discrimination against Women. See CEDAW
consumption tax. See tax
Convention on the Elimination of All Forms of Discrimination against Women, 78. See also CEDAW
cooperatism, 6–10, 38–43, 50, 56, 58, 62–64, 93, 122, 148, 158, 160–63
  affinity with productivism, 45–47
  decline of, 98, 100–102, 107
  under the DPJ, 145–46, 152, 155, 162

Council for Comprehensive Regulatory Reform (CCRR), 112–25, 126–29, 134, 136
Council for Regulatory Reform (CRR), 123, 126, 128–29, 152
Council for the Promotion of Regulatory Reform (CPRR), 112, 123, 126–28, 135–36, 149
Council on Economic and Fiscal Policy (CEFP), 10, 112, 115, 120–21, 123–24, 128, 142, 144, 152
course-based employment management. *See* employment management category
Crompton, Rosemary, 27
Crouch, Colin, 172n35
Crump, John, 94
Curtis, Gerald L., 42, 62, 170n1

Democratic Party of Japan (DPJ), 116, 118–19, 120, 122, 141–45
    gender equality, 82, 154–55
    in labor law making, 69, 71, 104, 130–40, 149–52
    vision and values, 145–49, 155, 162–63
    welfare reform, 87, 152–54
Democratic Socialist Party (DSP), 50, 54, 59, 116, 118, 143
Denmark, 14–16, 18–20, 27–28, 31, 66–67, 89, 166n7
deregulation panels, 10, 103, 115, 123–30, 140. *See also* Council for Comprehensive Regulatory Reform; Council for the Promotion of Regulatory Reform; Council for Regulatory Reform; Deregulation Subcommittee; Regulatory Reform Committee
Deregulation Subcommittee, 117, 123, 125–27, 129, 131–32, 178n12
discourse, 5–7, 11, 37, 59–60, 62, 98, 107, 110, 147, 158–61, 163. *See also* discursive analyses
discretionary working hour rules, 68, 99, 126–27, 130–31, 133–34, 137–39
discursive analyses, 6
dismissal
    doctrine of abuse of the right of/ doctrine of abusive dismissal, 21–22, 24, 57, 69–70, 104
    four requirements for dismissal for economic reasons, 22, 24, 57–58, 69–70

law/rules, 68–70, 102–5, 126–27, 133–34, 138–39
dispatched workers. *See* temporary agency workers
Dōmei, 40, 46, 57, 124
domestic and caring responsibilities, 84. *See also* family responsibilities
Dore, Ronald, 28, 158
Downsian spatial model, 122

Economic Strategy Council, 121, 180n17
employers. *See* Keidanren; Keizai Dōyūkai; Nikkeiren
Employment Insurance Law, 57, 63
employment management categories, 78–80, 82
Employment Stability Fund, 57, 63
Employment Stability Law for Elderly Workers, 68
Endō, Kōshi, 168n32–33
Equal Employment Opportunity Law (EEOL), 68, 78–80, 82
    equal treatment, 74–78, 90, 182n42
    principle of, 65, 72, 74, 82
Esping-Andersen, Gøsta, 3, 7, 17, 30–35, 183n11
Estévez-Abe, Margarita, 4, 7, 34, 166n1, 169n8, 173n39, 184n13
Evans, Peter, 145

family responsibilities, 24, 28–29, 66, 76–77, 79, 82, 92, 157. *See also* domestic and caring responsibilities
family wages, 27, 31, 33
Finland, 14–16, 18, 20, 67, 89, 166n7
Fiscal Structural Reform Law, 98
fixed-term contract, 18, 24, 68, 73–74, 82, 91, 99
Flanagan, Robert J., 109, 156, 179n44
Foote, Daniel, 21, 24
France, 14–18, 20–21, 25, 27, 31, 33, 67, 83, 87–91, 109, 166n1, 166nn6–7, 167n13, 178n10, 181n22
Fukuda, Yasuo, 128, 144–45, 154, 183n3
Fukui, Hideo, 83, 128–29
Fukushima, Mizuho, 151, 154–55
full employment, 7, 9, 38–39, 41–45, 47–48, 55–58, 148

Gao, Bai, 165n6
Garon, Sheldon, 5, 46, 170nn15–16, 171n14
gendered division of labor, 13, 26–29, 63, 76

gendered dual system, 2–3, 8, 12, 26–29, 63, 66, 68, 71, 74–75, 78, 83, 88, 92, 110, 146, 154–55, 159, 163
gender equality, 5, 8–9, 65–66, 78–80, 82, 92, 154–55
general unions, 106
 Haken Union, Rentai Union, Zenkoku Union, 150
Germany, 14–18, 20–21, 27, 31, 33, 66–67, 70, 87–89, 91, 166n1, 166nn6–7, 167n13, 181n22
Gini coefficient, 86–88
Goodin, Robert E., 34, 147
Gordon, Andrew, 24, 28, 44, 106, 167n17, 167n19, 168n29, 168n32, 171n17, 179n30
Gōshi, Kōhei, 40, 45

Hacker, Jacob S., 157, 165n8
Haken village, 1–2, 151
Hall, Peter, 4, 123, 185n2
Hamaguchi, Keiichirō, 72, 172n28, 181n20
Harvey, David, 60
Hashimoto, Ryūtarō, 62, 98, 115, 117–20, 122, 129–30, 132, 161–62
Hatoyama, Ichirō, 40, 42–43, 47, 51, 145–46
Hatoyama, Yukio, 118, 145–46, 148–49, 151–52, 154
health-care insurance, 48–49, 62, 91.
 See also National Health Insurance
Higuchi, Kōtarō, 121
Hiraiwa, Gaishi, 96, 117
Hiraiwa Report, 96
Hisamoto, Norio, 167n19, 179n30
Honma, Masaaki, 121
Hosokawa, Morihiro, 96, 115–18, 123
Hosokawa, Ritsuo, 152, 182nn39–40
Huber, Evelyne, 4, 35, 36, 109
human capital formation theory, 104–5

Iio, Jun, 182n45
Ikeda, Hayato, 43, 47, 51–52
Imai, Takashi, 97–98
Income Doubling Plan, 43, 51
incomplete contract theory, 105
individual labor disputes, 102, 107
Industrial Revitalization Law, 98
insider-outsider theory, 29, 65, 83, 85, 157, 163
International Labour Organization (ILO), 50, 72, 75, 83, 91
Ireland, 14–16, 18–19, 27, 32–33, 89

Ishibashi, Tanzan, 40, 42–43, 148, 171n18, 183n11
Ishida, Hirohide, 47–48, 50, 146
Ishida, Takeshi, 5, 41, 170n15
Italy, 14–19, 27, 31, 66–67, 87, 89, 166n1, 166nn6–7
Itō, Takatoshi, 142
Iwai, Akira, 48
Iwata, Kazumasa, 144

Japan Communist Party (JCP), 53–55, 57–59, 132, 150, 172n30
Japan Democratic Party (1954–1955), 39–40, 48
Japan New Party, 116–18, 143
Japan Renewal Party, 116, 118
Japan Socialist Party (JSP), 41–42, 48–50, 53–54, 57–59, 116, 118–19, 143, 172n30. *See also* Social Democratic Party
Job Security Law, 71, 126–27
Jōjima, Masamitsu, 104

Kahn, Lawrence M., 27
Kamei, Shizuka, 151, 184n14
Kamikawa, Ryūnoshin, 142
Kan, Naoto, 118, 148–49, 151–55
Kasza, Gregory J., 7, 36, 169n12
Katzenstein, Peter J., 165n6
Keidanren, 61, 96–98, 108, 117, 127
 Nippon, 73, 98, 101, 104, 108, 112, 121, 134, 142, 144
Keizai Dōyūkai, 45, 97, 121, 142
Kingdon, John W., 180n13
Kiriku, Takashi, 104
Kishi, Nobusuke, 40, 43, 47, 49–51, 142
Koizumi, Jun'ichirō, 69, 77, 86, 103, 112, 115, 117, 120–22, 124, 127, 129, 132–33, 136, 139, 141–43, 150–51, 161–62
 reforms, 77, 136, 141, 143–45, 150
Kojima, Noriaki, 103, 127–28, 133
Kolberg, Jon Eivind, 169n12
Komamura, Kōhei, 32, 90
Kōmeitō, 53–54, 59, 116, 118, 132–33, 138, 143, 150, 152–53
Korpi, Walter, 3–4, 6, 165n2
Kōsai, Yutaka, 170n10
Kouno, Yasuko, 39, 170n11
Kumazawa, Makoto, 28, 167n19
Kume, Ikuo, 102, 109, 172n28
Kuraishi, Tadao, 47–48
Kusakari, Takao, 128

Labor Big Bang, 112, 128
Labor Charter, 47–48, 146
Labor Contract Law, 70, 135, 137–38.
    See also monetary resolution system;
    work rules
labor market flexibility
    external, 3, 19, 23–24, 26–29, 65, 71,
        94, 110, 157, 159
    internal/functional, 2, 23–24, 26–29,
        65–66, 71, 83–85, 105–6, 110, 157,
        159, 163
Labor Standards Law, 68–70, 73, 79, 99,
    103, 126, 130, 133–35, 137. *See also*
    discretionary working hour rules;
    dismissal rules
Levy, Jonah D., 33, 36, 169n1, 172n35
Lewis, Jane, 27, 184n12
Liberal Democratic Party (LDP), 39,
    53–55, 58–59, 122
    gender equality, 154–55
    in labor law making, 104, 130–40, 150–52
    labor policy, 42, 47–48, 50, 144
    structural reform, 117–21, 142
    vision and values. *See* cooperatism;
        statism; productivism; neoliberalism
    welfare policy, 4–5, 49, 51–53,
        59–62, 144, 153–54
Liberal Party (1950 -1955), 39–41
Liberal Party (1998–2003), 104, 143
lifetime employment, 2, 43, 46, 55, 63,
    65, 68, 72, 93–94, 98–99, 104–7
Lijphart, Arend, 182n44, 182n46
Lisbon Strategy, 147
Luxembourg Income Studies (LIS), 86

Machida, Chūji, 39–40
Maehara, Seiji, 143
Maier, Charles S., 44
male breadwinner, 23–24, 26–27, 29, 31,
    33, 35, 76, 81, 92
Manow, Philip, 32, 166n1
market testing, 111–13, 126, 128
Marshall, T.H., 5
Mehta, Jal, 37
Miike coal mine strike, 46–47
Milly, Deborah J., 50, 171n26
Mimura, Akio, 144
minimum wage, 19–20, 25–26, 44, 48,
    50–51, 68, 89–90, 99–100, 126, 129,
    135–37, 144, 147
    law, 50, 68, 90, 126, 135–38
Ministry of Finance, 51–52, 60, 118–20,
    173n36, 180n6

Ministry of Health, Labour, and Welfare
    (MHLW), 69–70, 73–74, 76–77,
    80, 82, 84, 87–88, 103–4, 112, 123,
    128–29, 132–36, 149–50, 152–53.
    See also Ministry of Labour; Ministry
    of Health and Welfare
Ministry of Health and Welfare (MHW),
    49, 51–52, 60, 62
Ministry of Labour (MOL), 50, 55–57,
    63, 75–76, 78–79, 103, 113, 123–24,
    131–33, 135. *See also* Ministry of
    Health, Labour, and Welfare
Mitarai, Fujio, 142
Mitchell, Deborah, 19–20, 34, 35
Miyamoto, Tarō, 169n13
Miyauchi, Yoshihiko, 97, 124, 128
Miyazawa, Kiichi, 113
Mochizuki, Mike, 171n14
monetary resolution system, 103–4, 106,
    126–27, 135–36
Mori, Seigo, 22, 24, 167nn15–16
Mori, Yoshirō, 120–21
Morioka, Kōji, 84
Mulgan, Aurelia George, 139, 182n44
Murayama, Tomiichi, 117–19

Nagatsuma, Akira, 151–52
Nakakita, Kōji, 44, 171n21
Nakamura, Keisuke, 101
Nakano, Koichi, 6, 74, 116, 119, 122, 166n8
Nakasone, Yasuhiro, 61, 161
Nakayama, Ichirō, 45
National Council on Social Security, 144,
    154
National Health Insurance, 52. *See also*
    health-care insurance
neoliberalism, 7–10, 36, 64, 93, 163
    affinity with statism, 60, 62, 120, 145,
        172n35
    ascendance of, 9–10, 36, 115–16,
        121–23, 160–63
    declining appeal of, 141–45, 162
    reform, 120–21, 123–30, 159
    reformers, 98, 103, 116, 143, 146,
        161
Netherlands, 14, 16, 18–20, 25, 33, 67,
    84, 89, 166n1, 166nn6–7
New Frontier Party (NFP), 118–19, 142–43
New Growth Strategy, 147, 163
New Party Sakigake, 116, 118–19, 131
new public sphere, 148
new social risks, 2, 9, 66, 68, 88–92, 114,
    157

New Zealand, 14–16, 18–19, 27, 32, 35, 83–84, 89, 166n7
Nikkeiren, 44–45, 94–98, 100–103, 108–9. *See also* Keidanren
Nippon Keidanren. *See* Keidanren
Nitta, Michio, 45, 46, 56, 105, 168n29, 173n38, 179n31
Niwa, Uichirō, 142
Noble, Gregory, 166n8
Nomura, Masami, 171n16, 178n14
Norway, 14–18, 20, 28, 31, 67, 84, 89, 166n7

Obuchi, Keizō, 98, 120–22, 138, 183n8
Organization for Economic Co-operation and Development (OECD), 17, 20–21, 31, 33, 66–67, 87–88
Ōhira, Masayoshi, 59
Okuda, Hiroshi, 95, 98, 101, 103, 121
Orloff, Ann Shola, 27
Ōsawa, Mari, 31, 81
Ōtake, Fumio, 23, 83, 86, 167n16, 177n55
Ōtake, Hideo, 61, 170n10
Ōwaki, Masako, 175n23
Ozawa, Ichirō, 118, 143, 151, 154

Palier, Bruno, 109, 165n8
paradigm, 55–56, 58, 63, 98
shift, 57–58, 96–98, 123, 126–27
Part-Time Labor Law, 25, 68, 75, 77, 167n20
part-time workers, 23–25, 74–77, 80, 91, 135. See also *pāto*
pāto, 25, 27, 63, 81, 82, 85, 89, 132
Pempel, T. J., 169n3, 169n9, 177n9, 178n11
pension, 31–32, 48–49, 52–53, 62, 69, 81, 91, 97, 136–37, 143, 152
People's burden rate, 61–62, 159
People's New Party (PNP), 149–52
personnel assessment, 28–29, 105
Pierson, Paul, 109, 165n8
Polanyi, Karl, 10, 60, 141, 145, 162
Pontusson, Jonas, 165n2, 177n59
poverty rates, 3, 87–90, 153
power resource approaches, 3, 4, 8, 36
productivism, 6–7, 9, 38–48, 52, 60, 62, 160–61
    under the DPJ, 8, 10, 145–48, 155, 162–63
productivity First Guiding Principle of, 105

movement, 41, 44–46, 48, 101, 107
politics of, 44–47, 97, 101–2, 107, 145–46
Three Guiding Principles of, 45–46, 107
Public Services Reform Law, 112–13, 126

race to the bottom, 109–10, 147, 159
Recruit Scandal, 113
reformed capitalism, 39, 97
regime theory, 8, 30, 35–36
Regini, Marino, 17, 23
Regulatory Reform Committee (RRC), 103, 123, 126–27, 133
Rengō, 40, 64, 70–71, 79, 96, 100–101, 103–4, 131–37, 143, 146, 150–51. *See also* Kiyoshi Sasamori
Renhō, 155
Rinchō (Second Provisional Council for Administrative Reform), 61, 63, 124
Robbins, Gregory E., 108
Rueda, David, 176n46

Sainsbury, Diane, 27
Sakigake. *See* New Party Sakigake
Sako, Mari, 100
Sasamori, Kiyoshi, 106
Satō, Eisaku, 47, 52
Satomi, Kenji, 172n36
Scharpf, Fritz W., 19
Scheiner, Ethan, 4
Schmidt, Vivian A., 6, 19, 159
Schoppa, Leonard J., 92, 183n6
Schwartz, Frank J., 124
seniority wage, 104–5
Shibusawa, Eiichi, 40
Shimizu, Yasuaki, 153
Shinkawa, Toshimitsu, 3, 61, 102, 169n3, 172n33, 173n39
shuntō (spring offensive), 100–102
social assistance, 31–32, 51–52, 62, 85–86, 90, 136–37
    recipients of, 52, 62, 86
    take-up rate of: 32, 90
Social Democratic Party (SDP), 119, 122, 131–32, 142, 149–52
social expenditure, 14–15, 31–35, 52–53, 62, 121
social rights, 5, 31, 41, 59, 61, 155
Sōdōmei, 40–41, 46
Soeda, Yoshiya, 171n26
Sōhyō, 44, 46, 48, 50, 56–57, 78, 100, 124
Spain, 83, 88, 166nn6–7

spring offensive, *See* shuntō
staffing business, 110–13, 124–25. *See also* temporary agency workers; Temporary Work Agency Law
statism, 6, 38–43, 58, 60, 62, 120, 122, 160
    under the DPJ, 145–49, 155, 162
    See also neoliberalism
Stephens, John D., 3, 4, 35, 36, 109
Sugeno, Kazuo, 167n14, 173n7, 181n25
Sumiya, Mikio, 173n36
Suzuki, Bunji, 40–41, 183n10
Suzuki, Zenkō, 61
Sweden, 14–16, 18, 20, 28, 31, 34, 66–67, 87–89, 166n7, 167n13, 183n11
Swenson, Peter, 165n1
Switzerland, 14–16, 18, 33, 67, 89

Tachibanaki, Toshiaki, 86, 177n58
Takanashi, Akira, 172n28, 176n45
Takenaka, Heizō, 121, 142
Takeshita, Noboru, 113
Tanaka, Kakuei, 52–55, 58
tax consumption, 98, 119, 153–54
    exemption for spouses, 81–82
Taylor-Gooby, Peter, 6, 159
temporary agency workers/dispatched workers, 1, 24–25, 72–73, 88–89, 126–27, 129, 132, 149–52
temporary labor market, regulation of, 17–19, 66–67
temporary work agencies. *See* staffing agencies
Temporary Work Agency Law (TWAL), 2, 68, 71–72, 82, 110, 126–27, 129–33, 137–39, 149–52, 162
Thelen, Kathleen, 109, 157, 165n1
Three-Year Plan for Deregulation, 125
Three-Year Plan for Regulatory Reform, 134
Tiberghien, Yves, 98, 178n10, 180n9
Tominaga, Ken'ichi, 36
Toyoda, Shōichirō, 96
Toyoda Vision, 98, 127
Tsutsui, William M., 45–46, 171n13

unemployment
    insurance, 18–19, 20–21, 57, 91
    rates, 15–17, 90, 95
unions. *See* Dōmei; general unions; Rengō; Sōdomei; Sōhyō; Zenrō; Zenrōren

United Kingdom (UK), 14–16, 18, 20–21, 25, 27, 31–33, 40, 67, 83–84, 87–91, 109, 181n22,
    party system, 123
United States (US), 15–18, 20–21, 26–27, 31–32, 34, 36, 44, 46, 70, 83–84, 86–91, 109, 123, 166n7, 167n13
    employers, 22, 104
    government, 115, 117
    party system, 123
Ushio, Jirō, 121
Uzuhashi, Takafumi, 32, 34, 169nn2–4

veto
    player, 37
    power, 130, 140, 155
Vogel, Steven K., 98, 108, 177n1, 178n11

Weathers, Charles, 44, 72, 176n51, 181n31
welfare retrenchment, 52, 60–62, 64, 159–61
Westminster model, 139–40, 182n44
white-collar exemption, 126–27, 134–35, 138–39
Wilensky, Harold, 36
Wilson, J.Q., 111
working hours, 83–84
    unpaid overtime, 83–85
    See also discretionary working hour rules
working poor, 1–2, 85, 90, 95, 151, 183n7
work rules, 70–71, 99, 136
    doctrine of unfavorable changes to work rules, 70
work-family balance, 65, 79, 82, 92
work-life balance, 147

Yamada, Toshio, 167n19
Yashiro, Naohiro, 112–13, 127–28, 142
Yokomichi, Takahiro, 118
Yosano, Kaoru, 142, 154
Yoshida, Shigeru, 39, 42, 52
    anti-Yoshida conservatives, 39–42
    school, 43
Yoshikawa, Hiroshi, 121, 144
Yuasa, Makoto, 153, 183n7

Zenrō, 46, 50
Zenrōren, 173n8
zoku politicians, 115–16, 120, 139–40
Zysman, John, 165n2